NICE CHURCHY PATRIARCHY

NICE CHURCHY PATRIARCHY

RECLAIMING WOMEN'S HUMANITY FROM
EVANGELICALISM

LIZ COOLEDGE JENKINS

APOCRYPHILE
PRESS

AUTHOR'S NOTE

Parts of this book are based on my own recollection of events; others may remember things differently. Some dialogue has been recreated from memory. Many organizations' and individuals' names have been changed to respect their privacy; my intent is to share stories that illustrate larger issues at play, not to shame particular individuals or organizations.

Apocryphile Press
PO Box 255
Hannacroix, NY 12087
www.apocryphilepress.com

This cover has been designed using images from Freepik.

Please join our mailing list at www.apocryphilepress.com/free. We'll keep you up-to- date on all our new releases, and we'll also send you a FREE BOOK. Visit us today!

CONTENTS

PART II
Dismantling Misogyny's Power

DEMASCULINIZING SCRIPTURE

EXPANDING THEOLOGY

UNERASING HISTORY

RECLAIMING AGENCY

REIMAGINING AUTHORITY

WORDS OF INTRODUCTION

I stumbled on the evangelical stream of Christianity in college and stuck with it through my twenties. My relationship with evangelicalism was always a complicated one —more so as time went on. More so once I started working for my church. More so when it became clear that I couldn't work for said church much longer if I didn't get on board with the idea that gay relationships were sinful. More so when evangelicals voted Trump into the U.S. Presidency in 2016. More so when I went to seminary.

Over many years of deep involvement in evangelical communities, I found myself gradually and painfully becoming aware that patriarchy—that is, all the ways men hold more power than women and are valued more highly—operates in these spaces like a many-headed monster. Everything about my relationship with evangelicalism was influenced by my gender as a woman, especially as a woman in ministry. As soon as I began to notice and put words to one form in which patriarchy took shape, I would start to become aware of another. And another. And another. In some ways my twenties felt like one big slo-mo tumbling freefall into the miry depths of churchy patriarchy and how it impacts women—and how it impacts everyone.

I'm not talking about the worst of evangelical communities here. Not even close to it. I've been lucky—or some combination of wise and lucky, but mostly lucky—to avoid those. I'm talking about nice people. I'm talking about well-meaning leaders. I'm talking about humans I very much like and respect who have bought into twisted unjust systems that don't serve anyone well.

I'm talking about nice churchy patriarchy.

My particular journey into the bowels of nice churchy patriarchy ran a circuitous route through eleven years in a conservative complementarian context—the kind that explicitly believes that men and women ought to hold different roles in ministry and marriage—followed by a couple years studying at an egalitarian seminary and attending an egalitarian evangelical church—that is, a seminary and a church that (at least in theory) make no gendered distinctions between men's and women's roles. In these very different contexts, different faces of misogyny made themselves known to me. And some of the same faces reappeared, too, recast in slightly different forms. The first half of this book is all about naming these faces—noticing them and exploring how they operate, looking them in the eye, wrestling with them, viewing them from different angles to understand their form and function more fully.

These things are not easy to look at. But we aren't going to turn into stone if we do. In fact, we have to look. We have to face nice churchy patriarchy with directness and honesty. We have to name it, know it, and understand it, if we're going to be able to detach ourselves from it and learn together how to build something new. The second half of the book, then, is all about this "something new." Once we understand how patriarchy operates in subtle yet devastating ways, we can get to work—pushing for change in some cases and leaving and going elsewhere in others.

I'm here to speak of what I have seen of nice churchy patriarchy. And I'm here to suggest some ways we might, together, disrupt its power.

This book draws heavily on my own experiences in evangelical Christian communities and evangelical Christian ministry. I realize that, as a white woman from an upper-middle class background, there are lots of things I haven't experienced, lots of ways my perspective is limited. I'm glad I'm not the only one thinking and writing on these things. (I've included a list of suggested authors for further reading in an appendix, over half of whom are women of color.) Some of my stories will probably be most relatable to people with backgrounds similar to my own. I want to be upfront about that. I seek solidarity and partnership with women of all races and classes, as well as other realities like queer and trans identities, and I want to do so without trying to deny the societal power and privileges I hold. I want to be aware of these privileges so that I can lay them down in some cases and use them for good in others.

I think about the faith communities I've been a part of. They're complicated. I want to share some of the stories that nudged me along my journey of seeing and grappling with nice churchy patriarchy. But I don't really want to evoke pity. The faith communities I write about were good communities for me in a lot of ways, and I cherish them. I cherish the people I met there—even though I also wish things were different, and I feel strongly enough about this that I no longer wish to be a part of these kinds of communities.

I don't want to evoke judgment on the particular people and churches involved in these stories. It's not about them. It could have been any people, any leaders, any churches, any (patriar-chal) faith communities. It's not about anyone in particular. It's about what it's like to be a woman in church. It's about taking a clear-eyed look at the patriarchal dynamics that operate in so many faith communities, so much of the time—often in ways that are subtle enough to fly under the radar, ways that might not seem quite bad enough to make a fuss over. It's about shining a glaring light on these things, naming them, and considering them important—because women are important.

It's about learning, as individuals and as communities, to see that things are not okay. It's about refusing to accept the way things are. It's about refusing to think and feel, as many of us sometimes do, that there is something wrong with us, rather than something very wrong with the patriarchal systems we inhabit.

Some of my stories might seem like relatively small things. And they may be. But small, everyday things—the kinds of things that can so easily come to seem normal—add up to a lot. And they reveal a great deal about the attitudes behind them. None of these things should be normal.

My stories are far from the worst things that happen to women in our world and in our faith communities. (I'm sure the fact that I carry privilege in my body in pretty much every identity other than gender has a great deal to do with that.) But misogyny doesn't have to be physically violent, sexually violent, or even blatantly verbally violent to have an impact. It's worth paying attention to the subtle forms patriarchy takes in our daily lives, seeping into all levels of our psyches and communi-ties. The friendlier, gentler faces of misogyny are still faces of misogyny. Women will not be free—and faith communities will not flourish fully—until we root out misogyny in all its forms.

As you read these stories and my reflections on them, you

may not see everything the same way I do. That's totally okay. I have no interest in replacing one domineering and coercive worldview with a different worldview that is equally domineering and coercive. You are welcome in this space, in these pages, in these words. You are welcome to find yourself in the parts you resonate with. You are welcome not to relate to the parts you don't relate to. Some of my thoughts may call forth similar thoughts in you, and some might evoke total disagreement. That's all welcome here. I hope to spark reflection and conversation, and I want those things to take you wherever they take you.

Our fight is not against men but against the systems of imbalanced power that keep women and nonbinary people from flourishing in the fullness of our gifts and offering this world the best we have to offer. The biblical apostle Paul can be complicated (more on this later), but I like what he said about our struggle not being against flesh and blood but against powers and principalities, the cosmic forces of darkness.[1] Patriarchy is one of those dark forces. As is white supremacy. As is every other form of dominance and subjection humans have come up with. As we engage in this struggle, together with all women and on behalf of all women—not just upper-middle-class white cisgender heterosexual able-bodied women—we find that we are grappling not only with misogyny but with all the intertwining systems of oppression that keep us from flourishing together in beloved communities of equals.

The force of patriarchy lives both outside us and within us. And so this book is about changing churches, cultures, and systems at the same time as it's also about grappling with the internalized misogyny women often carry within ourselves. All of this is transformation. All of this is salvation—individual and systemic, personal and political, operating together as a unified whole.

And all of it is pursued together, in community. We are not the lone (male) hero slaying the many-headed monster. We are something else entirely. I didn't know until recently that the classic human "fight or flight" response to danger is actually a masculine phenomenon. I learned from Rebecca Solnit's *A Short History of Silence* that the original "fight or flight" studies didn't study female rats or female humans—and when researchers did study females, they found that we often gravitate toward other options: We "tend and befriend." We gather, support, nurture, and build social networks that help us cope with stressful situations.[2] That's amazing, and it feels right. But it doesn't have to be for women only; people of all genders can operate in these ways. Let's choose to do so. Addressing and eradicating patriarchal structures, systems, theologies, and narratives will take a community effort—collectively, together. An effort brimming with the full and necessary contributions of people of all genders, races, classes, sexualities, abilities, ages, experiences. Everyone has something to contribute.

As we see the stress induced by patriarchal ways of being, the danger it presents to us and our communities, we don't have to freeze, and we don't have to become violent. We can gather in supportive communities that heal together, tear down and build together, push together for change, hold one another gently as we do so.

Although I write from my experience, this book isn't really about me. It's about the Bible and how we read it; it's about Christian history and how we understand it;[3] it's about churches—how they are, and how they could be. And I hope it's about you. I hope you find some of your own story, heart, hopes, dreams, disappointments, and possibilities in these pages. Really, I wish you didn't have your own disappointments to process and heal from. But, if you're a woman in this world, I'm guessing you probably do. I hope this book brings some solace, perhaps a sense of being seen. I hope it's a companion in your journey, alongside friends and family and everyone who is important to you—the people who help you live with dignity, hope, and a stubborn insistence on your own full humanity, and on the full humanity of all humans.

If you're a man, thanks for joining us. Your journey through these pages is brave, on the one hand; on the other hand, it is simply as it should be. I invite you to listen, to engage in self-reflection and in reflection on your faith community. We need you in this journey alongside us. I remember the four men in my thirty-or-so-person Women in Church History class in seminary—how thoughtful and open-minded they were, how deeply I appreciated them being there, and also *how frickin' much* they had to learn. I also remember how badly I wished there had been more of them—many more. Thank you for being part of that "more."

If you're someone who doesn't fit neatly into the male/female gender binary, you have so much to offer these conversations. Even as I speak from my experiences as a woman, I want to listen to and learn from your experiences as a nonbinary person or any other gender complexities you might embody. Patriarchy impacts us differently. And I also hope you see yourself in these pages, grappling with oppressive gender roles and joining people of all genders to find a better way.

For everyone who wants to see faith communities live more fully into a vision of oneness, such that "there is no longer Jew or Greek, there is no longer slave or free, there is no longer male and female"[4]—I hope this book is one small piece of the puzzle in getting there. I hope it sparks reflection on your own experiences. I hope it fuels critique of your own churches. I hope it inspires dreams for your own communities. I hope it evokes ideas and provokes conversations around what it might take to move in the direction of these dreams. I believe that God, whose children we all are,[5] is with us on this journey.

Together, we can build new kinds of faith communities. We can build a new kind of world.

PART I

NAMING MISOGYNY'S FACES

THE SUBORDINATION

1

WHAT'S BEST FOR THEM

*W*hen I moved from the Seattle area to Palo Alto, CA to start my freshman year at Stanford, I visited five or six churches. I had no idea what to look for, no clue as to the kinds of questions I should be asking. Most of the churches I visited seemed reasonable to me. So I prayed about it, felt drawn to one of them, and began attending there regularly.

The church I chose was a medium-large nondenominational evangelical church with roots in the independent Bible church movement. Let's call it Faith Bible Church. I ended up being a part of the congregation there for eleven years, from age eighteen to twenty-nine. Coincidentally, or not, this is the exact age range some scholars have called "emerging adulthood":[1] the crucial young adult years during which we tend to try to figure out who we are, what we want to be about, who our people are and where we belong.

I liked Faith Bible. People were kind and genuine. I enjoyed the chance to get off campus once a week and be in a room with humans who weren't either between the ages of eighteen and twenty-two or college professors. Volunteers offered rides from campus, and the service didn't start until 11:15 am, which worked well for my wacky sleep schedule (or total lack thereof). Four different pastors rotated preaching—so if you didn't really connect with one of them, at least there were three others to balance things out.

I didn't think to ask any questions about gender roles in church leadership. I didn't really know what an elder was, let alone suspect that they might all be male. I could see that there were no women among the four pastors who did most of the preaching, but I assumed this was happenstance—coincidental, not intentional. The systematic subordination of women was not at all obvious to me when I first started attending Faith Bible.

I blame my initial obliviousness, in part, on the church I grew up in. (And by blame, I mean, I'm thankful for it.) For the first eighteen years of my life, I was a part of a large suburban PC(USA)[2] church. I'm sure sexism found ways to creep into this church, too, as it tends to do. But, to me, as a kid and teenager, things felt pretty equal.

I remember the female pastors: Rev. Danna VanHorn and Rev. Rosalind Renshaw. The senior pastor was a man, but there were always at least a couple of women who had important roles in the church's leadership—and, importantly, who preached, as much as any of the other male pastors did, on the senior pastor's off weeks.

Danna, when she preached, loved to talk about her grandchildren and show pictures of them. In a world that tends to demean and disregard older women (often called grandmas, whether or not they actually have grandchildren) as silly and irrelevant, Danna's choice to publicly embrace her role as a grandmother and her love for her family was brave and beautiful. She was both a loving grandmother and a gifted and insightful preacher, and there was no conflict between these two roles.

Rosalind, when she preached, often shared poems she had written. Her poems spoke of God in a way that was personal and intimate, and it was a vulnerable thing to share these poems with our large congregation. She, too, was brave. To the extent that poetry is sometimes feminized, and often under-valued in an efficiency-obsessed and money-driven society, Rosalind was courageous to offer her gifts as both a sensitive poet and a bold preacher.

No doubt these two female preachers helped women feel seen in church. They helped us see ourselves, in all our female-ness, more clearly in the scriptures and the life of faith. They helped us read the Bible in fresh and relevant ways—ways that the male senior pastor, speaking from his own masculine expe-rience, was unable to access fully.

Seeing these women behind the pulpit all those years taught me that female preachers are totally unremarkable. Because of Rosalind and Danna, I never quite believed what I ended up hearing so many times in my young adult years—that it was unnatural for a woman to preach. It felt like the most natural thing in the world. I never had that inexplicable, not-necessarily-logical, gut-level intuition that it just feels *wrong*— which is often the kind of thing that has less to do with actual right or wrong, good or bad, or biblical or unbiblical, and more to do with what we grew up with, what we're familiar with, what we've seen, what we've become accustomed to and comfortable with.

Because my home church had female preachers and this all seemed so normal to me, when I started attending Faith Bible in college, I didn't think to ask why the preaching pastors were all men. I didn't think to ask about the gender of the elders— the people who made up the governing board of the church. I did not expect, as a young woman, to feel limited or subordinated because of my gender in any way.

It was at least a year before I began to notice that perhaps all was not as I had assumed—before I remember feeling anything other than comfortable and happy as a young woman at Faith Bible. But I remember the moment this changed. I remember the first time I heard a man at Faith Bible say something sexist enough to catch me off-guard and make my insides boil with anger.

I was in my second year of college. This man, let's call him Dave, was in his thirties or so at the time, and he was one of a handful of adult churchgoers who volunteered with the college Bible study group every Wednesday night. Part of me wishes I could villainize Dave. How dare he say something that would hit me as a young woman like a slap in the face? What a jerk.

Unfortunately, Dave is not the worst. "Jerk" is not at all the right word for him. He's a generous person who genuinely cares about people. I like him, even though I disagree with him about a ton of things. He tends to be honest, and I find that refreshing. He was a dedicated college ministry volunteer for a long time.

Dave was not (and is not) a villain. But there he was, that evening, sitting across from me at a long rectangular table in the campus religious life center, as we all ate giant burritos from the campus eatery and talked about the Bible. The topic of the evening was women in ministry.

Someone must have said something along the lines of *why not let women lead or preach if they want to?*

Dave promptly replied, *yeah, but giving people what they want isn't always what's best for them.*

. . .

Giving people what they want isn't always what's best for them. In all of my naïveté, having grown up in a church where women were pastors and elders and no one felt the need to debate about it, this kind of statement was totally new to me.

I had no response. Just silent, roiling anger.

I had no words—and not nearly a strong enough sense of safety to be able to articulate any words I might have had, if I had them.

People continued to wax eloquent around me with various opinions about what roles women should or shouldn't have in churches. I slumped down in my chair, chewed on my burrito, and tried to look as small as I felt.

I didn't know, at that point, all the different arguments I would hear, both for and against women preaching and leading in churches, over the many more years I would spend in the evangelical world. I hadn't yet studied—and studied, and studied—the handful of Bible passages that seem to limit women's roles in ministry. I didn't know that, in the twenty-first century, there was still a need to debate about these things.

I also had no aspirations, at that point, of becoming a preacher or church leader myself. And so, if I was vaguely aware of any debates happening in the broader Christian universe, they didn't feel particularly personal or urgent to me.

But something about what Dave said that evening, in that Bible study group, did feel very personal—and very urgent. I may not have wanted to be a pastor, but I knew in my gut that something was wrong. I sensed something broadly applicable and broadly disturbing about a man saying that women don't know what's best for ourselves—about a man saying, in other words, that men know better than women what is good for women.

Beyond any particular questions about women in ministry, it's a statement that implies a certain kind of worldview. It's born out of a universe in which men are always the ones in power. Men are the ones who make all the choices—based, of course, on their superior wisdom and intelligence—about what kinds of rights and opportunities should or should not be "given" to women. Men are the benevolent demigods who control women's movements in the world—for women's good, of course.

I had not known, up until this point, that, as a young woman, I inhabited this universe.

If I could go back and put some words to that blood-boiling, shrinking, sinking, shocked, confused feeling, I might offer *patronized* or *infantilized*.

If I had the words, and if I felt safe enough to speak, I might have said that these sorts of statements made me feel that, as a woman, I was considered lacking in spiritual authority over my own life—lacking in the ability to seek and define my own sense of direction and purpose in the world. I was considered in need of men's permission—of men's generous "giving"— simply to be who I was, to follow God's calling in my life. I was considered in need of men to tell me what I should or shouldn't be doing. I was considered, in other words, not quite a full adult human.

Of course, in some cases it's true that what people want isn't really what's best for them.

Take children, for example. Maybe your kids want to eat candy all day, but you know that eating a vegetable or two is actually what's best for them. (I'm not a parent, but this is what I imagine parenting to be like: lots of time trying to persuade your kids to eat vegetables, with limited success.) Or your kids want to play video games all day, but you know they need to do their homework, because that's what's best for them—you know, learning and stuff. This is not always clear-cut; kids have wisdom too. Adults have much to learn from them. And it feels important to ask—and respect—what kids want for themselves. But, at least sometimes, as the parent—as the adult who takes care of your kids and really does know more than they do about many things—it's your responsibility to put some rules in place, to craft healthy boundaries that will help them grow and flourish.

Or, as another example, consider a supervisor/employee relationship. Maybe you're a manager, and someone under your supervision wants to take on a new level of responsibility. However, they're still pretty new at their job; you've been watching their work, and you know they still have some basic skills to develop before they're ready to take on something new. It's your job, as the supervisor, to do your best to set them on a path for success, which sometimes involves asking them to wait for something they aren't yet prepared for.

Shocker of shockers, though: Women are not children. And women are not subordinates under the management of men. As much as women have been infantilized in the popular (read: male) imagination in all sorts of ways throughout human history, we are, in fact, adults. We are, in fact, equal coworkers. We are fully capable of making our own decisions—about how we spend our time, what our gifts are, and how we want to use these gifts in the world.

Like men, we won't always make great decisions. We will make mistakes and course-correct, try and fail, learn and grow. But these are our mistakes to make. It's our growth to be had. It's our decision what kinds of roles we want to play in this world and who we want to be. No other human gets to act as a gatekeeper who decides whether or not to "give" us something they think is "best for us." If we're wise, we'll seek input from people we respect and trust, and we'll listen carefully to them. We'll make decisions in community, with community, for community. But ultimately the decisions are ours. Our lives are ours alone to live.

. . .

It feels important to me in this book to quote primarily from female authors. But I'll make an exception for Howard Thurman. Thurman was a Black pastor and theologian who wrote, among many other things, *Jesus and the Disinherited*—a book that deeply influenced Dr. Martin Luther King, Jr. and other Black freedom movement leaders. Thurman once said, famously, "Don't ask what the world needs. Ask what makes you come alive, and go do it. Because what the world needs is people who have come alive."

I think the world needs women who have come alive. The world needs women who refuse to allow men to tell us what's best for us. The world needs women who are learning to embrace our own full humanity, see our own visions, dream our own dreams, define our own priorities, set our own goals and take our own steps to try to get there. The world needs women who are learning to pay attention to the ways we are wired, learning to move toward the things that give us life and away from the things that exhaust and deplete us.

The world needs women who have come alive—and the world needs men who do not try to keep us from coming alive. The world needs men who refuse to tell women what's best for us. The world needs men who know that they do not know, better than women do, what is best for women.

The world needs humans who are stubbornly determined to see one another as equals, regardless of how centuries of misogyny and racism and other evil systems of domination have set things up and predisposed us to think. The world needs humans who commit to mutually healthy relationships with one another, the kind where we all help one another figure out what's best for us and for our communities.

In this kind of world, there is no way in which *giving people what they want isn't always what's best for them* makes sense—

because there is no power-hoarding group of people who think they have the right to give or take power from others. There is no room for systematic subordination of any group of people. There is only mutual honoring, loving care, simultaneous attention to our own needs and others' needs—giving and receiving, serving and leading, freely and with joy.

2

TELL ME, WHAT MUST I BE?

*B*y my senior year of college, I was, for the first time in my life, dating a Serious Christian Dude. Let's call him Charles.

In some ways, it was great. It was the first time I had been in a relationship with someone who shared my faith in God. We could talk about church, and the Bible, and how to love and care for our friends and dormmates. Plus, in the Bible study group I was co-leading, Charles was always game to share his thoughts and break any Long Awkward Pauses that might occur after I posed a (probably lackluster) question to the group. That was pretty much salvation, as far as I was concerned.

Like Dave, Charles was far from a villain. At the same time, he held some patriarchal views. If I were single now, and looking for someone to date and possibly marry, gendered roles and expectations would be among my top concerns. If I met a man who expressed any sort of doubt about whether women should be pastors, or who expected his wife to submit to him as the "head" of their marriage, it would be a deal-breaker. Same for a man who expressed doubts about women having their own careers, or who expected his wife to stop working and be a full-time mom by default if kids came into the picture. No more questions asked. I wouldn't want to waste my time or his.

But when I was twenty-two, dating Charles, somehow these things didn't seem like a terribly big deal. Maybe it's because there were other issues that felt more urgent—personality differences, cultural differences, commitment level differences, differences in how ready we felt to get married. (Me at twenty-one or twenty-two? Not at all ready.) And then there was the tiny detail that he was an international student who had received a generous scholarship from his home country in exchange for a commitment to return and work there for six years after graduation. Six whole years. These were the things I endlessly wondered about, prayed about, stressed about, and talked through with friends and mentors.

When it came to gender roles, I felt like we operated as equals, and that was what mattered. I felt respected by him. It wasn't clear to me that Charles' patriarchal beliefs made much of a difference in our day-to-day lives.

Looking back now, I feel like he bordered on controlling at times—was it really an issue for me to go jogging with other guy friends?—but at the time, I didn't really connect these mildly possessive tendencies with Charles' opinions about the Bible and gender. I thought it was just another set of differences in personality and preferences, another set of different assumptions about what being in a relationship meant.

On some level I probably assumed that, when it came to patriarchal views, Charles would likely change his mind over time. At the very least, we could negotiate these things together. We could figure out what worked for both of us.

Charles and I did talk about gender roles from time to time. After one of these conversations, he sent me two talks to listen to—kind of like a podcast, back before podcasts were a thing. The talks were titled *What He Must Be* and *What She Must Be*.[1] In them, a (male, of course) pastor spells out what he thinks the Bible has to say about gender roles in (heterosexual, of course) marriage. The vibe of husbands leading and wives submitting was strong.

I wasn't into it. Not that I had expected to be. I just listened to the talks because Charles asked me to. And we respected each other and wanted to understand each other, right? So, I sat down at my desk in my dorm room and put my earbuds in.

Now I had carefully chosen this dorm room with all my priority and privilege as a senior. It was located in the most visible and social spot possible. Dormmates were always passing by and saying hi, and I loved it. I may be an introvert, but I was also an evangelical student trying to "do ministry" in my place of residence—that is, trying to get to know people in the dorm, especially the freshmen, and love and care for them. (And, of course, trying to get them to come to the Bible study group I was leading.)

I tried to keep my door open when possible, and I kept a bowl of candy outside my door for a while, like the RAs and other dorm staff who were officially charged with looking out for freshmen and helping them have a good first year of college. I didn't mind when students forgot their key cards or were trying to visit someone in the dorm and pounded loudly on the lounge door nearby; I would happily hop up and let them in. I had a fantasy in my mind that I was some kind of secret, unofficial RA-type figure in the freshmen's lives. I'll confess I felt a small twinge of jealousy when, at the end of the school year, my dormmates voted one of the actual RAs "dorm mom," and not me.

As I sat down at my desk, earbuds in and door open, to behold the talks Charles sent me in all their unabashed patriarchal glory, several people must have walked by. I'm sure I gave them a friendly wave, as usual. They didn't know—and didn't need to know—about the degrading nonsense I was listening to because my boyfriend had sent it to me. I had my earbuds in. I could just smile and wave.

After I had been listening for a while, a freshman guy who lived next door walked by, saw me, and stopped outside the door. I waved, said hi, took an earbud out—after all, I wouldn't be terribly devastated if I missed a couple minutes of the talks —and asked him how things were going. He started to come into the room, then stopped, looked uncomfortable, mumbled something about having to go, and left.

That was odd, I thought. My freshman neighbor seemed to feel awkward, and I had no idea why. He had stopped by to chat plenty of times before and had never seemed uncomfortable around me. Oh well, I told myself—maybe he really did remember something he had to do. I put my earbud back in and turned back toward the computer.

It was then that I realized: My earbuds were not actually plugged into the computer.

I had been sitting there, in my highly visible, socially located dorm room, blissfully smiling and waving to everyone who walked by—all the while blasting these patriarchal Christian talks about *What He Must Be* and *What She Must Be*, out loud, for everyone to hear.

As I reflect on the Embarrassing Incident of the Unplugged Earbuds, I think about how Charles wasn't a bad guy—and how, at the same time, I am so glad we didn't end up getting married. Whatever mildly controlling tendencies he may have had while we were dating would not have magically gone away. And neither would his gendered expectations about what marriage should look like. We may have been in for a lifetime of fighting over what a man and a woman, a husband and a wife, *must* (or must not) be.

If we were part of a conservative Christian community, this would have been a hell of an uphill battle. I don't know how it would have ended.

I also think about the pastor who gave those talks. I don't think he meant ill. At the same time, though, as Brittney Cooper has written, "Impact matters more than intent."[2] Cooper was speaking of anti-Blackness—of white people's tendency to fail to recognize the full humanity of Black people. "The anti-Blackness at the heart of white fear," she writes, "is predicated on a misrecognition of the humanity of Black people. Whether that misrecognition is willful or unwitting matters less than its harmful outcomes."[3]

I hear and receive Cooper's words in their own right. And I also think they're true of sexism—of men's tendency to fail to recognize the full humanity of women. Patriarchal theology that casts men as leaders and women as their subordinates can be enormously damaging, whether "willful" or "unwitting"— whether or not it comes with ill intent on the part of the people who perpetuate it.

I think about this pastor, and I wonder: What gave him the right to speak as if there were just one thing a man *must* be, just one thing a woman *must* be?

If he felt that these prescriptive gender roles worked well for him in his own marriage, that's fine—I guess. If he wanted to share with others what's worked well for him, I guess that's his right, too. But he wasn't speaking in these terms. He wasn't just sharing his own experiences, his personal opinions. He was speaking of what God wants for all men and all women. He was speaking in terms of *must*. To him, this was not just his own perspective. It was *Bible*. It was authoritative—and, of course, perspicuously[4] clear. No room for different interpretations, dissenting voices, alternative perspectives. No room for thoughtful and nuanced conversations about the literary, cultural, and historical contexts of the Bible, and how these things might influence scripture's implications for present-day marriages.

Perhaps the idea of *what he must be* and *what she must be* was especially jarring to me because my parents didn't indoctrinate me with any such notions. My parents, like my home church, created a space of gender equity—of freedom to be who I was, unconstricted by culturally constructed gender roles or by anyone's opinions about what a girl *must* or *must not* be.

My mom and dad themselves embodied fairly traditional gender roles: my dad, the primary income-earner, an electrical engineer and then engineering manager; and my mom, a stay-at-home mom, after working for several years as a pharmaceutical rep. This was the model my brother and I saw, but it was never presented as the One Right Way. It was just what made sense for my particular parents in their particular situation.

My parents encouraged my first love, as a little girl of maybe four or five years old: dinosaurs. I read all the dinosaur books and knew all their names. I loved acing the dino knowledge quizzes at the Pacific Science Center dinosaur exhibit in Seattle. I collected a small army of dinosaur toys who fought each other, went swimming in the bathtub at bath time, and got tucked in nightly under a blanket on the floor. One particularly cunning Parasaurolophus had a habit of getting into a three-way fight with two other dinosaurs and then quietly walking away once the other two dinos were sufficiently busy fighting one another. It was a brilliant strategy. (At least in my five-year-old mind.)

I was never told that my interests were unfeminine—that I should prefer pink over blue, or arts and crafts over sports, or dolls over dinosaurs, or that I should want to grow up to be a wife and mom rather than a paleontologist or doctor. My activities and interests weren't limited because I was a girl. There were no gendered specifications as to *what I must be*. I didn't realize until much later how differently a lot of kids grew up, especially in conservative evangelical homes.[5]

It turns out that the Bible really says very little with any specificity about who we *must* be—and especially not in a way that's organized by gender. There are Jesus' commands that apply to everyone—*Love God with all your heart, soul, and mind, and love your neighbor as yourself*[6] comes to mind. And then there are verses—just a few verses, mostly in the apostle Paul's letters[7]—where we get some gendered instructions. But figuring out what to do with Paul's letters is always a complicated thing. He gives very different instructions to different churches. We find ourselves trying to sort out what was happening in these specific churches at specific times—trying to reverse engineer the situations Paul may have been speaking to.

After seminary, when I finally had time and energy to go back and read some of the female Christian authors my (mostly male) seminary professors hadn't assigned, I read Rachel Held Evans' delightful book *A Year of Biblical Womanhood: How a Liberated Woman Found Herself Sitting on Her Roof, Covering Her Head, and Calling Her Husband 'Master.'* Held Evans spent a year experimenting with what it would be like to take the Bible's commands for women quite literally—including many commands that even the most literalist of modern-day churches wouldn't dream of actually asking women to follow.

At the end of her year-long journey, Held Evans concludes this: "The Bible does not present us with a single model for womanhood, and the notion that it contains a sort of one-size-fits-all formula for how to be a woman of faith is a myth... Roles are not fixed. They are not static. Roles come and go; they shift and they change. They are relative to our culture and subject to changing circumstances. It's not our roles that define us, but our character."[8] Amen to that.

As most married people could testify, our ideas of *what we must be* change over time in response to the demands of life. Our expectations of one another, and the roles we play in marriage, shift in response to different challenges and surprises, different seasons of work and parenthood and empty nesting, different relationships and responsibilities. Job markets change, family situations change, living situations change. Couples might realize over time that he hates vacuuming less than she does, and she doesn't mind washing the car.

There is no good reason to put what Brené Brown calls "gender straitjackets" on ourselves or others. As Brown writes, "Until both men and women are allowed to be *who we are* rather than *who we are supposed to be*, it will be impossible to achieve freedom and equality."[9] Fullness of life is elusive until we learn to live authentically as who we really are. Dubiously biblical ideas about *what we must be* function as barriers to this authenticity.

In several places in the Bible, Paul dreams of churches that brim over with full, authentic life.[10] He writes of spaces of glorious freedom where all people, regardless of gender or other identities or social locations, exist together as equals— each person using their God-given gifts freely and graciously for the good of the community. No one controlling, no one subordinated, everyone free.

I imagine the ideal marriage being like this, too: a place where spouses learn together what their own gifts and passions are, what their partner's gifts and passions are, and how they can put all this together to be a strong team that loves each other, loves God, and loves the people around them as well as they can. A place where spouses operate according to their strengths and complement each other in their differences, which may or may not fall along the gendered lines various cultures draw. A place where each spouse gets to become more fully the person God made them to be, while also getting to help someone else do the same.

There is no *what he must be* or *what she must be*. I'm glad I didn't marry someone who thought there was. And I hope my poor freshman neighbor has long forgotten the Embarrassing Incident of the Unplugged Earbuds.

3

SOFT COMPLEMENTARIAN, HARDLY GRATEFUL

rom time to time, Faith Bible Church would host a "Theology Roundtable" on a particular issue. These were really not so much round table discussions as they were theology lectures with a bit of Q&A. A Faith Bible pastor or guest speaker would talk for an hour or so about a fun, light-hearted, non-controversial topic—like hell, or creationism, or violence in the Old Testament. (In the roundtable on violence in the Old Testament, I got to see a seminary professor just about get run out of the church for suggesting that perhaps, historically speaking, not everything in the Hebrew scriptures happened literally as written.)

At one point, there was a roundtable on women in ministry. This was where I learned the term "soft complementarian."

I sat and listened as one of our pastors explained some of the different viewpoints people hold. Some Christians are "complementarian," he said, which means they believe women and men ought to have different and complementary gender-based roles in marriage and the household as well as in church and ministry. Others are "egalitarian," which means they believe women and men are meant to be equal partners in marriage and church, with no gendered role distinctions or limitations for women in leadership.

And then he described a sort of middle category: "soft complementarianism." In contrast with—you guessed it— "hard complementarianism," "soft complementarianism" is the belief that there should be *some* gendered differences between men's and women's roles in the home and church—but not quite as much as "hard complementarians" believe. Faith Bible Church, our pastor told us, falls in this category.

Faith Bible's particular brand of "soft complementarianism" meant that female pastors were seen as legitimate—unless they preached regularly to the whole congregation. We had a female children's pastor, a female junior high pastor, and a female women's pastor, as well as a female volunteer counseling pastor. There were also plenty of other women on staff, working hard (and generally not getting paid enough for it) in various non-pastor roles, such as administration, communications, and finance.

If there was a gifted female preacher on the pastoral staff, the elders might ask her to preach occasionally (because God-given gifts should be honored and used)—but not very often, maybe two or three times a year at most (because women should absolutely not be determining the theological views of the church).

In *Fierce, Free, and Full of Fire: The Guide to Being Glorious You*, Jen Hatmaker tells a story about a time early in her career when she was invited to give a sermon at a megachurch. She was excited about the opportunity and had prepared extensively for it—in her words, "like it was my doctoral thesis."[1] Then, right before Hatmaker was about to speak, the (male) pastor stood up in front of the congregation and said this: "Ladies, you are in for a real treat today. Jen is here to share some stories with you, and I think you'll be tickled. And men? We will just peek over their shoulders this morning until we resume our sermon series next week."[2]

Yikes.

The male leaders at my church might not have said such egregious things so directly. But the same kind of attitude seemed to lurk behind the church's policies. Sure, women can preach, once in a while—but God forbid they might say something we find challenging, something that might cause us to see God differently. God forbid their words impact our theology, our practices, our lives. After all, we already know everything about God. Or if there is anything we don't know, surely we need a man to fill us in.

Faith Bible had an influential former pastor, let's call him Ted, who was well-known in certain conservative Christian circles. Former pastor Ted had been the main teaching pastor from Faith Bible's early days in the 1950s all the way into the 1990s, and long-time churchgoers looked back fondly on his leadership.

At the roundtable on women in ministry, I learned, to my surprise, that former pastor Ted actually did not have a problem with women preaching. He didn't believe it was in conflict with the Bible. Ted did not think that the scriptures prohibited women from taking greater leadership roles in his congregation. At the same time, though, he knew his people. He saw that the congregation was not ready to receive a sermon from a woman. And so, he did not invite women to preach.

Unfortunately, Ted wasn't wrong. The congregation really wasn't ready for it. I know this because I saw that people *still* weren't ready for it when I was there from 2006 to 2017. There were people in the congregation—both men and women—who refused to attend church on the rare Sunday when a woman preached. Meanwhile, the egalitarians among us kept attending church, week after week, dutifully listening to sermon after sermon preached by men and only men.

Former pastor Ted kept women out of the pulpit for many years, not because he believed it wasn't biblical for women to preach, but because he didn't want to split the church over it. He wasn't really against women preaching; he just felt it was more important to maintain the unity of the church.

When I first heard this, I thought it was kind of noble.

Now, I think it's a heaping pile of nonsense.

I'm sure Ted was doing the best he could, with what he knew, in the times he lived and led in. It's not about him. It's about all the church leaders out there, in all sorts of churches, who use unity as an excuse to trample over the gifts, well-being, and full equality of different subsets of their congregations— whether that's women, or people of color, or queer people, or anyone else.

As Maya Angelou famously said, "I did then what I knew how to do. Now that I know better, I do better." We can do better. Today's world demands more. Women deserve more, and the church deserves more.

There are things worth upsetting people over, things worth losing churchgoers over—things worth splitting churches over, if need be. And getting men in power to "take their feet off [the] necks" of the women in their congregations and "permit [them] to stand upright," as feminist and abolitionist Sarah Grimke wrote back in 1837, is surely one of those things.

Faith Bible's particular brand of "soft complementarianism" meant that, by design, they had no female elders. That is, there were no female members of the church board that was responsible for high-level direction and all sorts of important decisions. (I suppose this is the kind of policy you get when men in power are not quite convinced that women know "what's best for them," let alone what might be best for a congregation.)

The church's prohibition on female eldership meant, among other things, that I would sometimes hear church leaders lament about how hard it was to find people willing to serve as elders.

On the one hand, this made sense. It was a demanding role. People in Silicon Valley tend to work long hours and live busy lives. And it didn't help that elders were appointed for life, rather than a term of three or four years (as many churches do). It isn't hard to imagine that some elders might get a little tired over time, a little less excited and engaged than when they first started.

On the other hand, there was a clear solution to this problem—or at least a partial solution. There was an obvious way to double the pool of eligible people. But this solution was not one the elders were willing to adopt.

In faith communities where roles are limited by gender, women often find ourselves in a frustrating double bind. We want the good of the community. We want our churches to have leaders who are gifted, energized, involved, and committed. We want people of all genders—and all races, ages, and other identities as well—included in the decision-making body that is supposed to represent the whole church.

At the same time, any woman who expresses dissatisfaction with the status quo tends to be cast as power-hungry. I saw this happen to one woman at Faith Bible who tried to advocate for more egalitarian practices. Some (male) church leaders imme-diately became suspicious of her "agenda"—as if a human being who wants to be treated as a full human being is some-thing to be wary of.

The church had a hard time finding people willing to serve

as elders. But any woman who seemed interested was considered uppity, demanding, not to be trusted. Men who wanted to
be elders were acting out of noble and selfless interests,
wanting only to serve God and the church; women who wanted
the same thing were shamefully self-serving. Or, perhaps, no
one was supposed to have any particular leadership ambitions.
Everyone was supposed to be humble and look for ways to
serve others. But for men, this sort of humble service was
noticed and rewarded with respect and leadership positions;
for women, it was simply expected, regarded as the natural way
of things, not particularly associated with leadership qualities
or gifts.

When (usually male) church leaders talk about "soft
complementarianism," what I hear now is that they're asking
women to look around, compare our own subjections to other
women's greater subjections in "hard complementarian"
churches, and be grateful for the freedoms we have.

To be fair, as a young woman at my "soft complementarian"
church, there really was a lot to be thankful for. Many church
leaders and other men in the congregation were supportive of
me and of my dreams and gifts. They invited me to join leadership teams. They sought out and respected my perspective. For
a while I was part of a preaching feedback team, where we got
to read the pastors' sermon drafts and offer suggestions for
improvement. (As an Enneagram 1, this was right up my alley.)
Male church leaders welcomed me into the church's two-year
ministry training program, which they sometimes called "seminary lite"—and then encouraged me when I later expressed
interest in attending actual seminary. They hired me for college
ministry work without concerns about the appropriateness of a
woman leading and teaching college students. In those eleven
years, including two years on full-time staff at the church, I was

never sexually harassed, abused, or assaulted by any of the male church leaders. (I wish this went without saying. Unfortunately, though, these things are distressingly common.)

All in all, I could have spent my young adulthood in a much worse place. The church leaders were men who sincerely wanted to love God and love people, to lead the church faithfully. In a world full of embezzlers and liars and sexual harassers and power-hungry narcissists who call themselves pastors, the leaders at Faith Bible look like saints. They didn't intend to demean women with their "soft complementarian" views. Many of them just had a certain framework, more literal than logical, for reading scripture, and they were trying to do what they thought scripture required. Unfortunately, what they thought scripture required happened to look an awful lot like 1950s white suburbia.

I'm thankful for the good things about Faith Bible. But I'm not thankful for "soft complementarianism." Churches are either fully supportive of women, or they're not. They either encourage women to pursue whatever opportunities we find ourselves drawn toward, or they place gendered limitations on leadership roles for women. Women are either free to be completely who God calls us to be, or we are pigeonholed into a limited set of roles and functions.

In some ways, "soft complementarianism" is just a way of saying, *Yes, we think the Bible is patriarchal. Yes, we think God is patriarchal. And that is all The Way Things Should Be. But no, we're not bad people. We're not like those other complementarians over there—you know, the bad ones, the ones who oppress women and enable abuse.*

The message of "soft complementarianism" leaves women uncertain what to make of our possibilities. And it leaves men uncertain how to see women. Are we equal partners in life and ministry, fully human and gifted and complex? Or are we subordinate, less trustworthy, unsuited for leadership?

Complementarianism and egalitarianism are often both considered valid ways to see things. Plenty of women go to both kinds of churches. Women are often expected to be grateful for whatever crumbs men allow to fall from the table; we are often considered divisive and selfish if we advocate for full equality. I am no longer willing to be patronized in this way. I am no longer interested in calls for unity at the cost of the full acknowledgment of my humanity.

Churches *need* women to serve and lead in all the different capacities we are gifted and excited to do so. Churches that deny women opportunities to use our gifts miss out on so much.

I am grateful for many of the individual men I knew at Faith Bible, including those in leadership. But I am not grateful for the church's patriarchal policies and attitudes. I am not grateful for "soft complementarianism."

THE REDUCTION

4

STAND UP AND TURN AROUND

*F*or a tumultuous year in my mid-twenties, I served on staff with an egalitarian parachurch college ministry—let's call it Jesus Followers. One time, a local pastor reached out and asked our staff team if we would like him to speak at one of our weekly student fellowship meetings. This pastor, let's call him Aaron, had recently moved to the San Francisco Bay Area from overseas to start a new church plant. It seemed like a win-win situation: We got a free speaker, and Aaron got a free opportunity to spread the word about his fledgling church to fifty or so college students.

And so, one Wednesday evening, Aaron showed up to speak. He brought his wife with him, as well as a handful of other people from his church. Sporting super cool skinny jeans, Aaron stood up in front of our group of college students and began to talk. He spent the first couple minutes, as many guest speakers do, introducing himself and trying to build rapport.

In the course of these self-introductions, Aaron introduced his wife, who was sitting in the auditorium seats among the students. You could tell her apart from the rest of us (students and Jesus Followers staff alike) by her level of fashion. Her stylish stilettos were a far cry from the sneakers and flip flops that adorned the feet of most other people in the room. (Taylor Swift's commentary on footwear in her 2009 classic "You Belong With Me" comes to mind.)

Aaron told us he had been a youth pastor for a long time, and it's not exactly a lucrative career. There are a lot of things that are hard about it. But, he declared, God sees these sacrifices you make, and God rewards you for it all. How does God reward you? By giving you a "smoking hot wife." Aaron asked his wife to "stand up and turn around"—presumably so that our group of college students, who had come to hear a talk about Jesus, could see for themselves exactly how "smoking hot" Aaron's wife was, from all angles.

Believe it or not, in the moment, I didn't have a very strong reaction. I guess that's how you can tell that I was still mostly pre-feminist-awakening at this point in my life. I didn't really think twice about the "smoking hot wife," or the "stand up and turn around." I didn't know until many years later that the "smoking hot wife" thing is kind of a trope. (One friend read a draft of this chapter and quipped, "Do they teach pastors this in seminary?")

At the time, I didn't think the comment was particularly funny or clever, but I wasn't really offended by it either. I was more interested in seeing what Aaron had to say about life and faith and the Bible, and in seeing how students seemed to be responding to his message.

Aaron's statements about his wife didn't seem all that different to me, at first, from how other speakers would sometimes point out their spouse in the audience. It can be a sweet gesture. It shows the audience more of who the speaker is and who is important to them in their personal life. It honors the spouse for showing up and being supportive. Once, when I was in college, a female speaker pointed out her husband, asked him to wave, and said, "Isn't he cute?" I'll refrain from weighing in on his appearance, but as a couple they were indisputably cute. It was sweet that he was there to support her, and that she appreciated him being there—and that, after a few years of marriage, they still seemed to like each other. It was good for us mostly unmarried college students to have some relationship role models—#relationshipgoals, if you will.

So, I didn't think much about Aaron's "smoking hot wife" comment until our next staff meeting, when one of my colleagues announced that she would like to debrief something from the fellowship gathering.

I wasn't immediately sure what she was talking about.

I thought about the content of Aaron's talk, and how it had been a little different from the kinds of talks Jesus Followers staff tend to give. A little more authoritarian, perhaps—a little more along the lines of "these are *the* steps you need to take if you want to grow in your faith," as opposed to more of a story-telling approach, exploring models of what faith *could* look like and offering options for students to think and pray about.[1]

I also thought about how I had Googled Aaron's new church and ended up reading a handful of reviews on its Yelp page. In doing so, I stumbled on a review that said some positive things about the church and its pastor. Then I noticed that the name on the review was Aaron—no last name—and the picture was definitely of Aaron. He had left a review of his own fledgling church—including how great the pastor is—without revealing that he *was* that pastor.

My colleague went on, though, to share what she wanted to debrief. It wasn't the authoritarian-style teaching, and it wasn't the misleading Yelp review. Instead, she wanted to talk about Aaron's comment about his "smoking hot wife" and his request for her to "stand up and turn around." The whole thing had struck her as deeply offensive to women.

Ohh, I thought. *Yeah, there could be something there.*

My colleague explained that, in her view, Aaron was objectifying his wife, using her as a nice-looking prop rather than honoring her as a full human and an equal partner. Plus, Aaron had spoken as if pastors were always men, and women were nothing more than rewards for these (presumably heterosexual) men's good behavior. Not to mention the implication that a woman's physical attractiveness is her most important quality. And the implication that all pastors who want to be married will find a good (read: good-looking) partner, early on in life.

There were *so many things* wrong with what Aaron had said, so casually, as he began his talk. And I hadn't noticed any of them. My colleague had to spell it out for me—for all of us. As soon as she did so, though, I knew that what she was saying made sense. She was absolutely right.

"Stand up and turn around" is the kind of thing that's so *everywhere* that it almost starts to seem normal. But it should not be normal. Men treating women like objects rather than people should not be our norm.

In some ways, my conservative church community at Faith Bible felt like a refuge from all this objectifying nonsense. In most faith communities I've been a part of, men—especially male pastors—don't say stuff like that. Instead, they tend to be pretty careful *not* to (openly) notice or comment on a woman's body. I'm not saying all conservative churches are like this. But mine was.

On any given Sunday, with very few exceptions, I could feel pretty sure that most men at Faith Bible did not feel the need to assert their patriarchal dominance via leering or sexual comments. This was a luxury not at all guaranteed while walking around my neighborhood by myself ("Smile!"), or walking around another neighborhood with a female friend

("What's up, ladies?" "Not much. You?" "Just out here enjoying the view, heh, heh"), or shopping for groceries ("You look familiar. Did I see you at your boyfriend's the other day?").

If my young female body walking around or simply existing in the broader Bay Area world was an invitation to unwanted attention from male strangers, in church it was something else entirely. This "something else" was still public property. But in church it was public property of which to be wary—something dangerous and vaguely threatening. Something that needed to be eyed suspiciously and controlled carefully.

Not all men at Faith Bible treated female bodies in this way. Still, though, church leaders' anxiety about bodies and sexuality—which, in a male-dominated, heteronormative culture, means male anxiety about female bodies and female sexuality—had some implications for my life. Most people didn't go quite as far as the "Billy Graham rule"—recently made famous again by former Vice President Mike Pence—in which (powerful) men avoid one-on-one meetings with women entirely, on principle, to avoid any hint of impropriety. My church wasn't into that. I could grab lunch with a male colleague or meet a (male) elder for coffee to talk about our shared ministry, and that was all totally fine.

Other things, though, were less fine. For one thing, mentors were assigned in same-gender pairs. When I signed on for the church's two-year ministry training program, I was paired up with a woman who was (and still is!) a wise and amazing mentor, friend, human being, and person of faith. We took a walk together every other week for the entire two years. As we walked for an hour or so, I would tell her all the many things that troubled me in life, and she would listen well, ask great questions, and offer her perspective. I'm so grateful to have her in my life.

At the same time, though, when I was working full-time for Faith Bible in college ministry, I could have used a similar sort of mentorship from a pastor or elder—from someone who had an official leadership role in the church. There were pastors I respected and had good relationships with, including my supervisor, and I could go to them for advice about specific issues. But none of the pastors or elders was my designated go-to person for all-around mentorship—the kind of person who takes time to talk regularly about life and ministry, hopes and dreams, what I wanted in my career, what my gifts might be and whether I had opportunities to use them. Male anxieties about female bodies kept church leaders from assigning opposite gender mentor-mentee pairs.

I was very much in the "emerging adult" phase of life, trying to figure everything out: ministry, career, future plans, life in general—not to mention the confusing world of church politics and power dynamics. I could have benefited from an elder or pastor willing to meet with me regularly and help me navigate these things. I could have used a mentor who occupied the kind of position I might aspire to one day. But all of these positions were occupied by men. And this is one of the reasons they stay that way.

It may sound odd to speak of over-sexualization and mentoring in one breath. I hope it does sound odd—really, it should be odd. But this is what faith communities do when they insist on placing people in same-gender mentoring pairs. This is the reasoning behind it. So let's talk about that honestly. Maybe the icky oddness of it can help us reconsider.

It was clear to me that the male elders and pastors at my church were generally more careful around me than they would have been around a man in my place. Not me in particular—as if they thought *I* would try to seduce them—but me as an amorphous representative of the category "woman." That was, in effect, what I was reduced to.

I was subject to church policies that didn't impact my male peers. My supervisor, for example, always left the door to his office cracked open when we met there. This was fine, except when I wanted to discuss something sensitive—say, a tense conversation with a student leader, or (purely hypothetically) a sticky conflict with another churchgoer over meeting space. Sometimes you need a confidential place to talk with your supervisor. But, because I was a woman, nothing was really confidential. Anyone could walk by and overhear our conversation at any given moment.

Later on, I transitioned from full-time to part-time college ministry work, and the church hired another person to work with me. The powers-that-be decided that my new coworker and I would share an office. This was a little bit of a bummer, but totally understandable. I didn't expect that I, as a non-pastor, would always have the large corner office that I had to myself for a while—where I made myself a lovely personal prayer space, and where once I even took a nap on the floor during a particularly low point.

Now that I had a male compatriot, we were expected to share an office—but, goodness gracious, not *that* office. The corner office was much too private. My new colleague and I were asked to share a smaller space that was basically an awkward hallway between the main church office and a children's classroom. Its most salient feature was a huge window to the courtyard. Ain't no hanky-panky happening there. And also, no private prayer, and definitely no confidential conversations. (Or, for that matter, naps.)

I realize that, at their best, these sorts of policies are intended to protect women from the possibility of sexual assault. And there is certainly a place for safety measures that decrease the likelihood of assault on church grounds. But there is also a cost to limiting women's interactions with men across the board. There is a cost to assuming that every interaction between a man and a woman is fraught with sexual tension. This was not my reality. And I was limited by policies that assumed it was.

Aaron's "stand up and turn around" comment and Faith Bible leaders' tendency to tiptoe a little too carefully around female bodies were really two sides of the same coin. Both reduce women to object status. On the one side, women are to be celebrated, but only for our sexuality and visual self-presentation; on the other side, women are to be controlled, due to a fear of the power of that same sexuality and visual self-presentation. Both approaches make it difficult for women—and especially young women—to assert and express ourselves as fully human. Both mechanisms of reduction make it difficult for us to discover the complex and wonderful ways God made us, to figure out who we are and what God calls us to do in this world.

Neither the "stand up and turn around" comment nor the gendered anxiety at Faith Bible is remotely near the worst of what women experience in the way of objectification. But it's all connected.

Rebecca Solnit reflects on her experiences as a young woman in this way:

> You could be harmed a little—by insults and threats that reminded you you were not safe and free and endowed with certain inalienable rights—or more by a rape, or more by a rape-kidnapping-torture-imprisonment-mutilation, more yet by murder, and the possibility of death always hung over the other aggressions. You could be erased a little so that there was less of you, less confidence, less freedom, or your rights could be eroded, your body invaded so that it was less and less yours, you could be rubbed out altogether, and none of those possibilities seemed particularly remote.[2]

None of the stories I've told are stories of sexual assault. But it's all part of the same continuum. And it all matters. Daily experiences of objectification matter—even if none is worse than hearing a pastor talk about getting a "smoking hot wife" as a reward for good behavior. A little bit of objectification is still objectification. A little bit of reduction is still reduction. A little bit of erasure is still erasure.

I felt Solnit's words, when I read them, in my bones. I felt, as a young woman, "erased a little"—constantly subject to gendered restrictions and cautions, from sexualized compliments in one setting to sexualized-anxiety-driven measures of control in another. Possibilities for guidance and mentorship were erased a little. Possibilities for a private, confidential, prayerful office space were erased a little. Possibilities for my future at the church were erased a little.

My body may not have been subject to violence. But my sense of self, confidence, freedom, and rights—to use Solnit's words—was absolutely subjected to violence, and it was subjected all the time.

5

WHO'S LEADING THE COLLEGE MINISTRY?

J once had a conversation with a (male) stranger in the Faith Bible Church parking lot that went something like this:[1]

Male stranger (seeing me getting food out of my car, about to head toward the college ministry breakfast): "Hey, could you tell me, who's leading the college ministry these days?"

Me (with a friendly smile): "I am! What can I help you with?"

Male stranger: "No, I mean, who's *leading* the group?"

Me (smile fading a bit): "Right, that would be me…"

Male stranger: "No, no, I mean, who's the college *pastor*?"

Me: "Oh, well, Phil [not his real name] is the pastor who supervises me, but I'm the one responsible for leading the college group. Did you have a question about the group or anything?"

Male stranger: "Ah, okay, it's Phil. Great. Thanks!"

My new friend couldn't quite seem to wrap his mind around the fact that I—a young woman getting breakfast foods out of my car—was in fact the leader of the college ministry. This was how it often went during the two years I worked full-time at Faith Bible. So many people, from leaders to random dudes in the parking lot, assumed I knew less and did less than I really did.

I think about what John the Baptist once said about Jesus: *He must increase, but I must decrease.*[2] When (white male) evangelical pastors talk about this verse, they often take John's statement and apply it generically to all people everywhere. John the Baptist set a wonderful example for all of us to follow.[3] We all need to decrease so that Jesus might increase. More of Jesus, less of me. It sounds very holy and pious.

Unfortunately, it's also very problematic.

Pastors tend to speak as if diminishing ourselves is an equally important part of Christian spirituality for all people, across the whole spectrum of social locations. This way of thinking lacks sensitivity to the daily realities of women, people of color, queer people, and other marginalized groups—and this lack of sensitivity, in turn, worsens the inequalities that already exist in our world.

There was a pastor at Faith Bible—a person I like, respect, and look up to—who would often make self-deprecating comments and jokes, in staff meetings or otherwise. I appreciated his quick wit and his humility, and I think others did too. It took me a while to realize, though, that sometimes when I would make similar kinds of comments and jokes, they didn't work in the same way for me. The pastor-with-the-self-deprecating-jokes was male, older than me, and well-established in the structures of institutional power at our church. Given all this, I think his humble humor helped people feel comfortable around him rather than intimidated. It helped people see him as relatable and human.

I, on the other hand, was young, female, and not at all well-established in the church's leadership structures. I had to deal with things my male colleague didn't have to deal with—for instance, random men in the church parking lot not believing that I led the college group.

I was in a situation where I didn't really need to "decrease" more. I didn't really need to be any lower than I was already. I didn't need to reduce myself by downplaying my gifts or abilities. Doing so—through self-deprecating humor or otherwise—only hindered my ability to do my job, my ability to use my gifts fully and freely to lead the college ministry.

As a young woman fairly new to my job, with a lot of responsibilities but without the title of pastor—and all this in a church that did not fully approve of women in leadership—I needed to step forward and step up, bringing the best of my talents and passions into a challenging role. I needed to confidently embrace my own belonging and appropriateness in that role.

Well-meaning preachers can do a lot of harm by saying things like *we all need to decrease so that Christ may increase*—and, in so doing, communicating to the Black woman in the congregation that she should not ask for that raise she deserves, or telling the queer teen that they should just keep quiet about their identity so as not to make waves.

Not everyone needs to decrease, and definitely not all in the same way.

I led Faith Bible's college ministry full-time for a total of two years. My official title for the entirety of those two years was "College Ministry Intern."

That was fine by me when I first accepted the job. But as time went on, I settled into my role, and my responsibilities increased. Soon enough I found myself doing the same work most of the pastors were doing in their own areas of ministry: speaking and teaching, leading small groups and Bible studies, mentoring, organizing events, starting new initiatives, guiding a student leadership team, leading a volunteer team, and generally leading the ministry in every way.

One time, maybe halfway through those two years, one of the pastors casually asked if I might like a different title, one that better reflected the responsibilities I actually had. I said, "Thanks for asking, but I think I'm good. I don't think the college students know or care what my title is, so it doesn't really matter." He laughed and said, "Okay."

I had bought into the *I must decrease* mindset a little too much. I didn't care about things like titles. Or at least I didn't *want* to care. If I was holy minded enough, I wouldn't care...right?

For a while, this may have been true. But after two years of working full-time with pastor-type responsibilities and an intern title (and paycheck), I cut my hours down to part-time for a third year, and the church hired a second college ministry staffer. This was the male coworker, let's call him Trevor, with whom I shared an "office" that was more like an awkward hallway with windows the size of Alaska. When Trevor was hired, he and I were both given the title "College Ministry Director."

On the one hand, woohoo! A step up in the world!

On the other hand, Trevor was twenty-two years old and fresh out of college. His ministry experience was as a student Bible study leader on campus. By that time, I was twenty-eight, with three years of professional experience in college ministry, a couple more years of volunteer ministry experience, and the church's two-year ministry training program to boot. It didn't seem quite right for Trevor to be given a better title than I had had for the last two years.

No one would have admitted that any of this had to do with gender. And, in some sense, it didn't. I just happened to be in the wrong place at the wrong time. I happened to have been hired at a time when the church was using the "Intern" title a lot, and I happened to step down to part-time at a time when the church was transitioning toward using the "Director" title more broadly.

At the same time, I probably could have changed my title sooner if I had wanted to. A pastor asked. I said, "No thanks." And my lack of interest absolutely had to do with gender. Women are socialized not to advocate for ourselves. We are socialized to think only of the good of others—and to devote all our energies, often invisibly, toward this good.

No one seemed to wonder if perhaps it wasn't a great experience for me to be an "Intern" for two years and then suddenly find myself with a much less experienced male "Director" for a coworker. This lack of thought—about how things might come across to me and how I might feel my work was or wasn't being valued—was also absolutely about gender. Women are often expected not to care about things like titles and salaries. We are expected to decrease, and decrease, and decrease, and to accept this as the natural way of things.

As time went on, Trevor and I figured out how to lead the college ministry together. Then, just a couple months into working at the church, Trevor was invited to preach at the Thanksgiving worship service. It was a good opportunity, and I'm sure he did a great job. I was happy for him. But I was also a little confused. Preaching at a church service—even a special-occasion, smaller, less-formal service like Thanksgiving—was something that had never come up in any of my supervisor's conversations with me.

At the time, I didn't necessarily have a strong desire to preach. And yet, I was giving sermon-like talks to college students all the time. I had received instruction in preaching in the church's ministry training program, as well as in my previous experience on staff with Jesus Followers. It was something I very much would have been able to do. When my twenty-two-year-old coworker was invited to preach, I didn't love the fact that no one had ever invited me. It didn't feel quite right. And it did feel gendered.

I broached the topic—gently and tentatively, of course— with my supervisor, who replied, "Well, Trevor expressed interest in preaching, so I thought this would be a good opportunity for him. I haven't really heard you express the same kind of interest."

I thought about this. On the one hand, it's true. I never asked. I really had not expressed the same kind of interest Trevor had. On the other hand, it hadn't occurred to me that I *could* ask. It hadn't occurred to me that I could waltz into a new job—with a job description that involved teaching and leading college students specifically—and say, *hey, you know what I'd really like to do? I'd love to preach to the whole church sometime.*

I didn't really gain the confidence to consider myself a preacher until seminary. In my preaching classes there, I kept receiving surprisingly glowing feedback from classmates and professors. This hearty affirmation, which I didn't quite expect, helped me realize what my many years at Faith Bible had obscured from my sight. It helped me realize that I could, in fact, preach. And that I probably *should* be preaching—that it was a gift I should be using for the good of the church.

How could I have accurately discerned any preaching gifts I might have had, when women were only very rarely allowed to preach from the pulpit on a Sunday? How was I supposed to express interest in preaching if no one ever encouraged women to preach? How was I to know whether I had that interest? How could I have known that I could ask to preach, like Trevor did, when everything around me signaled that women should only be teaching small groups, or perhaps teaching other women or children?[4] How was I supposed to believe in my own potential enough to ask for opportunities, when my experience in church as a young woman was so entirely different from Trevor's experience as a young man?

A few years after I left my college ministry job, I was doing some apartment cleaning and came across a folder of old speaking notes from various talks I had given to the students at Faith Bible. I skimmed through a few pages and was struck by the thought: I was frickin' *good* at this.

It made me want to cry. Because it surprised me. And then I hated that it surprised me. *Of course* I had been good at my job —at least the teaching part of it, anyway. I *knew* that. And yet, I also didn't know it. There were just so many different ways, small and large, that I felt unappreciated for the work I was doing. And it made me feel—at least sometimes, in some ways —small and incompetent, when really, I was neither of these things.

It's easy to say, looking back, that I should have asked for a better title, or I should have asked for a raise, or I should have asked for different sorts of opportunities. But what would have happened if I had actually asked for these things? It would have been a trade-off. I might have gotten some of the things I asked for, and the workplace environment might have become a little more just and equitable because of it. But I'm sure there would have also been a backlash, a price (for me) to pay.

Other church staff may have judged. People may have thought less of me for failing to display the kind of *I must decrease* Christian humility they expected of everyone. Nobody likes a (Christian) woman who comes across as selfish, arrogant, or entitled—for doing, of course, the same things a (Christian) man does while coming across as responsible, confident, and competent.

There was also the constant fear that I would push things too far and be asked to leave. The thought of having to leave the community I loved—the community where most of my closest friends were deeply involved—was terrifying. I wish these fears hadn't had control over me. I wish I had been able to recognize that a community where I had to hold back was not actually a good community for me. I wish I had trusted that the people who were my true friends would keep being my friends, no matter what.

Mostly, though, I wish that things were different. I wish that all my fears weren't so very legitimate, because they absolutely were. I *was* being judged. And I was being judged differently from the ways a man would have been judged in my place. I would not have been looked upon kindly had I asked for a better title, higher pay, or more opportunities. I would have been asked to leave if I had pushed too hard for gender justice. The only way to continue in this environment was to participate in my own reduction.

For women in a patriarchal system, daily life is made up of ordinary instance after ordinary instance of being underestimated and underappreciated—and, if we suggest that this is happening in a gendered way, being doubted and dismissed. This can erode our confidence over time. Sometimes we come to underestimate and underappreciate ourselves.

This is the exact opposite of Jesus' impact on people who found themselves on the wrong side of the power structures of his day. Jesus lifted up people who had been cast down, centered people who had been marginalized, and restored to community people who had been rejected. He helped people know that God sees and loves them. He helped people see how valuable they are in God's eyes—and that it is through these eyes, rather than the belittling eyes of their oppressors, that they can see themselves.

John the Baptist played a particular role, in a particular time and place. He paved the way for Jesus. John's statement, *He must increase, I must decrease*, was not necessarily intended to apply to all of us—and certainly not in a gender-blind, color-blind, oppression-blind kind of way. Equal application of this sentiment across very unequal conditions only furthers a very un-Jesus-like kind of oppression. People on the underside of a patriarchal system, or any other structure of dominance, don't need to *decrease* any more.

I think Jesus longs to see us fully embrace our value as humans made in God's image. I think Jesus wants us to joyfully discover and use the gifts God has given us. I think he wants us to do all of this in the context of healthy relationships and loving community. I don't think Jesus wants to see oppressed people *decrease*. Rather, for people on the underside of power, Jesus increases when we increase. He empowers us to resist reduction. He delights in our wins. He rejoices in our growth. He longs for us to embrace the power God has given us and use this power for good.

I think Jesus wants us to find work, paid or otherwise, that we can look back on and think: I was frickin' *good* at this—and it just might have done something good in our world, too.

6

PREACHING IN JEANS

*E*ventually, once I moved to Southern California for seminary and got involved in a church there—let's call it Life Church—I ended up preaching every couple months. One Sunday morning, after I preached, a fellow female seminary student came up to me with something to say.

As usual, I hadn't thought a whole lot that morning about what I was wearing. I had thought *a lot* about the sermon—about what I wanted to say and how I wanted to say it. I had run through it a couple times at home that morning to solidify it in my mind, so as to leave more free brain space to connect with the congregation while I was preaching. I put on jeans and a reasonably nice shirt and headed out the door. It was a small church, after all—made up mostly of young adults, and pretty informal.

After the church service ended, my seminary classmate, who is a preacher herself, approached me and told me she appreciated my sermon. She then went on to say, "Sorry if this sounds weird, but I just wanted to say that I really appreciate your clothing choices. It's so liberating to see a woman preach in jeans!"

So liberating! I loved that.

But I also hated that this was the case—that female preachers still need this kind of liberation. I was in a church that placed no gendered limitations on women's roles, a church that believed in female leaders and female preachers. I had now become one of those female preachers. And I was learning that affirmation of women in ministry is not enough to make things actually equal.

At Life Church, our (male) pastor preached in jeans and a nice shirt all the time. I'm pretty sure he didn't think twice about any of it. I, on the other hand, had the nerve to do the same, and it was nothing short of "liberating" for my classmate. It broadened her image of what a female preacher could look like. It reminded her, in a world that keeps shouting at us otherwise, that the way a woman presents herself physically is not the most important thing about her.

Regardless of the opportunities that may be open to us, women are still subject to objectification, still subject to reduction. We are subject to others' constant appraisal of our clothing choices, and other aspects of our physical self-presentation, in a way that men are not. Things are not equal, and we are not free.

Years before I had any particular plans to preach, I remember reading a female pastor's blog post describing her (extensive) thought process in choosing what to wear. No detail escaped this pastor's attention as she embarked on her Sunday morning quest for the unattainably perfect combination of attractive (but not *too* attractive), modest (but not frumpy!), formal (but not inaccessible), and simple (but not so simple as to be distracting in its very plainness). And it had not escaped her attention that male preachers don't have to think about these things. Dress pants, respectable shirt, good to go.

At the time, I wasn't sure what to think. On the one hand, I totally got it. Everything a woman wears communicates something about herself. And people are always paying attention to a woman's appearance. On the other hand, could this pastor have been overthinking things just a wee bit? Can't a woman just be herself and wear what she likes and feels comfortable in? (The answer, of course, is yes and no. It's complicated.)

Clothing, for most women, is complicated—even for women who, like me, aren't that interested in it and would rather have it be as uncomplicated as possible.

A good clothing day, in my book, is one where I feel comfortable. I'm not thinking too much about what I'm wearing. My body doesn't attract unwanted attention from random men. I am approximately the right temperature for the day's weather. And I embody a more-or-less appropriate level of formality for the occasion. (That disheveled genius look, à la Albert Einstein or Mark Zuckerberg, is a luxury women don't have.) Beyond these basic things, I've never been one to pay much attention to self-presentation as mediated by clothing.

When I was in high school, this meant that I would wake up in time to shower (very important—I may not care much about clothes, but I do like to be clean), throw on jeans or sweatpants with my brain half-awake, eat breakfast (also very important), and make it to school for "zero period" jazz band at the crack of 6:30 am. I'd wake up when I had to, not a minute sooner.

For the most part, people didn't really seem to care. Then, at the beginning of my sophomore year, I became first chair clarinet in Wind Ensemble. A junior, let's call him Evan, was second chair. On the other side of Evan, in the third chair, sat a senior girl, let's call her Abby. I may have prevailed over Abby in the clarinet seating audition, but there was no competition when it came to fashion. Abby showed up to school every day with perfectly curled, perfectly dyed hair, complemented by perfectly done makeup and a wide array of trendy outfits.

Abby was also less than thrilled to find herself sitting in the third chair rather than the first one, upstaged by a sophomore. I don't remember her ever being mean to my face, but every now and then she would gossip quietly to Evan, just out of my hearing, about how the first chair clarinet player should *really* be putting more of an effort into her appearance. After all, I was the one sitting right up *front*, for *everyone* to see. (Whom exactly this "everyone" entailed, I was never quite sure. It wasn't as if our daily high school band rehearsals attracted an audience.)

Rather than critiquing my clarinet skills or anything else about me, Abby took offense at my makeup-less face, pony-tailed hair, and swim team sweats. (I knew this because Evan would turn right back around and tell me everything Abby told him.)

Abby did what we are trained to do: When a woman makes you feel threatened, you play the appearance card. Brittney Cooper writes about this in *Eloquent Rage: A Black Feminist Discovers Her Superpower*. She recalls that in college, on two separate occasions, she was winning an argument with a male classmate—and he responded by calling her unattractive. Cooper reflects, "When they were left without anything of substance to say, they both did what men learn to do when they can't dominate a woman intellectually—they berate her physically."[1] Sometimes people feel threatened by a woman's success —as if they are losing something, or fear losing something, because of it—and so they fall back on the old standby of saying nasty things about her appearance. In Cooper's words, this is one persistent "way [that] patriarchy shows up."[2]

I learned from Abby back in high school that men aren't the only ones who can invoke patriarchy in this way. Women do it to one another, too. I doubt Abby would have whispered the same sorts of nasty things about a male student in my place. If

Evan were first chair, who would have cared what he looked like? No one would have expected him to spend an hour on his appearance every morning.

Patriarchy takes a whole brilliantly diverse world of women and tries to criticize, mock, shame, and otherwise reduce us into a horrifyingly narrow mold of the One Right Way to be a woman: makeup, (blond) hair dye, trendy clothes, and all. (Not to mention fair-skinned and slender, both of which are whole other cans of worms.)[3]

In my college psychology classes, we learned about studies that show that women who wear more makeup are regarded more positively by others, male and female alike. Women who wear makeup are seen as more competent and capable at work. And—somewhat surprisingly, at least to most of us minimally-made-up students who put some stake in a "natural" look and assumed others did too—beyond the college bubble, the more makeup, the better.

This kind of thing makes me sick to my stomach. It also makes me want to say "screw the whole misogynist system" by wearing no makeup at all.

Different kinds of communities have different expectations for women's physical self-presentation, different understandings of what is appropriate and acceptable. Even within the realm of U.S. American evangelicalism, there are the go-getter, make-friends-and-influence-people kinds of Christians who think you should try to look your best as a sort of spiritual practice— after all, it's all part of giving the "outside world" a positive impression of what being a Christian is like. And then there are the Christians who go for a literal reading of Bible passages like 1 Timothy 2:8-10: "I desire, then, that in every place the men should pray, lifting up holy hands without anger or argument; also that the women should dress themselves modestly and decently in suitable clothing, not with their hair braided, or with gold, pearls, or expensive clothes, but with good works, as is proper for women who profess reverence for God" (NRSV). (When this passage came up in one of my seminary classes, a male classmate looked around the room at the women in our class, trying to assess whether any of us were actually following these instructions about not wearing gold. "Look around," he said. "How many women in this class are abiding by these rules? Maybe just Liz?" I pointed to my wedding ring and said, "Nope, I've got gold too!")

I have a bone to pick with both extremes—both the baptized version of what Abby used to say about me in high school band class, which is that Christian women need to be presentable and attractive to others to give a good impression of Christianity, and the literal interpretation of some Bible verses taken to mean that modern-day women are holy in inverse proportion to how much jewelry and makeup we wear. Like the overt objectification of "stand up and turn around" and the more subtle control mechanisms of same-gender mentor pairs and offices in hallways, these, too, are just two sides of the same coin. They are just different ways of judging and pigeonholing women—different ways of saying, "Well, God may have created all different sorts of amazing, strong, beautiful women, but *I* say there's only One Right Way for a woman to be."

Women will not be free until we refuse entirely to do what a patriarchal society keeps telling us to do. We will not be free until we refuse to look around and judge each other. We will not be free until we refuse not only to be reduced but also to reduce one another—and refuse especially to reduce women who are on the underside of other power structures like race, ability, sexuality, class. We will not be free until we are able to see the soul-deep, mind-deep, heart-deep, spirit-deep, breath-taking beauty in one another, totally unrelated to how any of us chooses to present ourselves physically. We will not be free until we know, really know, that there are four billion different amazing ways to be a woman on this planet right now, and counting.

The point is not to figure out *how* we should judge female appearance and self-presentation, but to learn—together, over time—to *stop* judging entirely. To make space for one another to be who we are and present ourselves as we wish. To choose, in a world that refuses to do so, to see past self-presentation to the whole, complex person inside—which is to choose to see one another the way God sees: not the outward appearance, but the heart.[4]

As we refuse to participate in patriarchy's reductive logic, we liberate one another as we liberate ourselves.

THE UNEVEN GROUND

7

AT THE CHURCH PICNIC

I remember standing around one afternoon at a Faith Bible Church picnic at the local park, chatting idly with friends and enjoying the August sunshine. The delightful smell of burgers wafted up from several grills. The potluck side dishes were plentiful. Everything was set for a fun afternoon.

Then, out of nowhere, my male friend, let's call him Ed, brought up 1 Timothy 2:8-15. This is the passage of scripture that includes the (in)famous line, "Let a woman learn in silence with full submission. I permit no woman to teach or to have authority over a man; she is to keep silent."[1] I just wanted to eat my burger and talk about the weather or how work was going. But Ed was asking questions—important questions. And I had some thoughts about what the answers might be. He wanted to know what I thought, so I reluctantly shared some of what I had been learning.

I don't remember exactly what I said. I may have talked about the context of these verses within the book of 1 Timothy. It seems that a group of particular women in a particular church are being "idle, gadding about from house to house; and...also [being] gossips and busybodies, saying what they should not say."[2] I speculated that, in this context, Paul[3] may simply want these particular women to be silent—in the sense of choosing not to gossip about others in harmful ways.

I may have mentioned some of the relevant translation issues. The Greek word for "authority" used in this passage is unusual in the New Testament, and it may mean something more like "usurping authority" or "domineering authority," not just any kind of authority. It also feels worth noting that Paul literally writes "I do not permit a woman" (rather than "I permit no woman," as the NRSV has it, for example)—which leaves open the possibility that he's thinking of one particularly domineering (or gossiping) woman, rather than all women everywhere.

Ed listened to what I had to say. Then he replied, "Well, I don't know about all that, but I feel like in the end I kind of have to just take the Bible at face value."

I think I suggested going back to talking about the weather.

I remember taking a week-long summer seminary class with some of my fellow Faith Bible Church staff. Our male professor was trying to demonstrate how we might set up a theological discussion among people at our churches. He had us do a sample discussion in the format he suggested. The sample topic? Whether women should be preaching.

We were split up into two sides arbitrarily, such that some people ended up representing what they actually believed, and others were asked to come up with the best arguments they could think of from the opposing view.

It was an interesting discussion format. But the conversation made my heart beat loudly and palms get sweaty in a way I doubt it did for any of the men in the room. It was a stressful experience, a loaded topic—and the brunt of the emotional load fell on the women in the room.

. . .

I remember eating breakfast one sunny morning at our yearly church camping trip. (Maybe I just don't like to be drawn into unexpected debates about women in ministry during otherwise pleasant mealtimes.) I was sitting at one end of a long set of picnic tables, when my ears began to pick up pieces of a conversation at the opposite end.

One of the church elders started discussing the topic of women in ministry with a female college student. The college student held her own, asking great questions and patiently hearing him out. I asked her later if the conversation bothered her, and she said it didn't. But it bothered me. I don't think the elder ever bothered to ask the student what she thought, and why. He just seamlessly assumed the role of the older, wiser, benevolent teacher, explaining to a young, bright, eager learner The Way Things Should Be.

In the evangelical church world, I could never quite be sure when these conversations would pop up. Gender roles in leadership are still a live topic of discussion in many churches. They're debated all the time—everywhere from youth groups, to casual conversations among friends, to seminary classes, to elder boards and pastoral ministry teams. Whether or not women should be subordinated to men is an open question—up for discussion at any time, often without warning.

For women, this can be exhausting. It was exhausting for me in my twenties, in my complementarian church. And it's still exhausting today. As with any discussion about a particular marginalized group, it's so much more wearying for people who are members of that group than for people who are not members of that group.

As a white person, I don't necessarily experience conversations about race and racial justice as exhausting. Sometimes it's energizing to feel like I'm advocating for others' equal rights, for the recognition of their full humanity. It's the right thing to do. It feels good. And if others think I'm wrong or foolish for doing so, at least they don't think I'm selfishly pushing my own agenda.

It's all these things for me because, ultimately, the conversation isn't about *my* full humanity, *my* personhood, *my* rights. It can stay on an intellectual level, discussing what makes sense. It can stay on a theological level, discussing what the Bible says and how Christian tradition has interpreted it. It can stay on an academic level, discussing the latest sociological and psychological scholarship. It can stay on a theoretical level, discussing what should or should not be. It can stay on a moral level, discussing right and wrong. The outcome of the conversation will likely not significantly impact my own rights and limitations, my own subordination or freedom.

For many people of color, on the other hand, as I understand it, these discussions are exhausting. They take a different kind of toll. Likewise for me when it comes to women in ministry. Every conversation takes a toll. I think these conversations will always feel that way for me; after all, they will always be, essentially, debates about my full personhood. They will always be debates about whether or not I am actually a complete adult human being created in God's image. The feeling that this is up for discussion is deeply demoralizing.

And yet, these conversations keep happening. And they need to keep happening.

They need to keep happening because many people and many churches still regard women in ministry with ambivalence at best. Many women inhabit faith communities whose policies still limit them from certain leadership roles, whose people are still divided in their minds and spirits. Avoiding the topic doesn't help anyone. We need to keep talking about these things.

But I think we also need to talk about *how* these conversations go down.

For one thing, could women get a heads-up before these conversations happen? Women deserve the chance to be mentally and emotionally prepared. We don't deserve to be blindsided while enjoying an innocuous-seeming burger or breakfast. We deserve to opt in and out of these conversations as we choose, rather than feeling coerced into talking about things we don't have time, energy, or desire to discuss.

I would also suggest that we stop having these conversations "for fun"—the kind of debates people have for sport, just because they like to argue. I'm not interested in talking about these things with people who are intellectually intrigued by the topic but have no intention of actually changing their views—and often very little recognition that their views might impact someone else's life negatively. I think of Julie Rodgers' words from her memoir *Outlove: A Queer Christian Survival Story*: "I wanted someone to acknowledge how shitty it was for people to debate about LGBTQ people as if it were a sport."[4] I hear that. And I feel the same way about women in ministry. Debating about us is not a fun sport. It involves real humans, real lives, real stress hormones coursing through bodies, real acknowledgment of (or failure to acknowledge) shared humanity.

Women's subordination was not an appropriate topic for a fun, casual "sample debate" in a classroom discussion. Our professor could have easily chosen something else. We could have debated, say, pews versus chairs, or communion every week versus once a month, or wine versus grape juice. Something, anything, that wouldn't take a disproportionate toll on the already-exhausted female ministers in the room.

. . .

One last memory: I was hanging out with a few friends after our weekly church young adults' group gathering, and we were joined by a male church planter our church was supporting. The topic of women in ministry came up. Before I had a chance to weigh in with my own views, the church planter started explaining to me that, in the world of theology, there are things contained in a primary circle, like Jesus' resurrection from the dead, and things contained in a secondary circle, like women in ministry. Christians should agree about the things in the primary circle but could disagree about the things in the secondary circle. He drew circles in the air with his hands. He kept on talking. I couldn't find the space or the words to tell him as politely as possible that I already knew everything he was saying.

I remember that moment with anger. Even if we ignore the mansplaining and pretend he was actually teaching me some-thing—who did he think he was, to place things that impacted my life more than his in a secondary, outer circle? Who gets to decide what is or isn't okay to disagree about? Women should be involved in that decision. I was the only woman in the conversation, and he had no interest in involving me. His deci-sion was already made. I could tell that anything I might have said to push back against it would be met with the same conde-scending smirk he wore on his face as he explained the whole two-circle scheme in the first place, assuming I was unfamiliar with it.

We can do better than relegating these issues to a secondary circle of not-really-essential things. If recognizing the full humanity of every person in a congregation isn't essential, I'm not sure what is. And, in all these conversations, we can do better than letting men talk and expecting women to listen and "learn." We can moderate these discussions to make sure women's voices are heard. We can refuse to allow men to dominate debates on questions that impact them less. Women's voices should be front and center when it comes to policies and attitudes that disproportionately affect our lives—just as queer folks' voices should be centered when it comes to things that impact them most, and people of color's voices should be centered in discussions that disproportionately affect them.

Women deserve to be in church communities that embrace our gifts gratefully rather than debating them endlessly. But when these debates do happen, we deserve to be heard. We deserve to be taken seriously. We deserve for the topic to be treated seriously, with an acknowledgment that it impacts real human lives drastically—an acknowledgment that it is not a fun topic for casual debate. And we deserve to be able to step in and out of these conversations as we choose.

I wish I had known these things at the church picnic. At the summer seminary class. At the breakfast table on the church camping trip. In the one-sided "conversation" with the church planter and his air circles. In all the times and places where the question of women's subordination rears its necessary but complicated head.

8

WHAT CAN WOMEN DO?

*C*onversations about women in ministry are often framed in terms of what women "can" or "can't" do. In an essay called *Sister, You Can Be Anything God Desires You to Be,* Kara Triboulet recalls a discussion in her theology class at her Christian college. When the professor opened up the floor and invited students to express their views on women in leadership, these are some of the things her classmates said:

> "I believe women can be in leadership, just not as pastors."
>
> "Allowing women to teach other women and children isn't limiting. At least they have a place to serve."
>
> "Women can be directors, but not pastors."
>
> "The Bible is *very clear*...women can't teach or lead men because men were created first. It's just the way God ordained it, and we all just need to accept that."[1]

All the language of "can" and "can't" sticks out to me like a sore, maddening thumb. Women can be in leadership, but they can't be pastors. Women can be directors, but they can't be pastors. Women can't teach. Women can't lead. That's just how God ordained it.

My beef with these statements is not just that I disagree with them. It's also that, regardless of my own opinions, these statements are simply not true.

It might sound odd to put it like that. But this is the truth: Women *can* be pastors. Women *can* teach mixed-gender groups of adults. Women *can* be in church leadership. If you look in the right places, women are doing all of these things. There are female pastors. There are women who teach mixed-gender groups of adults. There are women in church leadership.

I know women *can* do these things, because they already *are* doing these things.

When people make statements about what women "can" and "can't" do—unless these people have buried their heads so deep in the (quick)sand of their own conservative evangelical circles that they really aren't aware of any churches where women lead freely—I think what they really mean is something more like this: "I am not comfortable with women preaching." Or perhaps: "My understanding of gender roles in the Bible places women under men's authority."

They are not really speaking about what women are or are not able to do. They are speaking about their own comfort, their own familiarity, their own current understanding of the New Testament and its interpretation.

Fortunately—for women, and for anyone who thinks we're all better off when the whole church is free to express their gifts fully—the reality is that only God can decide what people "can" or "can't" do. God gives gifts. God puts passions in people's hearts. God gives people a desire to lead and serve in particular ways. Churches and denominations can choose whether or not to recognize, encourage, support, acknowledge, and embrace these things. But only God gives these gifts. Only God determines the *can* and *can't*.

This might seem like semantics. It might seem like verbal nitpicking. But I think it's important. It's important for the women involved in these discussions to know that the opinions of their classmates, colleagues, friends, professors, and pastors have absolutely nothing to do with what they *can* or *can't* do. These women *can* do whatever they believe God is calling them to do. It's just a matter of finding a faith community that supports this calling rather than opposing it.

People and churches can—and do—put up roadblocks that make women's journeys a thousand times harder. They can—and do—place limits on women's titles, functions, salaries, and more. They can—and do—look down on women, belittle women, laugh at women, exercise their patriarchal authority and express their misogyny in a million ways—some subtle, some blatant; some well-intentioned, some malicious.

They can—and do—do all these things.

But we, as women, have agency even in the midst of this. We can stay in patriarchal contexts and work for change. We can leave. We can find church communities that impose no gender-based limitations on us. We can find spiritual homes that greet our gifts with gratitude rather than a suspicious side-eye.

We can say, *you may have your opinions about what I should or shouldn't be doing, and that's fine for you; but as for me, I* can *preach, and I* can *teach, and I* can *lead.*

These days, when someone says, "I don't think women can lead," or "I don't think women can preach," I want to press them to be more precise. What exactly are they trying to say? There are (at least) a few possibilities.

Maybe they feel uncomfortable following a female leader

or listening to a female preacher. If so, that's something we can talk about. We can explore what exactly makes them feel uncomfortable. Maybe they grew up in a church without female leaders, and that makes it hard to imagine what it might be like to follow one. Maybe the pastors they look up to have expressed discomfort, and they hesitate to form a different opinion. Maybe they had a bad experience with a female leader, or they carry baggage from their relationship with their mother or another important woman in their life.

Or, maybe it's more of an aversion to change. Maybe their church has always done things a certain way, and they don't see a need to try something different. I get that. Change is hard. It's often unpleasant, even scary. Change involves loss—even just the loss of a kind of comforting familiarity. These, too, are things we can process together. We can explore our feelings about change and why we might be resistant to it. We can also talk about some of the ways the status quo may not actually be working as well as it seems. We can talk about some of the reasons change might be worth the struggle and loss.

Or, for others, maybe it's all about the Bible. Maybe they've been unable to find a way to read scripture that affirms women in ministry. Maybe they don't really have a personal issue with female leaders, but they aren't sure how to square their egalitarian intuitions with what scripture says about women. If so, we can talk about that. There are plenty of relevant resources for biblical interpretation.[2] People might not have been exposed to these resources, and their conservative pastors may act like they don't exist. But they do. If the issue is biblical interpretation, there are all sorts of things we can talk about. The Bible is full of women who *can* lead and preach and teach and minister;[3] we can talk together about how we might reconcile this with the handful of passages that seem limiting. We can dig deeper into questions of culture and context and see what we might find together.

There is no shame in acknowledging these kinds of questions, feelings, thoughts, and hang-ups. We can talk about them. But when we fail to acknowledge them—when we hide behind *can* and *can't*—it's impossible to have an honest conversation about the real issues at play.

Conversations about women in ministry—about whether or not women should be subordinated to men in the life and leadership of faith communities—are an ongoing reality. They can be exhausting, frustrating, contentious, church-splitting, friendship-breaking, demoralizing. But as long as religious communities continue to exclude women from leadership, these conversations will continue to happen.

I hope to see a day when women's leadership is no longer up for debate. Until then, though, women deserve for these discussions to be courageous ones, fair ones, honest ones. We deserve conversations that get at the real issues involved, the real things that keep some Christians from fully supporting women in leadership. We deserve better than language that subordinates by implication before the discussion has even begun. We deserve better than the vague authoritarianism of *can* and *can't*.

9

SOME WEIRD STUFF ABOUT BLOOD MOONS

*O*nce, while I was on staff at Faith Bible, I was invited to attend an elders' meeting. It was one of those random things where I happened to be tangentially connected to someone who was visiting from out of town and speaking to the elders, so I was invited to sit in and listen. Unrelatedly, at the same time, the elders were looking for a new high school pastor, and they were far along in the interview process for a particular candidate. And so I found myself sitting around a big table in a Sunday school classroom with this group of powerful men, listening to them discuss whether or not to make a job offer to this candidate—let's call him Matt. I got to hear about the interviews the elders had done with Matt, everything they learned about him, and all the great things he had to offer— and also some of the things they weren't totally sure about.

I listened with fascination as the elders talked things over. Most of the conversation was what you might expect. Some elders mentioned things they liked from Matt's application and from their (many) interviews and other interactions with him. Others had been present at a recent youth group meeting, where Matt had given a sort of try-out talk (no pressure!), and they expressed a positive impression of his interactions with the teens. Matt had a lot going for him.

Then someone mentioned that, in one of the interviews, Matt had said something about blood moons—something they didn't really understand. Others agreed—yes, come to think of it, at a couple of points in the interview process, Matt had said "some weird stuff about blood moons." Apparently, Matt seemed excited about this blood moon stuff. Did anyone understand what he was talking about? No, not really. Was it a big deal? Nah, probably not.

And the discussion moved right along. The elders went back to talking about Matt's many promising qualities that could make him a wonderful high school pastor.

I didn't really know what the blood moon thing was, either. But I went home and did some Googling. It turned out to be a fringe end-times theory, promoted by a couple of pastors who wrote some books about it a few years ago. The general idea was that we were in the middle of four lunar eclipses, coinciding with Jewish holidays, which marked the arrival of the end times.

Never mind that Jesus said, *no one knows the day or the hour*.[1] Or that *so* many people throughout history have predicted the time of Jesus' second coming and have been wrong. Never mind that the people who do these things are often scary cult leaders who promote a lot of other messed up stuff and leave a wake of havoc behind them—or that the people who follow them tend to be vulnerable and easily misled.

These are all serious things. These are all things that could have come up in the elders' conversation about good ole Matt and his blood moons. But they didn't. The elders didn't discuss what, if anything, Matt's fringe beliefs might imply about any other aspects of his life or ministry. It seems to me like the sort of thing that might warrant further conversation. It could have been worth digging a little deeper. Would Matt want to talk about end times prophecies with the teens all the time, since he was so excited about it? People tend to get excited about the things their leaders are excited about. Would the high school students get the idea that following Jesus was all about trying to predict his second coming—rather than about, well, following his actual life and teachings? Would some of the more skeptical teens think the blood moon stuff sounded bonkers and see it as another reason to want nothing to do with Christianity?

For that matter, what other cult-like beliefs might Matt buy into that didn't come up in the interview process? What about other sorts of conspiracy theories—perhaps dangerous political ones? Was there something about Matt's personality or background that made him prone to believing these things?

The elders treated Matt's blood moon interest like a curious but harmless personality quirk, like running ultramarathons or growing carnivorous plants. (*Well, that's unusual, but it seems fine...I don't think I would do it myself, but I guess I get the appeal.*) And they moved forward in the hiring process.

Blood Moon Matt ended up turning down the job offer, so I'll never know how all of this would have played out. At the time, I found the whole thing mildly annoying and a little disconcerting. But Blood Moon Matt didn't end up joining the church staff, and I moved on to worry about other things.

Some time later, the elders at Faith Bible Church began discussing whether they might offer me a pastoral staff position —like the one they offered Matt, but for college ministry. As an early step in this process, they asked me for my thoughts on several topics: women in ministry, LGBTQ+ affirmation, the charismatic movement, social justice, and hell. You know, just a casual assortment of super chill, low-stakes, non-controversial things.

It was clear that, if I wanted to be offered the job, I would need to step through these five minefields very carefully.

Instead, I went merrily skipping along, writing down some thoughts and doing the best I could to be totally honest. I wrote up some reasons why I believed women should not be restricted from leadership roles in church. I outlined some reflections on charismatic Christianity, some of the things I thought about hell, and some of the reasons I thought Christians should absolutely care about social justice.

And, last but not least, I wrote down some thoughts about the Bible and same-sex relationships. I wasn't (yet) fully affirming. I was just unsure. I was uncomfortable teaching college students that same-sex relationships were straight-up sin, when the Bible didn't actually seem all that clear about it. I wrote down some of the reasons I thought the scripture passages often used to condemn gay relationships may not actually apply to modern-day, loving, committed couples.

This turned out to be a deal-breaker. Even my *uncertainty* about LGBTQ+ affirmation was enough to stop the conversation from moving forward.

There were plenty of other areas in which I thought differently from most of the elders. I was told, for example, that some elders had raised concerns that my "ministry was motivated too much by social justice." (Yes, thank you, I will take that as a compliment.) But this wasn't the deal-breaker. Likewise, with women in ministry—the elders were willing to recognize that my position was a legitimate one, even though many of them disagreed with it.

But LGBTQ+ affirmation fell in a different category. For many of the elders, it was not something Christians could legitimately disagree about. It was certainly not something a pastor should express uncertainty about. For them, the Bible was clear, and we needed to stand by it doggedly.[2]

As these conversations unfolded, I thought sometimes of Blood Moon Matt. I remembered how his "weird stuff about blood moons" barely provoked a second glance from the elders. My uncertainty about same-sex relationships, on the other hand, was an immediate deal-breaker.

It felt like a bit of a double standard.

Of course, it wasn't just about gender. But gender was definitely involved.

I think of Ijeoma Oluo's reflections on race: "Something can be about race, and that doesn't mean that it is *only* about race."[3] White people sometimes argue that people of color say things are about race when they're really more about class, or gender, or something else. But, as Oluo writes, something can be about race, *and also* about many other things. Just because there are other factors involved in the mix—which there usually are, because everything is interconnected—doesn't mean that race isn't an important part of it.

Analogously, the double standards I experienced absolutely had to do with gender—even when they also had to do with other things. Whatever else they were about, they were almost always *also* about gender. What is or isn't a deal-breaker for a pastoral candidate? Which is a bigger red flag: a male pastoral candidate's enthusiastic belief in fringe end-times prophecies, or a female pastoral candidate's uncertainty about same-sex relationships? Apparently, the latter.

On the one hand, this makes sense. It's about which issues are highly debated, visible, and controversial—which issues have been irrationally elevated to the status of a litmus test for whether someone takes the Bible seriously.[4] It's also about a conservative church wanting to hold onto its uniqueness, keep itself separate from the surrounding liberal Bay Area culture, and help Christians live lives that feel really distinct. It's about holding on to a stable sense of identity in a rapidly changing world.

On the other hand, it doesn't make any sense at all. What were the actual ministry implications of these two potential deal-breakers—of Matt's blood moons, and my uncertainty around LGBTQ+ affirmation?

Blood Moon Matt could have infused a whole generation of young people with some false ideas about the end times. He could have led them on wild goose chases for prophecy fulfillment. He could have set an example that encouraged teens to glom onto other sketchy fringe groups, or to buy into dangerous conspiracy theories. (Certainly there are plenty of those to go around.)

Consider my uncertainty about LGBTQ+ affirmation, on the other hand—focusing on the practical ministry context, on the real lives of real college students at Faith Bible. What would the consequences be? Imagine a group of Christian students whose pastor simply isn't interested in telling them that same-sex relationships are wrong. LGBTQ+ students might feel more loved and accepted, just as they are—more able to be fully themselves in the community. Fewer LGBTQ+ young people might experience the depression, anxiety, and suicidal ideation that often come from being told there's something deeply wrong with you. Non-LGBTQ+ students might benefit from knowing a Christian leader who thought differently from the dominant conservative voices of evangelicalism. Does anyone really benefit when church leaders pretend there's only one way to think?

Maybe it's overly optimistic to think we could have made it work. But I would have been willing to try.

. . .

To the church leaders, though, the possibilities for Blood Moon Matt were much more promising. No doubt their belief that women should not set the theological direction of the church had something to do with all of this, however subconsciously.

Church leaders would often talk about how our church had, or wanted to have, a "big umbrella" when it came to theology. They would talk about how there are many things we can disagree about and still remain in community together. There is room for people who think all sorts of things, as long as we can agree about the main things. (Remember the air circles?)

Don't get me wrong—I like a big umbrella. But, at Faith Bible, sometimes it felt like this umbrella was only "big" in one direction. Its conservative side splayed out as far as the eye could see, but the liberal side was cut short after a centimeter or two. People could believe and teach as many patriarchal things as they liked, even things that were too patriarchal for many of the elders' tastes. But leaders were constantly on guard against anything that might possibly be perceived as drift in a liberal or progressive direction.

They had, correctly, sniffed me out as someone moving in that direction, and they cut off the potential for a long-term working relationship. With Blood Moon Matt, in contrast, they caught a glimpse of some differences and said, *Okay, no worries, this seems fine. No big deal. Let's focus on all Matt has to offer and the things we have in common.*

It was not *only* about gender. But it *was* about gender.

It was about (male) leaders being more likely to downplay a male candidate's questionable views.

It was about my empathy, as a woman who faced unequal treatment because of my gender, for my LGBTQ+ siblings' struggle for equal rights.

It was also about an idea, in some leaders' minds, that egalitarianism is a "slippery slope" leading to LGBTQ+ affirmation. There are plenty of Christians who have egalitarian views when it comes to women in ministry but conservative views when it comes to LGBTQ+ affirmation. But it is also true that a certain logic links egalitarianism with LBGTQ+ affirmation. Conservative Christians, when they argue that the Bible prohibits same-sex relationships, often find themselves going back to Genesis 2 and claiming that Adam and Eve were given different gendered roles in their relationship.[5] They then contend that same-sex marriages aren't valid because same-sex relationships don't have these different roles. Thus, it makes sense that egalitarian heterosexual marriage—between a woman and a man who consider themselves equals, and whose roles in the marriage are based on interests and gifts rather than gender—is indeed threatening.

Rebecca Solnit addresses this in her essay *In Praise of the Threat*. "The term 'marriage equality,'" Solnit writes, "is ordinarily employed to mean that same-sex couples will have the rights different-sexed couples do. But it could also mean that marriage is between equals. That's not what traditional marriage was. Throughout much of its history in the West, the laws defining marriage made the husband essentially an owner and the wife a possession."[6] Marriage equality threatens this history, this tradition, this worldview—a worldview that carries forward into complementarian relationships that would never describe themselves as between owner and property but nonetheless insist on gendered roles and power differentials.

Women who see ourselves as men's equals—including women who have the nerve to seek pastoral ministry positions —are, by nature, a threat to a certain conservative Christian perspective. Simply by existing, I was a threat. And so I walked into our hiring conversations with dramatic, highly visible question marks over my head. Was I really one of them? If I had already indicated that I believed in women's equality in a church that did not support this, would I toe the party line on other matters? My gender was a sneaky unspoken complicating factor that influenced everything.

Blood Moon Matt and I were never on a level playing field. And sure, it was about all kinds of things—including the explosiveness of conversations around LGBTQ+ affirmation in evangelical churches. (As Barbara Brown Taylor writes, "If there were anything simple about these debates, they would not still be going on."[7]) It was about a lot of complex things. And it was *also* about gender.

It was about double standards in the hiring process. It was about who gets the benefit of the doubt, and for what. It was about how far that big umbrella extends, and in which direction. It was about who gets to participate in shaping the theology of the church. It was about a woman's aspiration to a pastoral position setting off red flags in the minds of the church leaders: grill her more thoroughly, be more careful to make sure she's one of us, that she's conservative enough for us. It was about the heightened threat level evoked by a woman who dares to disagree.

THE DISMISSAL

10

IS IT PERSONAL?

*W*hen the Faith Bible Church leaders decided that my unwillingness to declare gay relationships sin was a deal-breaker for a long-term pastoral position, they instead offered one more year of working in college ministry: a "year of mutual discernment."

On the one hand, this was a nice gesture. When I told a college minister in a different faith community what was going on, he less-than-half-joked that he was surprised the elders didn't run me out on the spot. The leaders at Faith Bible were open to continuing to talk about things.

On the other hand, the "year of mutual discernment" felt like a polite churchy way of saying, *You can keep working here as long as you try really hard to realize the error of your ways. And if you don't succeed at changing your mind within a year, you can't work here anymore.*

As far as I could tell, the discernment was not actually mutual. The church leaders knew their own position and showed no signs of reevaluating it. They didn't seem to be studying the relevant Bible passages or talking with and listening to queer people. They didn't seem to be reading any of the many helpful books that had come out (so to speak) in recent years, like Matthew Vines' *God and the Gay Christian*, or James Brownson's *Bible, Gender, Sexuality*, or David Gushee's *Changing Our Mind*. They didn't seem to be reading the stories I was reading about LGBTQ+ people's horrifically traumatizing experiences in churches. It felt like the church leaders wanted me to keep thinking about things until—if I wanted to keep my job—I came around to their view.

I did keep thinking about things. Unfortunately for my job prospects, though, the more I thought—and read, and studied, and prayed, and listened to people, and read and studied and prayed and listened some more—the more LGBTQ+ affirming I became.

I agreed to keep leading the college ministry for another year, but not as a year of supposed "mutual discernment." I told my supervisor that the discernment didn't quite feel "mutual." But I wanted to stay. I didn't want to abandon the new fellowship group I had just started at Stanford. I wanted to provide some sort of continuity for students as the church searched for someone to take my place. From what I had seen, these searches often took many months; I didn't want to leave the college group leaderless in the interim. I asked if I could stay for another year to help with the transition, reducing my hours from full-time to part-time while starting seminary. The church leaders agreed.

To my surprise, my replacement appeared quickly, in the form of "Trevor"—who, office-with-all-the-windows aside, was a wonderful colleague and very capable of leading the college ministry without me. I started to think that maybe I didn't need to stick around for the whole third year. I would no longer be leaving the college group adrift or abandoning the new ministry I had started.

Then November 8th, 2016 happened.

In all my white liberal naïveté, I was shocked and shaken to the core. I began election night ready to be distressed and depressed that it was anywhere near a close race. I ended that night in disbelief, mourning, and horror.

I went to work at church the next day to find many of the office staff, mostly women and people of color, in a similar state of anguish and grief—and many of the (mostly white male) pastors walking around smiling and going about their business like nothing world-changingly awful had just happened.

I was shocked and shaken once again when I learned just how many white evangelicals voted for Trump. And then for a third time when I learned that there had been pushback from people at my church when one of the pastors—the one woman of color on our pastoral staff—led the congregation in prayer the Sunday after the election and expressed sympathy for all those in mourning or fear because of the results. That's all she said. She didn't even say that she was one of those people. She didn't say that their mourning and fear was justified. She just expressed sympathy, asking God for comfort on their behalf. And people didn't like it.

Up until that point, I don't know if I had fully allowed myself to imagine that there really might be Trump supporters in my faith community. When I talked with church friends about the election, they were all either voting for Clinton, abstaining, or voting for third-party candidates. I'd even talked with one church leader who told me, *I'm not telling many people this, but I'm voting for Hillary.*

The 2016 U.S. presidential election changed something in me. After the election, I felt I could no longer keep quiet about the human rights issues that mattered to me. Up until that point, as a paid ministry leader on the staff of a conservative church, I had felt like I should try to be somewhat neutral—offering forums for discussion without taking controversial sides, helping students think through things without weighing in with too many of my own unasked-for opinions.

After the election, this no longer felt tenable. I craved the freedom to speak what I really thought. I didn't want to feel like I had to hold back to keep the peace. I didn't want to muzzle myself in order to faithfully represent an institution that in many ways no longer represented me.

So, because of all this—and also because Trevor was hired so quickly and was so capable, and also because I just kept becoming more and more LGBTQ+ affirming the more I thought about it—I decided to leave my job. I stepped down in December 2016, after the first quarter of my third year in college ministry at Faith Bible.

When I stepped down, I thought the college students deserved to know why. And I was no longer on staff at the church, so I could speak freely...right? I wrote a letter and emailed it to the college ministry list. I told the students that, after a lot of thought and study and prayer, I had become LGBTQ+ affirming—and that, while I loved the church, this was why I wouldn't be able to work there long-term.

My hope, beyond practicing a basic degree of transparency, was that the letter might open a door to fruitful conversations with any students who wanted to talk about these things but weren't sure if it was safe. I hoped my openness might spark deeper thinking for students who wanted to sort out their own views, and I offered myself as one person to talk to in that process. And I hoped that students who identified as queer but felt stuck in the churchy closet might find my affirmation encouraging—that in some small way it might help them feel less alone, less afraid, less rejected.

Some of these things happened. I ended up having some great conversations with students, the kinds of conversations we hadn't been able to have before. Some students were LGBTQ+ affirming themselves; others weren't sure; others just wanted Christians to be free to have different perspectives on complex questions. Several students expressed appreciation for my words and stance. Good things came out of it. (And if nothing else, *I* certainly felt better—freer and more honest.)

Then, some of the church elders read the letter.

They were less than enthusiastic. My supervisor, "Phil," who was also an elder, asked me to meet with him along with another pastor, let's call her Vicky.

Phil invited Vicky out of kindness toward me, I think. I had mentioned at one point that sometimes it's intimidating to be a young woman, without much institutional power, in a room full of older men (the elders) with all the institutional power in the world. It can be difficult to articulate a minority viewpoint in that context, especially when these men are so sure of themselves—so willing to exercise the full weight of their numbers and their churchy authority to try to convince me they're right about everything and I'm just out in left (pun intended) field. We had talked about these things, and so I think Phil was hoping to make the conversation less intimidating for me by inviting a female pastor to join us. It was a nice thought.

Unfortunately, though, the femininity Vicky and I shared did not even begin to bridge the ideological divide between us. She was an outspoken advocate for women's equality in the church but firmly on the non-affirming side of LGBTQ+ questions. Early on in our conversation, Vicky suggested that I was "undermining the pastoral leadership" of the church by expressing a different viewpoint and inviting students to talk more about it with me. It was a rough conversation.

At another point, Vicky asked, "Liz, is this personal for you?"

In the seconds that followed, my brain did a lot of processing. *Liz, is this personal?* What the hell did that mean?

My first thought: Is she asking if I'm gay? I had just married my husband, Ken, in this same church building, no more than a couple months before. She couldn't be asking about my sexuality...could she? And even if she was—because sexuality can be complicated, and just because you're married to a person of the opposite gender doesn't mean you aren't also queer—what kind of a question is that? How was it relevant to the conversation? The implication: Maybe I just care about these things because they affect me personally. Otherwise, it makes no sense to take such a subversive stance against everything the church teaches.

My second thought: Maybe she isn't asking about my own sexuality so much as whether I have a gay family member. Maybe she half-expected a teary-eyed, *yes, I was raised by two moms, and they mean the world to me, and how could their love possibly be wrong in the eyes of God because they're perfect and wonderful?* Or a weary-eyed, *yes, my sister is gay, and she's not a Christian anymore because the church wouldn't accept her, and it breaks my heart.* The implication, in that case: Love clouds judgment. Love is inferior to reason and must bow down to it. Maybe if I had a close family member who was queer and my judgment was clouded by my love for them, it would explain my otherwise inexplicable rebelliousness.

My third thought, and this one came as I reflected on the conversation later: How is it *not* personal for you? How were these two pastors not personally impacted in some way by the pain the church inflicts on queer people? Their job is to care for people in God's name. I thought, *if you were paying any attention at all to queer people, if you listened to their stories and the trauma they have endured, it would be personal for you, too.*

.   .   .

Liz, is this personal for you?

With this one question, Vicky and Phil dismissed my views entirely. They tore legitimacy from the long intellectual, emotional, and spiritual journey I had been on, as I slowly came to realize that the Bible actually did not speak against gay relationships in the clear and condemning way I had thought it did. They took my study and prayers and anguished processing and threw it back in my face—as though, if I just studied and prayed and processed more, or better, then surely I would see things as they do. So this must be personal for me.

All I could do in the moment was venture, stammeringly: "Um, is it personal in the sense of having a close family member who's gay or something? No, not really. I mean, I have friends who are, and they matter to me, so I guess it's personal in that sense."

I've thought about this a lot since then. And I've decided I'm no longer interested—if I ever was—in a Bible, a theology, a church, a faith, that is *not* personal.

None of us actually reads the Bible objectively. Our interpretations are always affected by our own pasts and personalities and cultures and feelings and experiences. More than that, though, I don't know why we would *want* to read the Bible in a way that isn't personal. That doesn't sound very relevant or interesting at all.

Or rather, I do know why people would want that. It's a way of asserting power and control. *Read the Bible like me; otherwise, you're not a real Christian. You're out. I have the power to kick you out, and I will use it if you do not conform to my way of seeing things.* This is patriarchy; this is white supremacy; this is spiritual abuse.

White male supremacist discourse often aspires to the (unachievable) ideal of purely intellectual discussion, where

emotions are checked at the door. It assumes that white men—
and only white men—are capable of truly rational, objective,
unbiased thought. White men are the singular, special kind of
humans who do not see the world from a particular, biased
perspective.

I now see this mindset as wrong in at least two ways.

First, white men, like all humans, do indeed see the world
with a particular set of biases and blinders. (Often, in their
case, a particularly damaging set.) They are not objective. They
have only been conditioned by patriarchal white supremacist
culture to believe that they are. For white men, it takes a lot of
learning (and unlearning) to start to see and divest from the
ways they were taught history that centered people of their race
and gender, the ways seminary reading lists are dominated by
theologians of their race and gender (and thus so are pastors'
sermons), the ways television shows and movies consistently
feature people of their race and gender as heroes. White men
are not cultureless or bias-less, and their belief that they are
has set the stage for all sorts of oppression and abuse.

Second, the ideal itself is a false one. Not only do white men
fail to live up to the stated goal of unbiased, unemotional ratio-
nality, but why is this considered the standard in the first place?
Pure intellectualism that dismisses any consideration of human
compassion or feeling is terrifying. There is no actual value in
trying to push emotions out of important conversations and
decisions. Humans process things on many levels—including,
very powerfully, our feelings and our gut. We need our
emotions to help us make holistically good decisions. Our intuitions are important. Trying to remove emotions from group
discussions only results in these emotions getting pushed
below the surface, never actually being processed in a healthy
way.

. . .

I used to be offended when men said or implied that women are more emotional than men, and, for this reason, we aren't the best people to lead a church. Who did they think they were, to make such sweeping generalizations based on gender? Did they really believe that men don't have emotions and women can't think?

Now, I'm still offended—but not just at the unfair and untrue stereotypes. I'm also offended that emotion and intuition are devalued and dismissed as avenues for engaging with scripture, God, and one another, when they're actually essential. Who do we think we are, to try to cut our feelings off from God—to say "thanks but no thanks" to the God-given gift of emotions, pretending that the only proper way to engage with faith is through intellect alone? For that matter, isn't faith itself a nonrational thing? What kind of hubris is it to reject the whole complexity with which God made us, embracing one part and throwing the rest away?

The patriarchal circular logic goes something like this: Rational thought is the One Most Valuable Thing, and emotions are fickle and untrustworthy; women tend to be "more emotional" than men, and thus are deficient in that One Most Valuable Thing; thus, women are deficient and inferior in general, as is anything associated with femininity; thus, because emotions are associated with women, emotional modes are less valuable than rational ones (and at odds with them); thus, rational thought is the One Most Valuable Thing, and emotions are fickle and untrustworthy. And on, and on, and on.

These days, I want to make things personal. Or rather, I want to recognize that things *are* personal. I want to be part of communities where we engage our most important conversations with our fullest selves. I want us to learn, together, how to bring our thoughts, feelings, and intuitions into our disagreements and debates—and into our learning and teaching, our church committee meetings, our Bible studies, and everything else we do. I want us to learn, together, to stop trying to check our emotions at the door, and to stop expecting others to do the same. People of all genders are better off if all of us can breathe, be our full selves, and examine and articulate any emotions that arise in the process, rather than shoving them aside.

I want to be part of communities for whom the election of an openly, brutally racist and misogynist president is absolutely personal—communities who lament this sort of thing together, because even if we don't think we're personally impacted by it, we know and love others who are. I want to be part of communities where we mourn with those who mourn, even if we don't yet fully comprehend the reasons for their mourning.

Questions like LGBTQ+ inclusion absolutely should be personal—even if we don't identify as LGBTQ+ ourselves, and even if we don't have a close friend or family member who does. These things should be personal because we care personally about the people our churches have hurt and continue to hurt; because we want to stop the cycles of pain and abuse and marginalization; because we know we are personally deprived of LGBTQ+ people's gifts when our churches shut them out.

Likewise, with women in ministry. There should be no one for whom this is not personal. Likewise, with people of color, when they are marginalized in church and in our society. Likewise, with every other group of people whose stories and needs and gifts have not been centered, who have not experienced church as a place of full welcome and freedom.

Is it personal?

These days, I sure hope so.

11

HE NEVER QUITE FIGURED IT OUT

*B*y the time I started thinking seriously about seminary, I was pretty pissed off about the situation of women in conservative churches. I was ready—long past ready—for something different. So, I intentionally chose an egalitarian seminary.

At first it seemed clear that the school I chose—let's call it United Evangelical Seminary—checked the box definitively. The seminary's website features a lovely statement of commitment to women in ministry. Equal welcome. Equal opportunity. Equal calling. Equal encouragement. Equal resources. It's all very nice-sounding.

And in some ways, United Evangelical is a great place for women. My experience there really was different from my experience in complementarian environments. It was, in many ways, a big, glorious gulp of fresh air. After spending eleven years at a church whose policies and practices were openly patriarchal, I was excited to finally be in a Christian environment where this was not the case.

Sure, there weren't many female faculty members at United Evangelical, especially not in the theology department. But at least women were not specifically, deliberately prevented from working as professors, preachers, teachers, or researchers because of their gender. And there were plenty of fellow female students—although we were fewer and farther between in the Master of Divinity (MDiv)[1] program, and I *felt* that in some of my MDiv-specific classes.

Unfortunately, despite all these promising things, it was often still difficult to be a woman in seminary. Perhaps in part because of the strength of United Evangelical's rhetoric affirming women in ministry, it took me a while to become aware of some of the ways United Evangelical was still a hard place to be a woman. Once I began trying to articulate these observations, though, I found that other women at United Evangelical agreed emphatically. Not many women I knew there felt that it was a totally easy and comfortable place to be.

In contrast, I got the feeling that a lot of the (male) students and faculty at United Evangelical considered egalitarianism to be kind of a moot point. As in, we settled that debate back in the 1970s, when the school first allowed women to pursue the same theological degrees as men. Problem solved, right?

Many people seemed to think that if an institution expresses verbal support for women in ministry, and if students and professors are required to be on board, then we're all good. Women must feel fully supported and included. Everything is fine.

I realized over time—slowly and painfully, as usual—that, for me, everything was not fine. Casual misogyny would pop up its gnarly head at unpredictable times, often just when I was starting to relax and enjoy a class—just when I was starting to feel, as a woman, at home in seminary.

One professor told our class a story about his parents' church in a rural community. The story went something like this:

There was a man who was a well-known drug dealer in the community—an all-around bad, violent dude. No one would have ever expected him to go to church.

But, one day, he did. Against everyone's expectations, he showed up at my parents' church. And, against everyone's expectations, he gave his life to Jesus that day. No one expected the change would last. He was too far gone.

But, sure enough, God transformed this man's life. He stopped dealing drugs, stopped dealing in violence, and turned his whole life around, dramatically. What an amazing testimony to the power and goodness of God!

He may have never quite figured out how to treat women...but his life was dramatically transformed. The whole community saw God's grace and love in a very tangible way.

A wonderful, heart-warming evangelical conversion story...right?

The professor even paused for effect after the part about not figuring out how to treat women. The class chuckled right on cue.

I looked around the room, wondering if anyone else was thinking, *what??* I wasn't sure. But I had a hard time paying attention to the rest of the lecture. Was this story really supposed to be a testimony of God's goodness? What were women supposed to take away from it—regarding the kind of treatment we can expect from men in church, and the value we have as humans? For that matter, what were *men* supposed to take away from it—regarding how much it matters that they treat women well?

Is a man's continuing abuse of women really just a cute little aside, an incidental footnote in the story of God's miraculous whole-life transformation—stuck in a story to get a chuckle from its hearers, and to show that this is a real, flesh and blood, fallible human, and the story is set in our real, imperfect world? Is that what women are worth?

He never quite figured out how to treat women. Isn't that the story of too many men in the church—and, especially, too many pastors and other powerful men? I wished my male seminary classmates were being taught something different. I wished they were being taught to take men's mistreatment of women seriously. Instead, stories like this encouraged them to laugh it off as just part of how (some) men are, and how they will always be.

Another professor began a lecture on Thomas Aquinas by saying, "I think you'll find that Aquinas was a very humane thinker." I laughed a little. (Thankfully, quietly.) I thought my professor was being funny. After all, he had a subtle sense of humor that could pass you right by if you weren't paying attention.

Unfortunately, I was wrong about this one. It wasn't a joke.

I laughed at the "humane thinker" label because I had been struggling through the assigned parts of Aquinas' *Summa Theologica* the night before, and his choice words about women were fresh in my mind. Aquinas believed that females were basically deformed, defective males. As my professor explained later on, Aquinas connected Aristotelian ideas about women being smaller and therefore naturally less active and powerful than men with biblical ideas about the created order of things, attaching a lot of meaning to the fact that men were created first in the Genesis story. Aquinas approved of women as queens and in other secular leadership roles,[2] but argued very strongly that the priesthood should be reserved for men.

A humane thinker?

Sure, Aquinas approached many areas of life and ministry with a great deal of graciousness and pastoral sensitivity. As my professor went on lecturing, it became clear that this was what he was talking about. But when it came to women, Aquinas spoke in no uncertain terms.

To my professor's credit, he taught us about this, too. He didn't gloss over it. But when it came to assessing Aquinas' overall humaneness as a thinker, my professor seemed to find the demeaning stuff about women easy enough to overlook. For me, this was not so easy.

Another time, I got to take a whole seminary course on Dr. Martin Luther King, Jr. It was awesome. We read a ton of Dr. King's essays, speeches, and sermons, and I learned so much. And yet, sometimes—ironically, for a class that was all about justice and kinship and the dream of a beloved community of equals—it was hard to be a woman there, too.

One day, in class, a fellow female student raised her hand and asked a question about Dr. King's alleged unfaithfulness to his wife. To be honest, I hadn't thought about it much until that point. But, once she asked, I was curious. I had heard similar rumors and didn't know whether they were true. But it seemed worth addressing—especially as our professor waxed poetic about what a great role model Dr. King was and how we as Christian leaders should follow in his footsteps.

Our professor replied, "That's not what we're talking about today, but we'll get to it later."

Fair enough, I thought. It wasn't in the lesson plan for the day. That's okay. I didn't blame my professor for preferring to wait for another time to address a sticky topic.

The quarter went on, and I waited for us to "get to it later." I waited class session after class session. I began to wonder if my professor didn't actually plan on coming back to it, or if perhaps he had forgotten.

In the meanwhile, I thought about things more. I wondered,

did the possibility of Dr. King's marital infidelity cast a shade of doubt on his lofty words about integrity and justice? Surely it did not make these words any less true or compelling—or take anything away from the brilliant, prophetic, courageous leader Dr. King was—and yet, as a woman, it was something I couldn't help but think about and be bothered by. How do we hold these tensions and acknowledge the complexities of Dr. King's legacy? It felt worth a conversation in class.

Finally, one day, near the end of the quarter, the topic came back up. Another student asked about it, or maybe the same student again. In reply, our professor said something like this: "Okay, so what you have to understand is that Dr. King became a really big name, an important man, someone people really idolized. Women flocked around him when he traveled to a town and signed books or led a campaign. You have to understand that he traveled a great deal, apart from his family, and women were basically throwing themselves at him."

Once again...*what??*

That was it. End of discussion, as far as I can recall. *Women were throwing themselves at him.*

Was the implication that any extramarital affairs Dr. King might have had were consensual, and therefore not all that bad? That if a woman initiates an affair, then the man is not also responsible for it? Of course, consensual affairs are a whole different matter from coerced sex—and, rage-inducingly, plenty of (mostly male) Christian leaders have committed sexual assault in its various forms. So I guess Dr. King, if he was cheating on his wife with women who were *throwing themselves at him*, was worlds better than many. But that doesn't make it okay.

So what if women were throwing themselves at him? He didn't have to give in. I believe that men are capable of resisting women's inappropriate advances. I believe that husbands are capable of being faithful to their wives, and that this matters—

because the marriage matters. Because the wife matters. Because the husband's integrity in staying true to his promises matters.

I get that, when it comes to Dr. King, this is complicated. I think I understand why my professor seemed annoyed when a female student brought up the topic. After all, people have done all sorts of twisted things to try to distort Dr. King's work and malign his legacy. That totally sucks. Accusing Dr. King of marital unfaithfulness can be just another way to do this— another weapon deployed by white people, especially white women, to try to discredit Dr. King.

This strategy, though, operates out of an odd sort of logic— the sort of logic in which everything Dr. King did for racial justice and equality is somehow negated by any sexual indiscretions he may have had. I like to think we don't have to operate out of this logic. I like to think that, just as married men can do better in the face of women's sexual advances, white women can do better than this sort of dismissal. I like to think that, in our classroom, we could have had an honest and thoughtful conversation about Dr. King's alleged unfaithfulness and what it might mean. Maybe we could have come to some more nuanced conclusions.

Dr. King's alleged affairs are certainly not an excuse—for those who are always looking for one—to discard Dr. King's life and work. And yet, they are also not inconsequential. I don't think we do any good by glossing over them. Dr. King has an incredible, complicated legacy. He was an incredible, complicated person. We could have talked about these things.

At another point in my class on Dr. King, we were allowed to choose a book among several options. I chose the only book on the list that was written by (and about) a woman: *Ella Baker and the Black Freedom Movement: A Radical Democratic Vision*, by Barbara Ransby. I hadn't heard of Ella Baker before but was delighted to learn about this incredibly brave and wise woman whose career spanned many decades of fighting for racial equality—and for economic equity, and for the voice and agency of every person involved, especially young people. Inspiring stuff.

Part of Baker's story is that she worked behind the scenes in the Civil Rights movement, including a stint with the Southern Christian Leadership Conference under Dr. King's leadership. During this time, she felt that Dr. King and other male leaders were dismissive of her gifts and her status in the movement due to her gender.

A female student (braver than I) brought this up in class, and our professor addressed it very briefly. He suggested that the author had her own sets of biases, and that Ransby's account of Baker's life was not the only side of the story.

This strikes me as one of those things that may be true but not necessarily helpful. We all have biased perspectives. But that doesn't mean there isn't truth in those perspectives. If Ransby says that Baker experienced Dr. King's leadership as oppressive because of her gender, we could have had a conversation about this. We didn't have to dismiss it. We could have looked at Ransby's account and also at another account of the same story; if there were multiple sides to it, we could have talked about some of those different sides. We could have talked more about what it was like to be a female Civil Rights leader in that time. I like to think there could have been a way to talk about these things without putting Dr. King on trial for sexism and dismissing his entire body of work if found guilty.

I have no interest in "canceling" Dr. King. We have so much to learn from him. *I* have so much to learn from him. But we could also acknowledge that maybe there were things he missed, areas he could have grown in. Maybe an honest conversation about his flaws could lead us to explore together how to recognize the things *we* tend to miss, whether in the areas of race, or gender, or something else.

I realize it may not be my place, as a white person, to write about these things.

On the other hand, I think about the long and brutal history of white feminist leaders placing their white feminist concerns ahead of the concerns of women of color. I see this as a grave and costly injustice, and I want it to change. But in order to have any chance of change, we need to have some honest conversations about these white feminist leaders' racism and how it impacted their work. If there were a seminary course about one of these leaders, it would need to include the complicated parts of her legacy, not just the awesome and inspiring parts. We would really miss something if we ignored or made excuses for her racist tendencies.

There must be a way to refuse to dismiss legitimate concerns about Dr. King when it comes to gender—while also refusing to dismiss his vast contributions to our world. I respect and admire his work so much. He was the leader his time needed—and, in so many ways, the kind of leader our time still needs. I want to hear what he said and read what he wrote. All of it.

These conversations may not have been easy ones. But I think it would have been worth a try.

All three of these professors—the "he never quite figured out how to treat women" one, the "humane thinker" one, and the "women were throwing themselves at him" one—are egalitarian. All three are fully committed to supporting female seminary students. All three are committed to equal partnership between men and women. I *like* all of them and learned a ton from each. I'm so grateful for their classes, for their knowledge and their dedication to teaching. None of them intended to belittle women, make female students feel uncomfortable, or act in a way that was casually dismissive of gendered concerns.

And yet, all three are men who live and work in a male-dominated world. And there were things they missed. One apparently failed to see that men mistreating women is not a particularly funny joke. Another didn't seem to realize it might be hard for the women in his class to look past a theologian's very inhumane comments about women when assessing this thinker's humane-ness as a whole. And the third didn't seem to be able to acknowledge a need for a more nuanced conversation about Dr. King, race, and gender.

My seminary's affirmation of women in ministry couldn't save me—or other female students—from the sexist things professors would say. It couldn't save us from the ways (male) professors were sometimes unaware of and other times actively dismissed women's concerns. Even professors I liked and respected. Even professors who didn't strike me as particularly patriarchally-minded in general. Maybe these instances were especially jarring *because* I didn't expect this sort of thing from these particular professors—because their misogyny was so clearly unintentional. But it still left me reeling, every time.

12

THIS IS WHY IT'S HARD TO TALK
ABOUT MONEY

*A*nother seminary professor, let's call him Dr. Jones, devoted multiple class sessions to the topic of fundraising. He lectured at length on his fundraising philosophy, which, as I understood it, is basically that it's all about the giver. Whether you're fundraising for a church or nonprofit or other cause, it isn't primarily about the needs of the people the organization serves—often people living in poverty. It's more about the giver's heart. We need to be attentive to the heart, mind, and spiritual life of the donor or potential donor. We want to invite them to see how worthy the cause is, to be excited about contributing to it. We want them to feel good about giving, not to feel like they were guilted or pressured into it. As we ask them to give, we care for their souls.

I felt tension when I heard this. On the one hand, it sounds nice. I'm all for removing guilt, pressure, and manipulation from the equation. And I agree that donors are lovely and important people who deserve to be cared for well.

On the other hand, people with material needs—people who will receive and benefit from donors' gifts—are equally lovely and important. Don't they too deserve to be cared for well? Don't they deserve their needs met? Dr. Jones' emphasis on the heart of the giver—over and above the concerns of people living in poverty—was disturbing to me. Sure, I thought, giving is about the giver—but it is also about the recipient. It's not just the attitude with which something is given that matters; the gift itself also matters. It matters because the recipient of the gift matters.

I want people to be generous with money not just because it makes them feel warm and fuzzy inside, but also—more primarily, more fundamentally—because they recognize that wealth is distributed unevenly and unjustly in this world. I want them to give out of an acknowledgment that this unjust distribution, where the rich get richer and the poor get poorer—and the poor suffer from a lack of adequate societal safety nets—is wrong. And, as followers of Jesus, who stubbornly cared for impoverished people throughout his life, Christians are called to help make things right.

Back in the day, Jesus turned over the moneychangers' tables in the temple.[1] And, still, today, Jesus takes everything wealthy people often believe about money and turns it upside down: the belief that we earned it, that we deserve it, that we're more important than others because of it, that we can do with it whatever makes us feel good, that it's all about us.

Christians are descendants of the early church community described in the book of Acts as always selling stuff, sharing money and other possessions, making sure no one was in need of anything.[2] We are meant to be people who share generously. We are invited to see our money as not just—or even primarily—our own, but as belonging to the communities we are a part of, to the poor who have been robbed of it. We are invited to see our money as belonging to God in the form of Jesus—the God who identifies with the prisoner, the hungry, the naked, the thirsty, the stranger, the sick, the least of these.[3]

. . .

As you may have gathered, I have some thoughts. And I have some feelings.

I have some opinions that aren't exactly aligned with the donor-centered vision of charity that Dr. Jones was teaching. I think this vision has done harm in our world. When (relatively) rich people make the act of giving all about themselves, poor people suffer. What is given often does not match what is actually needed. Sometimes it's insulting to the dignity of those who are poor. And it's always a deviation from the life and work of Jesus.

Jesus centered the impoverished and brought comfort to the weary. He saw and favored the marginalized; he named them as important, loved by God, worth healing and restoring to mutually life-giving forms of human community.

And so, there in that classroom, I took a breath, and I raised my hand to voice some of these concerns.

With the benefit of time and hindsight—and without a whole roomful of eyeballs staring at me—I am able to be more articulate now than I was in that classroom at that time. But I tried. I tried to challenge the premise that the giver's heart is the most important thing. I suggested that perhaps this perspective privileges the needs of the rich over the needs of the poor. It was no easy thing to speak up in class and push back against what a professor was teaching. I don't have the personality type that enjoys that kind of thing.

I mentioned the idea of a "preferential option for the poor" —a phrase I assumed my classmates would be familiar with. Dr. Jones asked me to explain the term, which caught me off guard, because in my mind it seemed self-explanatory. It's a Catholic social teaching originating from Latin American liberation theology, saying that the Bible consistently prioritizes the well-being of the poor and oppressed. In the moment, I wasn't quite sure how to say this. I fumbled for the right words. Fortunately, my brilliant classmate Grace came to my rescue with a clearer explanation. I nodded along—a little embarrassed that I had needed her to fill in the gaps, but also grateful.

Dr. Jones heard us out. He listened to my attempt at a critique, as well as what Grace added as she backed me up. He let us finish. Then he took a step back, laughed a bit, and said, "Remember what I said about how it's hard to talk about money in church? This is why! People get angry and upset about it so easily. Am I right?"

The class, dutiful as always, chuckled and nodded along. I nodded, too.

But on the inside, I was stewing. Dr. Jones went on with his lecture without addressing my concerns; meanwhile, my insides coiled into a mixed-up soup of confusion, humiliation, and, as Dr. Jones had correctly named, anger. I was livid. Not just about the rich-person-centered philosophy of fundraising, but now also about being laughed at and labeled as overly emotional—about the way Dr. Jones casually dismissed my concerns.

Sure, I made my points imperfectly. I was still working out what I thought. I was figuring out how to articulate what wasn't sitting well in my gut. I struggled for the right words and needed Grace to rescue me. My cheeks probably turned a little red in the process, and my heart thumped in my chest, and my hands shook a little with the nervousness of publicly challenging a professor. But isn't the classroom supposed to be a space where students can speak imperfectly—a space where we can bring our whole flawed selves, unpopular viewpoints and partially baked ideas and all? This is how we learn.

I had been unable to hide the emotions that came along with my words. And I felt as if, in doing so, I had forfeited any of the power my words could have had.

It can be stressful to express a dissenting opinion, and of course there is emotion that goes along with it. But this is part of what it means to be human, part of what it means to care about something. And Dr. Jones had a choice: to respond as if I deserved space to express a different viewpoint, or to write me off as an overly emotional woman who didn't have anything serious to say—whose words were nothing more than an inappropriate outburst that just goes to show how people get upset so easily. He chose the latter.

It seems to me, upon further reflection, that Dr. Jones' reaction wasn't just about me. It wasn't just about my particular modes of emotional expression. If a professor responds that way—so callously, so dismissively—to a student's dissenting opinion, perhaps there's something else going on for that professor in that moment.

I can't help but wonder if, even if I had spoken as dispassionately, articulately, calmly, and generously as anyone could, Dr. Jones would still have found another way to write off my concerns. My hunch is yes. I wonder if the real issue was that Dr. Jones didn't like the feeling of being contradicted. My guess is that he felt threatened—and that he would have felt threatened no matter how gently I had said what I was trying to say.

I also can't help but wonder if Dr. Jones would have responded to a male student in the same way. I can't know for sure. No one else really challenged him on anything, as far as I remember. (Which seems in itself a sign of a less-than-wonderful classroom environment.) But I can imagine a male student raising his hand, expressing some similar concerns, and Dr. Jones saying, "That's an interesting point. Thank you for bringing it up. Let's talk about that. What do others think?"

I could be wrong about this. I know the suggestion of a preferential option for the poor rubs many evangelicals the wrong way. It could have been about that, more than it was about gender. But part of what is so stressful about being a woman in subtly patriarchal environments is that unintentional sexism is always an open question. Would this person have responded to me in the same way if I were male? The answer is often unclear. But it's a question we spend time and energy worrying about, where men don't have to. We can't help but wonder.

In this case, I can't help but wonder if it was especially galling to Dr. Jones that two female students challenged his ideas. I'm sure if you asked him he would say, *Of course I treat my male and female students the same way*. But it sure felt like Grace and I set off his "hmm, this doesn't feel right by the patriarchy" radars—you may know the ones—and he responded in kind. It felt like he did what men with power often do when women without power challenge them. It felt like he demeaned us, dismissed us, painted a picture of us as irrationally emotional and angry, pushed us to the margins of the discussion, and moved on without us.

It didn't matter that we weren't really challenging Dr. Jones personally. I didn't say, "Dr. Jones, you jerk, I can't believe you don't care about the poor. You're an awful person." Maybe in his own mind that's what he heard—but it isn't what I said. I simply expressed concern about where some of his views might lead, and my female classmate backed me up. We were pushing back on an idea. And he chose—in front of a bunch of seminary students who were looking to him as an example of good leadership—to laugh off the discomfort of the moment, rather than responding to a serious concern with appropriate seriousness.

I was left feeling confused, frustrated, belittled. None of this was explicitly about gender. But when it comes to perceiving and talking about people's emotions and the way we express these emotions, gender is almost always at play. Women are expected to stuff our anger and frustration down deep and pretend they don't exist. If we do this successfully—which many of us do, much of the time—we may succeed in making things easier for others around us, but we pay the cost in our bodies. We pay the cost in our health, in our holistic well-being, in our closest relationships, in our confidence, in our peace of mind.

When it comes to emotion, patriarchy runs deep. Even when everyone has the best of intentions, the reality is still far from equal. If a woman speaks out about something and comes across a little flustered, with a little emotion behind her words, people tend to see this as a sign of irrationality, of emotions getting in the way of logical thinking. If a man does the same thing, people tend to see it as a sign of his passion. *Isn't it wonderful that he has such a big heart for the cause?*

I have no regrets about trying to speak up in class that day. Who knows, maybe something Grace or I said stuck with someone. It was worth a try.

The world is a less interesting, less equitable, and less wonderful place when women's perspectives—even and especially the ones that contradict dominant perspectives—are not spoken and heard. Patriarchal people in power might not want to hear it. But our churches—and classrooms, cities, communities, governments, societies—desperately need women's opinions. Even, or especially, the outspoken ones, the emotional ones, the passionate ones.

Kaitlin B. Curtice writes this:

Power distorts the soul. Empire distorts. Oppression distorts... But oh the liberation that waits on the other side of knowing! Oh the wholeness, the togetherness that comes with healing! ...This is why the anger of Indigenous people, Black people, and other people of color is so important. It's why the anger of *women* is so important. Something must change, and when it does, it will bring us all closer to our own humanity and to the holy mystery of God, a closeness only birthed through the journey of pain.[4]

Something must change, indeed. And the anger of women, as well as the anger of people of color—and others' willingness to take this anger seriously and not dismiss it—is an essential part of the process.

Our patriarchal ways of being are deeply intertwined with violence, militarism, colonialism, and many other harmful systems of dominance and subjugation. This is not to say that all male leaders are violent and awful, and all female leaders are peaceable and amazing. Reality tends to resist these kinds of stereotypes. But there are patriarchal ways of seeing and engaging with the world, and especially of seeing and engaging with women, that lots and lots of men have bought into— whether or not they're aware of it, whether or not they want anything to do with it. And we need to figure out how to do things differently.

This is (part of) why, as Ruth Bader Ginsburg said, "Women belong in all places where decisions are being made." Women belong in these places. Women need to speak up in these places. And others in the room need to listen to what these women are saying. We would all be better off for it.

I hope someday to stop fearing so much what others will think and how they will respond if I express a dissenting opinion. But it's not all on me. I hope that someday people's responses to emotional expression will be less gendered. I hope that someday people will see women who are passionate about something as just that—passionate and powerful—rather than overly emotional and irrational, easily written off. I hope that someday people—especially men, and especially men in power

—will choose to stop using imperfect communication as an excuse to laugh off important words. I hope that someday they'll find the courage—and the basic respect—to engage rather than dismiss.

That day could be today. There is no reason to wait.

13

HAVE YOU CONSIDERED THERAPY?

*W*hen my husband Ken and I moved across the state so that I could study at United Evangelical's main campus, we needed to find a new church. And we were definitely looking for an egalitarian one. Sure enough, just as United Evangelical checked the egalitarian box convincingly, so did "Life Church."

I first met Life Church's pastor, let's call him John, at a church fair hosted by the seminary—you know, like other schools might have activities fairs. John asked me what I was looking for in a church. I had a several-point checklist, and I gave him the rundown. Multiracial. Multi-socioeconomic class. Involved in serving the local community. LGBTQ+ affirming. And, of course, supportive of women in ministry.

John listened patiently and then told me where Life Church stood on all these points. Of the several pastors I talked with that day, he was the first who actually seemed to care about who I was, what I thought, and what I wanted, rather than accosting me with a lengthy prepackaged spiel detailing all of the wonderful things about their church. That counted for a lot. Among other things, I learned that Life Church was part of a denomination that supports women in ministry. And while John was the only pastor and he was a man, he was also vocally pro-women in ministry. Women were on the church's leadership team, and women often served as guest preachers.

Ken and I started attending Life Church soon after moving to Southern California. Since it was a small church, and a lot of people there were fellow grad students, it wasn't terribly difficult to meet people and make some friends. We got involved in a grad student small group, where Friday evenings were full of good food, goofiness, warm hospitality, board games, music-making, and come-as-you-are honesty.

It was clear from the beginning that some things about the church weren't exactly what I had hoped and dreamed of—most notably, the church, and John, were not LGBTQ+ affirming—but the fact that I could see myself building a sense of community there overrode a lot of these concerns. I told myself we didn't all need to agree about everything; I just needed a supportive faith community.

At first, this seemed to work fine. But over time, I became increasingly frustrated. Maybe I should have seen a screaming fluorescent red flag early on, when I was talking with John about my LGBTQ+ affirming views—it was important to me that I didn't feel like I was trying to hide anything—and he asked me to consider how I would want a person with strong complementarian views to engage with our church community. It felt like a heavy-handed attempt to persuade me not to "proselytize" his community with my heretical opinions. But the analogy was not right. Others' desire to contribute to my oppression was not at all a fair comparison to my desire to contribute to my LGBTQ+ siblings' liberation from oppression.

Over time, it became clear that my theological differences with John went well beyond our perspectives on gay relationships. Seminary was helping me rethink a lot of things. It was helping me think about things more deeply. I was learning to see scripture differently, learning to see the church differently, learning to see the gaping holes in dominant U.S. American evangelical theology. I was becoming increasingly convinced that the ways evangelicals have interpreted the Bible are not working.

My paradigms were shifting. And John was preaching a lot of the very same things that I was coming to find wholly inadequate. It got to a point where his sermons often left me quietly thinking, *I don't think John and I believe the same things, on a pretty basic level.* Other people took notes and seemed to nod along in agreement as he spoke; I felt alienated.

At one point, I tried to communicate my frustrations to John. I wanted to share with him some of my seminary journey—how I was rethinking things, how I was having a hard time with some things that were being preached. I thought it might be helpful feedback—especially since there were other seminary students at our church, and I knew that the paradigm shifts I was experiencing were not uncommon among my classmates. I had things to say that I thought John as a pastor might want to hear.

These aren't easy things to talk about. It isn't fun to hear that someone finds your sermons vaguely upsetting. And it isn't a blast to tell someone that, either.

Recognizing this, I tried to err on the side of being less confrontational. I wanted to give John every possible opportunity to respond productively rather than defensively. So, I used "I" statements. I spoke of my perspective and my experiences. I talked about how I found myself feeling a little frustrated sometimes, how I didn't necessarily agree one hundred percent with everything he was preaching, and how this sometimes felt a little unnerving for me. I shared that I had had some difficult church-related experiences in the past, so it was easy for me to be reminded of those things and feel negatively about it.

I kept it personal. But on some level, I figured John might understand that this was not *just* about me—that maybe I wasn't the only one with some of these frustrations, and I might be sharing something that could help him lead our church community. I hoped the conversation would be thought-provoking for him. After all, my concerns were hardly original ones. I thought I might be able to offer some insight into how my generation thinks about things, insight that might help John preach more effectively to us.

Maybe this was too much to expect. I'm sure I could have articulated some of these things more clearly. But I tried. And I tried to do it in a non-accusatory, non-threatening way.

John heard me out. Then, he asked me: "Have you considered therapy?"

Have you considered therapy?

In the moment, I took the question at face value. I didn't think too much about it. I just answered directly, and the conversation moved on.

It didn't really hit me until later that the question "Have you considered therapy?" can be an insidious one. In effect, it turned the conversation away from my frustrations with the church—from our different ways of thinking about things, from any productive discussion of generational differences and how those might relate to preaching. It turned the conversation, instead, toward my own personal issues. It moved the focus away from what might possibly be wrong in the church and toward what might be wrong with *me* such that I was having trouble with it.

The question about therapy isn't—or shouldn't be—offensive in and of itself. I'm all for therapy. I'm all for throwing out any shame or stigma that might surround it. I'm all for making space in our lives to sort out some of our complex hurts with guidance from a skillful and caring professional. All these things are good.

And yet, to suggest therapy for me, in this context—when I had been trying to communicate my frustrations with Life Church in a non-threatening way—is exactly what was driving me bonkers about evangelical theology in the first place. Everything felt so individualized. I felt like the message was: It's all about me. Faith is between me and God. I sin and God forgives, and I sin again and God forgives again, and then God wants me to go out and tell everyone else how good it is that I sin and God forgives. It's all about *my* Jesus time. *My* prayer life. *My* evangelism and ministry (or lack thereof). I felt like there wasn't a very strong sense of *us*—of faith being about the flourishing of the community; of sin and forgiveness and transformation being more complex and more collective than just me and my own conscience before God; of people and communities often needing liberation from others' sins as much as we need forgiveness for our own; of justice-seeking not just being a matter of personal righteousness but also of belonging to one another as kin.

If faith was all about *me*, then clearly any issues I might have with the church's teachings were just that—*my* issues with the church's teachings. Just things in *my* past and *my* psyche that caused me to react in a negative way to normal church stuff. My frustrations were clearly cause for *me* to seek therapy —not for the church (or its pastor) to consider some self-examination.

Brené Brown puts helpful language to this. According to Brown, growing away from debilitating shame and toward healthy resilience often involves turning away from three particular movements that tend to reinforce shame: "Individualizing (I am the only one); Pathologizing (something is wrong with me); and Reinforcing (I should be ashamed)."[1] We can move away from these things, Brown writes, and instead learn to "Contextualize (I see the big picture); Normalize (I'm not the only one); and Demystify (I'll share what I know with others)."[2]

Responding to someone's church-related frustrations with the question "Have you considered therapy?" strikes me as a quintessential example of individualizing and pathologizing. It feels like a way of saying: *You are the only one. I don't think anyone else feels the same way you do. I don't think you have any legitimate concerns. These are just your individual issues. You should probably try to work through these issues individually, in therapy. These are your wounds speaking, your particular pathologies. I am not willing to consider any broader wisdom your experiences might have to offer the church, or any insight your perspectives might have to offer my theology.*

In time, Ken and I started thinking about checking out other churches. But we still liked a lot of things about Life Church, and we liked a lot of people there. Our frustrations weren't quite enough to push us to leave. Plus, I was graduating soon and we didn't plan on staying in the area after that; it didn't seem to make sense to look for a new church just a few months before moving away.

Then, something happened that propelled us out the door for good.

A man visited Life Church and interacted with two different young female leaders in ways that made them feel uncomfortable. The two female leaders did a little research and found that this man had a criminal history involving felony stalking charges and possession of illegally modified guns, and he was currently awaiting trial. They also had some conversations about the man's situation that left them with the impression that he was legally required to stay put where he was living— that he wasn't supposed to be at church.

This surfaced some questions that our relatively young church hadn't had to deal with before. How do we weigh the need to protect the physical safety of our congregation against the desire to welcome any person who would come to worship? To the two female leaders, the situation was clear: The man posed a danger to our whole congregation, and especially to the women in it. To John, it seemed, the situation was equally clear in the opposite direction: Anyone and everyone should be welcome to worship with us. Concern for women's safety was secondary to this man's feeling of comfort and belonging in church.

For me, it was hard to think about these things without remembering a Sunday morning four years prior, when white supremacist Dylann Roof sat through an entire church service at the Mother Emanuel AME Church in Charleston, South Carolina, before shooting and killing nine of the Black church-goers who had welcomed him so warmly into their community.

It was also hard not to think of the Saturday just days before this man's visit to our church, when a young man walked into the Chabad of Poway synagogue near San Diego, opened fire, and killed one person and injured three.

Our congregation was not majority African American or majority Jewish, so, as a group, we were not necessarily targets for white supremacist violence or anti-Semitic violence as these other two congregations were. But what about the very real threat of misogynist violence? Five years prior, Elliot Rodger penned a highly disturbing misogynist manifesto and then went and killed six young women and injured fourteen others at a sorority near UC Santa Barbara. According to a newspaper article, the man who visited our church had expressed admiration for Rodger.

I felt deeply disturbed by the way Pastor John handled the situation—or, really, as far as I could tell, refused to handle the situation, by refusing to take the female leaders' concerns seriously. But I had heard the details secondhand, and I didn't want to jump to conclusions or assume I knew everything after hearing just one side of a complex story. So I decided to meet with John and hear his perspective. We grabbed some coffee and plunked ourselves down at a picnic table outside the seminary coffee shop.

It was a frustrating conversation, to put it mildly. One of the most frustrating things was the way John talked about the two female leaders. At one point, John brought up the fact that both young women were survivors of sexual assault.

What?

For one thing, it was a huge breach of trust. John shared a piece of sensitive information about these women's histories— something each of them had chosen to entrust to John, likely under the assumption that the conversation was confidential.

On top of that, how exactly was a history of sexual assault relevant to the present situation? John seemed to be suggesting that these women were bringing their own personal histories of trauma into the current situation in a way that muddied their judgment and decision-making. Perhaps they were overreacting, playing up the danger in their own minds because of their own not-fully-healed wounds. Perhaps if these women had been whole and healthy and able to see things clearly and logically—as, of course, John did, as a man—they would not have felt afraid, threatened, or uncomfortable around our church guest, even knowing his criminal history and his current status awaiting trial.

. . .

At one point in the conversation, John used his own wife as a counterexample. *She* wanted to welcome the man into our congregation, he said, and she was willing to accept whatever risks might come from that.

Again...*what?*

I respect John's wife's right to have her own opinion. But I hate that it felt like John was using her to make a point: *My wife thinks the way I do about this, and she's a woman; therefore, any woman who thinks differently must be operating out of her own issues.* I felt that John was trying to use his wife's perspective to invalidate the perspectives of the two younger women. He seemed to be trying to frame the whole situation as if, some-how, the two younger women's desire to protect women in the congregation from violence was less holy, less compassionate, less faith-filled, than his wife's desire to welcome the poten-tially dangerous man to worship.

None of this was right. Of course the man awaiting trial was a valuable human being, made in God's image. But so were the women to whom he was a real physical danger.

Valuing women in a congregation means choosing not to subject them to harassment and violence. This is one of those things that feels like it shouldn't need to be said. It is not right for (male) church leaders to expect women to take risks with our bodies and lives that they do not themselves take, risks that we do not freely choose to take. If John's wife wanted to take those risks, that was her decision. But she did not deserve to be used as a foil against other women in John's attempt to dismiss and discredit their concerns.

I felt from the beginning that the two female leaders were right to be concerned. And I felt angry at John's dismissal of them, his readiness to discredit them and cast doubt on their judgment, his unwillingness to consider that his own judgment may have been wrong.

Only much later did I find out what became of the man awaiting trial. He was eventually convicted of murder, for a crime he committed just a few months after he visited Life Church.

The danger was real. The two female leaders' assessment of the situation was anything but alarmist or hyper-sensitive. It was absolutely reasonable. They were completely right to be concerned. Pastor John, as far as I know, never acknowledged this.

Individualizing and pathologizing. In my case: You have complaints about sermons and frustrations with evangelical theology; therefore, you should consider therapy. In the case of the other two young women: You have your own history of sexual assault; therefore, your perspective can't be trusted.

It's easy to individualize. It's easy to pathologize. It's harder to acknowledge that something might be wrong—that a mistake may have been made, or that something could be changed to make things better. It's easy to dismiss women who are brave enough to act on their concerns, and by this dismissal, harm not only these women but also others in the congregation who did not know enough to speak up—not to mention future generations of women who may be involved in the church for years to come.

At Life Church, no one ever said directly—as people sometimes say at complementarian churches—that women were less rational than men, less capable of being entrusted with important decisions. But, the way I saw it, John used his male pastoral privilege to bulldoze over the valid concerns of two female leaders in his congregation. And he used this same privilege to ignore my own valid concerns by suggesting therapy.

Life Church was part of a denomination that affirms female leaders. John himself was vocally committed to supporting women in ministry—and, in many ways, he really did. Maybe I was naïve, but I had hoped I wouldn't experience the same kind of sexism from John that I had experienced from (male) religious leaders in other contexts. And, indeed, I didn't experience the same kind of sexism. But I did experience a different kind. Individualizing and pathologizing are just subtler ways to discredit women's experiences and devalue our perspectives. They're just nicer, more egalitarian-sounding ways to tell us we don't know what's best for ourselves, to tell us what we *must* be, to put and keep us in our place—subordinate, timid, unobtrusive.

THE LOW BAR

14

YOU DO YOUR OWN LAUNDRY?

*W*hen Ken and I got married, we never quite got around to combining our laundry and making it a shared chore rather than an individual one. This wasn't necessarily a conscious decision, at least at first, but it works fine for us. He has his own laundry basket, and he washes his clothes when he runs out of clean shirts; I have my own laundry hamper, and I wash my clothes when I run out of clean underwear. Simple enough.

When we moved to Southern California and into a small apartment in my seminary's student housing, the laundry room was in the building next to ours. Whenever one of us needed to do laundry, it was a full body workout: carry the heavy laundry hamper down the (long) hallway, then down two (long-seeming) flights of stairs, then across the outdoor courtyard to the laundry room in the other building. We missed the in-unit laundry in the townhouse we had shared with housemates in the Bay Area. But the shared laundry room in student housing really wasn't bad. There was usually an available machine or two, and the machines were only sometimes broken.

One time, Ken was in the laundry room, and he met a

woman who turned out to be a seminary student's mother. As they were both doing their laundry—or, come to think of it, was she doing laundry for her grown-up kid?—she started making conversation with Ken.

"Are you a student here?" she asked.

"No, I'm not," Ken answered, "but my wife is."

The woman replied, "Wow! And you're doing the laundry? You're a good husband!"

Ken said, sheepishly, "Well, I'm really just doing my own laundry..."

Without missing a beat, she replied, "Well, you're still a good husband, for doing your own laundry!"

I'm sure the woman in the laundry room was just being friendly, trying to say something nice. (And who knows, maybe she was doing laundry for her adult kid, wishing her kid were more like Ken.) And don't get me wrong: Ken is indeed a good husband—a good partner.

At the same time, though, it got me thinking about how low the bar sometimes is for men. Doing your own laundry—isn't that just what grown-up people do? Nobody gives women any medals for doing their own laundry. Women often do their whole family's laundry without getting any medals for that either. (Just plenty of gendered shame if we're not keeping up with it perfectly all the time.)

The laundry room interaction with the well-meaning mom was kind of funny. The low bar for men, though? A little less so. In some ways, it's just a subtler, more egalitarian-friendly version of the same double standards that take more explicit forms in complementarian communities.

People back at Faith Bible Church felt free to say things like "women shouldn't be elders," or "the husband is meant to be the leader of the family." Gendered roles and expectations were often spoken of freely. At a place like United Evangelical, on the other hand, I don't think anyone would have said, "wives should definitely be doing their own laundry, but if a husband is doing his own laundry, that's remarkable." We just make these assumptions based on what we've seen—in our families, in movies, in advertisements. Wherever we look, really.

Over the course of my time in seminary, one particular gendered set of assumptions started to drive me bonkers: people's reactions upon learning that Ken had followed me to seminary. We moved to Southern California because I wanted to pursue a degree at United Evangelical, and Ken had been willing to uproot his life in the Bay Area to join me there. This was a fact that never failed to impress people.

Ken had been willing to move across the state, give up his job and find a new one, and leave the network of friends we had built over many years. I don't mean to take any of this lightly. It wasn't all sacrifice—it was also an exciting new adventure together—but it was more of a sacrifice for Ken than for me. People weren't wrong to acknowledge this. They weren't wrong to be impressed with Ken as a partner.

What did strike me as wrong, though, and disturbingly so, was how gendered all of this was. There were *so many women* who had done the exact same thing as Ken. They gave up jobs and support networks to move across the state, or across the country, or even overseas, so that their (male) spouses could study at United Evangelical. They set back their own careers, gave up educational opportunities, left hometowns and churches, sacrificed proximity to friends and family. They put their own hopes and dreams on hold, at least for a time, to support the hopes and dreams of their husbands. So many of these wives had sacrificed so much. But I didn't often hear people singing these women's praises.

Each one of these women did everything Ken did for me—minus the glory, minus the awe-filled responses from others. People seemed to assume that this is just what women do. This is what wives do. Wives sacrifice. Wives put their husbands' needs before their own. Wives consider their own careers less important than their husbands' careers. Wives endure the pain of moving to an unfamiliar place, put on a brave and smiling face, and make new friends and build new communities. Wives take the risk of unemployment, or of taking a job that isn't what they studied for and hoped to do. All of this was so expected, so common, so normal—even at a place like United Evangelical, where women are supported and encouraged in ministry, and where wives and husbands are, in theory, equal partners in marriage.

Few and far-between were the husbands who had been willing to make the same sorts of sacrifices. And these husbands struck people as immensely praiseworthy.

Maybe all this struck a chord because it brought up questions for me. Was I being selfish? Had I asked too much of Ken, to consider giving up his job and moving away from all our friends? Was I expecting too much, as a married woman, to hope that I might be able to freely pursue my sense of calling and take the right next step for me in my vocation?

I wondered these things, sometimes.

But then, I also wondered: Did my married male classmates think any of these sorts of thoughts? I would be surprised if many of them did. I doubt many of them spent much time worrying about whether they were being selfish or asking too much of their wives. Men often tend to assume that, when they get married—and even, often, when they have kids—nothing substantial will change about the course of their careers and the rest of their lives. Women rarely have this luxury.

Couples often need to make choices about whose career to prioritize at different points in time. And the societal default is to prioritize the man's career. Anything else is swimming upstream.[1] The man is considered exceptionally praiseworthy, and the woman, perhaps, selfish—selfish, of course, being a word often applied to women in response to behaviors that might be described in a man as motivated, purposeful, focused, ambitious.

When I was single and thought about marriage—that is, whether I wanted to get married, and if so, to what kind of person—I was thinking about partnership. I was thinking about a shared life together. I was thinking about personality compatibility, common values, strength of character. I was thinking about commitment, problem solving, conflict resolution, enjoying each other's company and being by each other's side in the difficult times. I was thinking about love and support, mutual and equal.

These are all good things. They're what I want for my marriage and for all marriages.

I didn't think much at all, though, about what it would mean to become, specifically, a wife.

It turned out that when I married Ken, I not only became a spouse, an equal partner—as Ken and I wanted it to be—but I also became a wife. A wife, with all the baggage this word carries in our society, all the controversies it holds within the Christian world. A wife, with all the accompanying gendered norms and expectations, even in places that in theory reject these things. A wife, with all the complications the word turned out to hold within my own mind and being.

When I intentionally chose to become Ken's life-long committed partner, I unwittingly became the person societally assumed to do his laundry. I became the person presumed perpetually willing to sacrifice my dreams and career for his. I became the person deemed responsible for decorating our home and making it a warm, comfortable, and tasteful space—things I'm not good at and don't have much interest in—and the person responsible for keeping said home clean and tidy, which is also not my strong suit.

Ken and I consider ourselves equally responsible for all these household tasks—the laundry, the home decor and furniture, the cleaning, the cooking. And this is, mostly, how we operate when it's just the two of us. We really do have the kind of equal partnership I imagined we would.

But when other people come into the picture, sometimes it gets harder. I *feel* the gendered expectations. Even if no one ever says anything. Even if it's all in my mind, deeply seated there. I wonder what people think of me—of *me*, not Ken, and not us as a couple—if the floors haven't been swept, or if there's a pile of sweatshirts and jackets on the "chairdrobe" because they didn't quite make it into the closet, or if the furniture doesn't match.

When I got married, I inherited a world full of gendered expectations that go along with the title of "wife." It takes regular conscious effort to learn how to just be a partner, how to just be a spouse, how to just be a human.

I think about this sometimes when I read books by female authors. There are so many amazing female writers out there. They're interpreting scripture, theologizing, reflecting on what it means to be a person of faith, offering their lives and experiences to encourage and teach and challenge others. I love them all. So much. And, at the same time, I see gender roles pop up in their writing. I've been struck by *how much time* many of these amazing female authors are spending in the kitchen. (And, for that matter, doing laundry.)

I was simmering a stew, one female pastor writes, *and I real-*

ized something about God. A second female author shares: *Here's a trick I use for keeping up with my family's laundry.* Or a third: *One time, while I was making a chicken dish, my kid came up to me and said something incredible.* You get the idea.

On the one hand, this is awesome. I love that these women are writing with real life in mind. They're bringing their theology into the real world and the real world into their theology, refusing to keep God-talk sequestered in ivory academic towers. Cooking is an important and time-consuming part of many people's lives, and especially many women's lives. It's a breath of fresh air when writers reflect on food preparation as deeply spiritual work. Surely it is exactly that. And in reading about it as such, there is a feeling of being seen, a sense of being affirmed—that our daily work of feeding ourselves and others is holy, that it reflects something about who God is, that it matters to God. That is a beautiful thing.

On the other hand, though, I can't help but wonder: *Where are the men?* Many of these female writers are married to men. What are the husbands doing while these women are spending *so much time* cooking and cleaning and doing laundry? It feels like these female writers are the ones solely, or at least primarily, responsible for meal prep in their families. These women— these awesome, brilliant, powerful women who are helping the whole church rethink theology and biblical interpretation and a million other things in a billion desperately-needed ways— are still assumed to be the ones doing all the laundry. I get the impression that their husbands—even their egalitarian husbands—are always off busy working outside of the home.

I don't mean to criticize these amazing women who are working and writing and cooking and parenting and doing an amazing job. I don't know their lives. Maybe they like to cook and their husbands don't. Maybe their husbands do other equally time-consuming work around the house. Maybe this is the division of labor they've discussed with their spouses and mutually decided makes sense. If so, that's great. But it's still hard, sometimes, to get the feeling that these women are responsible for the things women are always assumed responsible for, while their husbands can focus more freely on their work, with less responsibility at home. People seem to assume that this is just the way things are, even in egalitarian churches and families.

In egalitarian settings, people might not say, "as a wife, you really should be doing the laundry," or, "as a wife, you really should be willing to uproot your life and move to another city if your husband wants to, but my goodness is he a saint if he does the same for you." People might not say, "you should be ashamed, as a wife, if your household isn't clean and beautiful all the time."

But I still *feel* these things. And I think I'm not alone. The gendered expectations don't stop where the explicitly patriarchal environment does. The bar is still, in many ways, very high for women, and very low for men.

15

MEN CAN DO BETTER

*a*t age twenty-nine, I did something I hadn't done since high school. I joined a swim team.

My efforts to stay in shape (or, let's be real, to get in shape) in my twenties had mostly consisted of jogging, and a few workouts here and there on the free Nike Training Club app. But the neighborhood near my seminary wasn't a great place to jog. It was a fairly crowded, urban-ish environment, and I didn't love the idea of *so many people* seeing me red-faced and sweating up a storm as I jogged slowly along. Plus, there were busy streets everywhere. I would have spent half my time waiting at corners for traffic signals to change. And there was so much car exhaust. I didn't want to breathe in any more of that than I had to.

So, I started to look into other fitness options. At some point, while poking around at the websites of various over-priced and uninspiring gyms, I remembered something I had first heard of as a kid: Masters swimming. Actually, come to think of it, my parents may have inception-ed me with this thought from a young age. I remember my mom pointing out the Masters group as I was on my way to or from swim practice, saying things like *Look, those are the Masters swimmers! Isn't it great that swimming is something you can do your whole life?* It took a couple of decades, but I guess my parents' not-so-subliminal messaging finally kicked in. I found a Masters team that swam nearby and wasn't really any more expensive than most of the local gyms.

I had swum on a year-round team as a kid and then on my high school team and a summer league team as a teenager; I had never been a great swimmer, but at least the world of swimming was familiar to me. I still had some ancient caps and goggles, knew how to find a workout swimsuit, and vaguely remembered how to follow a pace clock. I figured that, with some time and work, I could probably hold my own in the water. Plus, being new to Southern California and not knowing many people in the area, I liked the idea of having a group of people to work out with.

The Masters swim team I joined ended up being all of these things and more. It was a major highlight of my two years in Southern California. The coaches were amazing, and I was grateful to have a social circle outside of the (sometimes very small, and sometimes very odd) seminary universe. I made great progress toward being friends with people from different faith backgrounds (or lack thereof) without feeling like I was supposed to convert them to evangelical Christianity. It was gratifying to work hard at getting back into swimming shape and to see quantifiable results from this effort. Over the course of two years, I went from being hopelessly exhausted after swimming a couple of laps in the 50-meter pool—which, in my defense, is a *very* long pool—to being able to race as fast as I ever did in high school.

As I got into the habit of swimming several times a week, and often doing "dryland" workouts[1] with a handful of team-mates afterward, I found myself noticing muscles I hadn't had in years, if ever. My previously non-existent triceps gradually took shape. I learned that the big lat muscles in the back are super important for swimming—and that I hardly had any of them. Slowly, over many months, I began to feel stronger and more powerful in my body.

I hadn't realized how much I missed this. I wonder if, as women, we are often socialized to think it isn't important. We aren't supposed to be strong. We—or at least the white women among us—are supposed to be weak, helpless damsels[2] in need of a man to open jars for us and do the heavy lifting around the house. Women's bodies exist to please the male gaze, not to make us feel powerful in a way that might be threatening to men. We're supposed to be small, unobtrusive, slim to the point of disappearing.

As Roxane Gay writes, "This is what most girls are taught— that we should be slender and small. We should not take up space. We should be seen and not heard, and if we are seen, we should be pleasing to men, acceptable to society. And most women know this, that we are supposed to disappear, but it's something that needs to be said, loudly, over and over again, so that we can resist surrendering to what is expected of us."[3] We have to talk about these realities, these often-unspoken assumptions, so that we can understand their gravity and learn to resist them. So, say it again, Roxane. And I will, too.

Sometimes women don't want to build too much muscle for fear that we might appear "too masculine." This should raise some questions. Who is telling us that strong equals mascu-line? What gives them that right? What does it mean to look masculine, anyway, and why is this a bad thing for a woman? Who gets to decide what a woman should or shouldn't look like —what kinds of strength she should or shouldn't have?

Women deserve to be strong and healthy, to the extent that our genes and circumstances allow. We deserve to take time to care for our bodies, as much as we're able to. We deserve to find activities we love that will bring us the physical and mental benefits of regular exercise—whether that's swimming, or yoga, or strength training,[4] or walking or jogging around the neighborhood, or playing pickleball, or whatever it might be.

I reflect on the Masters swim team here because I think exercise is important, and it's definitely undervalued in our culturally-imposed notions of femininity. It's one of the things we often cut out first when life gets too busy and something has to give. I also reflect on my swim team experience, though, because of something else I noticed early on there. Joining the swim team as a twenty-nine-year-old woman made me very aware of a simple yet mind-blowing truth: Men *can* do better.

I realized, not too many practices in, that I could walk around on the pool deck in a swimsuit, and none of the men gave my body a second glance. This was surprisingly healing and liberating for me. There were men all around—men swimming, men getting in and out of the water, men standing around chatting after a workout, men lifeguarding, men coaching, men socializing in the hot tub—and none of them looked at me in a way that made me feel uncomfortable. I was wearing so much less clothing than I would have worn in any other public place. I was basically pantless. And the clothing I was wearing—a one-piece workout suit—was so much thinner and tighter than any other clothes I would have normally worn. It was basically the equivalent of a really thin and tight tank top and underpants. Did I mention no pants?

At first, I felt self-conscious about my body in a swimsuit, especially after all those years passed (and pounds gained) since high school. And I felt self-conscious about how men might stare—the way men often stared in other contexts, when I was wearing form-fitting jeans, or a not-super-baggy sweater, or anything, really.

I was surprised and delighted to find that my male teammates' eyes met my eyes when we greeted one another. It turns out that adult men and women can be swim teammates together without the men being inappropriate or gross about it. Who knew?

I realized, too, that the fact that I was *so* surprised and *so* delighted suggested that, perhaps, there was still something in me that believed that a man's objectifying gaze is somehow a woman's fault—that the way a woman dresses, or carries herself, or speaks, or moves, or breathes, causes men to take notice of her in a sexualizing and objectifying way. After all these years and all the feminist convictions I had come to hold, there was still something in me that was surprised to see that men were actually capable of treating a woman in a swimsuit as a teammate, a human, just another person at the pool. Apparently, my bar was lower than I had been aware.

In my two years on the team, I never felt objectified by or uncomfortable around any of the men. (Well, there was one older man who sometimes made me feel uncomfortable by inviting me a few too many times to his Latter-day Saints church, but it was more the *oh no, I think he's trying to convert me* variety of uncomfortable[5] than the *oh no, I think he's hitting on me* variety.) I felt like the team was a safe space to be a human. And I needed that. It helped me remember that men are not the helpless sex-crazed monsters conservative churches sometimes make them out to be. It helped me remember that women are more than sexual stumbling blocks for men, and men are more than stumbling nincompoops who can't help but objectify women.

I don't mean to imply that swim teams, Masters or otherwise, are paradisiacal places where sexual harassment or assault never happens. I just mean to say that, for me, for those two years, my swim team was a safe place. It was a place where

I didn't feel objectified or othered or leered at—or, for that matter, given a skeptical side-eye or looked down on—because of my gender. And I want that kind of space for every woman.

I wish churches were such liberative places. And I think some are. But unfortunately, many are not. My hope, then, for women who choose to stay in faith communities that feel less than liberating, is that they might find spaces that feel like freedom outside of church.

Secular spaces aren't necessarily any better than churchy ones. Sometimes they're just different, and sometimes they're worse. But there are some spaces that are healthy and perhaps surprisingly healing. It's okay—it's good!—for Christians to recognize the good things about communities and organizations outside of church, and to join in with these things.

I believe that God was in the good things about my swim team—in the relationships, in the people, in the strengthening of the human body, in the skill and care of great coaches, in the support of teammates who cheer each other on. I believe that God is present in all of the spaces—whether sports teams, workplaces, neighborhoods, community service organizations, schools, or anywhere else—where people of all genders regard one another as fully human, as equals. Sometimes churches try to build walls around the places God can and can't be. God honors no such boxes. Sometimes churches and Christians feel threatened by the thought that there could be good, life-giving communities outside of church. But there's no (good) reason to be afraid of this, and every reason to embrace it with joy.

I want people of all genders to find—and to create—the kinds of spaces where women are not reduced to object status. The kinds of spaces where *no one* is reduced to object status. I want us to know what these spaces feel like, to see how they work, to gain a sense of what we're working toward. I want this because I think it will help us get there in our churches. I also want it for the sake of our own well-being in the meanwhile. Because these things matter. Because *we* matter. No one is served when the bar for men is so low that we don't expect, seek, and demand these kinds of spaces. Men can, in fact, do better.

16

THANK YOU, MR. VICE PRESIDENT

*O*n October 7, 2020, on a Wednesday evening, fifty-eight million people watched as Vice Presidential candidate Kamala Harris, a woman of color, debated incumbent Vice President Mike Pence, a white man. Fifty-eight million people watched as Harris repeatedly asked for and did not receive equal time to speak.

Pence did not interrupt Harris with the mannerisms of a toddler having a temper tantrum, as Donald Trump repeatedly interrupted Joe Biden in their presidential debate the previous week. Pence was not openly belligerent. His manner was calm, cool, and collected—sometimes eerily so, as when a fly landed on his head and stayed there for two whole minutes without Pence flinching one bit. And his disrespect for Harris was complete and brutal.

The moderator—Susan Page, a white woman—seemed unprepared to deal with it. Pence casually disregarded her many attempts to hold him accountable to the debate format and timeline. Page kept repeating "Thank you, Mr. Vice President"—which, I imagine, is a nice way of saying what the rest of us were yelling at our screens: "Shut up, poop face!" or something similar but with more profanity. Pence, unphased, just kept talking, calmly bulldozing over both Page and Harris with a non-stop barrage of White House-fabricated lies.

If you ask ten different people what they saw as they watched the debate, they might give you (at least) ten different answers. But this is what I saw.

I've thought about that debate a lot since then. I've thought about where I might find myself in it.

As icky as it feels to admit this, in some ways, I find myself in Pence. I have a lot of beliefs, and I tend to feel very strongly about them. So strongly that—while I do think that Pence was shamelessly lying his face off when he kept telling Harris she was "entitled to her own opinions, but not her own facts," and I don't mean to give him a pass for that—I can relate to the feeling of believing in something so doggedly that anyone who sees things differently must be totally mistaken. Sometimes I have viewed people who disagree with me with disdain rather than trying to understand where they're coming from. I don't often bull-doze over people in conversation—that just isn't really my style, and my voice is too quiet for it anyway—but some-times my mind holds the same sort of contempt that gets you there.

On top of that, whenever I hear a right-wing evangelical Christian like Pence talk, I have to remember that, once upon a time, I was (kind of) one of them. I used to think like them about a lot of things. I used to think Christians were a perse-cuted minority group in the U.S. I used to think being Christian meant opposing gay marriage and abortion rights. I used to think these two issues were the major moral concerns facing our society, and a Christian's vote should be used primarily toward these ends.

To be clear, I no longer think any of these things. And I was pretty young when I did.

But though I was young, I was also thoughtful and well-intentioned. I cared about people and wanted to do good in the world. There was a time in my life when all these things were true, *and* the Religious Right made sense to me. That feels significant. I don't want to dismiss it just because I was young.

If I totally distance myself from someone like Pence, I am distancing myself from part of my own past. This is exactly what white U.S. America tends to do: We sugarcoat, manipulate, and rewrite our collective history, and this keeps us from experiencing real healing. My denial of my personal history—like our collective denial of our society's history—serves no one. I need to remember my past, acknowledge it, learn from it, transform out of it into something new.

Conservative evangelicalism, destructively married to right wing politics, is a part of who I have been. And so, even though my political beliefs have done a one-eighty since then, I still have to see myself—or at least a part of my past, which is a part of myself—in Pence.

As a woman, I also see myself in Harris.

It may take many more years before I'm able to say—assertively and very appropriately, as Harris said to Pence—"excuse me, I'm talking," when men interrupt me. But although my reactions may be less developed, poised, and confident than hers, I share with Harris the near-universal female experience of being talked over by men. As most women—and, as I understand it, women of color more than white women—can attest, men interrupt us often, in all sorts of settings. Harris found her own statements contradicted by a calm, low, authoritative-sounding male voice that may have seemed to carry more weight than hers, not because of the truth of its statements but because of society's subconscious perception of its credibility. This kind of scenario is disturbingly familiar to most women.

When this happens, our options are limited.

We can allow ourselves to be interrupted—and, in so doing, make ourselves complicit in the silencing of our own voices.

We can wait for the interrupter to finish, and then, after he's done, come back to what we were saying. That way, our thoughts are still heard. But something is lost. The interrupter is never held accountable for his disrespectful actions. He might be unaware of them. Plus, the conversation may have already moved on, following the thread of the interrupter's thoughts, such that going back to a previous thought can feel jarring—like a step backwards, or just no longer as relevant.

We can convey the rudeness of being interrupted. If the interruption (justifiably) evoked a flash of anger, we can express that anger. We can say something to convey the hurt and frustration we feel. But there is a cost. We are labeled as reactive, volatile, overly emotional. We confirm men's (however subconscious) suspicions that we were not to be trusted as equal partners or important decision-makers. They may use our anger as an excuse to devalue and dismiss our perspectives and arguments.

Or, we can say something like what Harris said. Her "excuse me, I'm talking" statements were restrained, dignified, and not unkindly or harshly spoken. They were also firm. She did not allow herself to be interrupted, and she also did not return violence for violence. She responded in calm, measured tones, giving Pence the chance to acknowledge his "mistake" and stop talking. I don't know how Harris did this so well. Or, rather, I think I do—I think she's a remarkable person, brilliant and tough and quick-witted, and has probably developed this practice over many years of experience. I admire her for this, even as I wish things were different.

In the no-win situation of being interrupted by a man,

Harris's response was about as perfect as it could have been. And yet, she was still labeled as condescending and arrogant.

When we stand up for ourselves as women, people deploy negative labels to try to keep us in our place. We can go to great pains to speak calmly, measuredly, and respectfully—and sometimes, as Harris did, we succeed—and in return we get stuck with the same dehumanizing, silencing labels we would have gotten if we didn't bother to try so hard to be kind. For simply insisting on our own dignity and humanity, we are treated as though we had actually been rude, angry, arrogant, demanding, overly emotional, irrational, disrespectful, insubordinate, a troublemaker, not a team player.

Like Harris, I often find myself saying things that I think are true and important—while a man attempts to talk over me, saying things that are less true or less relevant. And there is no way to respond that will uphold my dignity without risking a backlash of irrational misogynistic criticism. I see myself in Harris.

Ultimately, though, as a white woman, if I'm being quite honest, I have to see myself in Susan Page, the debate moderator.

As a white woman, I don't get to identify only with the woman of color who gets talked over. I don't get to pretend that her experience is the same as mine—that we're on the same footing in this world because we both experience sexism, and that other intersecting identities like race have nothing to do with it. I need to examine how race and gender dynamics played off each other during the debate, and where I might find myself in all of it. I need to think about the ways I might find myself in Page's position, and to figure out what to do with that.

Because, ultimately, I am not really like Pence. I am not the white man with privilege and power who gets to run roughshod over others and bully my way into commandeering far more than my allotted share of time. But I am also not really like Harris. I am not the woman of color who, in a racialized world, experiences intersectional oppression—double marginalization by gender and race, as well as a whole set of complex interactions between the two.

I am not at the top of the power structures of our society, but I am also not at the bottom. In our white supremacy-soaked society, my race gives me privilege. And in our misogyny-soaked society, my gender marginalizes me.

And so, here I am, like Susan Page, trying to navigate this sometimes strange social location as a white woman—a location that I did not choose but I do need to reckon with. Sometimes men with power trample all over my efforts to do well in the roles I find myself in, just as Pence trampled all over Page's efforts to moderate a productive and fair debate. And sometimes, like Page, I have the opportunity to fight to make room for the voices of women of color. Sometimes I miss that opportunity.

Sometimes, in the face of white supremacist patriarchy, all I have to offer is "Thank you, Mr. Vice President." And it is not enough. Like most white women, sometimes—however unintentionally—I side with white supremacist patriarchy rather than practicing solidarity with women of color. Women of color should not have to turn to me, as Harris turned to Page, and say, "I would like equal time." I should be proactively doing everything in my power to make sure their voices are heard.

Just as men can do better, white women can do better.

I write about these things because I think faith communities, whether or not they realize it, desperately need to make space for women—and for all sorts of women, not just upper/middle class white women—to speak and be heard. It is not enough for white women to be at the table if our sisters of color are excluded from it. It is not enough for just some women's voices to be heard.

I don't want to be part of a white-centered feminism that, in Mikki Kendall's words, "since its inception...has been insisting that some women have to wait longer for equality, that once one group (usually white women) achieves equality then that opens the way for all other women."[1] I don't want to be part of a feminism that, as Kendall writes, "fails to show up for women of color."[2] In order to be truly pro-women, and not just pro-wealthy-white-women, white women need to see and feel that the lives and freedom of women of color are intimately connected to our own. We need to refuse to settle for an ineffective "Thank you, Mr. Vice President."

White patriarchy claims to offer certain protections and advantages to those of us who play along with the system. We need to resist the temptation to believe those offers. For white women, our whiteness can obscure our view of what life is like for women of color. It's easy to be aware of our shared marginalization and oppression as women. It is more difficult to be aware of the kinds of marginalization and oppression we do not share. The empathy comes less naturally. The understanding will never entirely be there. We are called to listen, though, and to try to learn the things we do not know. This is a life-long and difficult process, but a necessary one.

The male-dominated world is always trying to control women's voices. Sometimes white women may feel like a polite "Thank you, Mr. Vice President" is all we have to offer a woman of color whose voice is being trampled. After all, anything stronger would cross a line of propriety that we are not always prepared or willing to cross. We don't want to be labeled as bitchy, aggressive, or controlling. But I want to become willing to be labeled these things when necessary. I want more and more white women to become willing to be labeled these things when necessary, so that all women's voices can be heard.

Men in power in patriarchal white supremacist structures sometimes, in effect, pit women against one another—as if there is only room for so many voices, only so much power to go around. Sometimes we internalize this destructive mindset. Sometimes we compete and tear each other down rather than lifting and building each other up. I appreciate Kathy Khang's words: "Encourage others to find their voice as you find yours. Part of learning to speak up is also about encouraging others to do the same."[3] Amen to that. There is enough to go around.

We are all better off when everyone's voice is honored. Making room for all sorts of women to speak does not mean there is less room for the women whose voices are already heard. It doesn't have to mean that. It doesn't need to be a zero-sum game. That is a lie patriarchy tells to keep us all from moving forward together. I'm learning, I hope, to stop believing it.

WORDS OF TRANSITION

These are the stories and reflections I wanted to share from my eleven years in complementarian evangelical communities and two years in egalitarian evangelical communities. It might feel like a lot. It *is* a lot.

These stories may have surfaced some feelings. You may find yourself reminded of your own experiences, or the experiences of people you know and love. There may be some difficult feelings. That's okay. I invite you to notice what's surfacing and explore it. Stay in the place of whatever sadness or anger or excitement or hope or energy or frustration you find yourself in. And be open to the possibility that something good could come out of whatever complex feelings you might have—in time, as the Spirit who lives in you leads.

When you've had enough time, I invite you to keep reading. We're making a turn, here. We're moving beyond reflecting on what patriarchy looks like, and into exploring how we might build a new kind of world together. Beyond noticing the forms patriarchy takes, and into the realm of dismantling patriarchy's power. Beyond acknowledging the impact that even the subtler faces of misogyny have had on us and on others, beyond understanding the ways verbal commitments to egalitarianism can sometimes mask deeply seated misogyny—and into the realm of dreaming together about the way things could be, informed and inspired by scripture and history. We're looking to take practical steps to change the conversations in our communities, prioritize our own holistic well-being, and be willing to leave communities that are not healthy places for us to thrive.

We're going to get into some Bible. We're going to get into some history. We're going to get into some liturgy—how we speak about God in church and in private, in prayer and in song. We'll explore what it might look like to read scripture in ways that are less male-centered. To expand our theology to consider God's feminine sides and not just God's masculine sides. We'll look to Christian history for inspiration and hope as we uncover women's stories that have often been ignored. We'll explore how we might reclaim our God-given agency as women—and our anger, too. And we'll reimagine what spiritual authority could look like in a world not presumed to be dominated by male churchy leaders (even the nicest of ones).

I think of Pentecost, when Peter and the other apostles preached about Jesus, and people responded, *What then shall we do?*[1] The scripture says they were "cut to the heart" when they heard the truth the apostles came to speak. If the stories I've shared have you feeling "cut to the heart" in any kind of way—whether in an *oof I relate to that and I join you in your anger* kind of way, or in an *oof I have perpetuated these misogynistic systems and I see how wrong that is* kind of way, or a little of both—then the chapters that follow seek to answer the question, *What then shall we do?* These are some of the ways we might—together, communally—dismantle misogyny's power in our churches.

PART II

DISMANTLING MISOGYNY'S POWER

DEMASCULINIZING
SCRIPTURE

17

SUBMIT TO ONE ANOTHER...BUT MOSTLY IN ONE DIRECTION

"Submit to one another out of reverence for Christ." —Paul[1]

"Now as the church submits to Christ, so also wives should submit to their husbands in everything." —Also Paul[2]

"But every woman who prays or prophesies with her head uncovered dishonors her head." —Paul[3]

"Women should remain silent in the churches." —Also Paul[4]

"If a man ever tries to use the Bible as a weapon against you to keep from speaking the truth, just throw on a head covering and tell him you're prophesying instead." —Rachel Held Evans[5]

In some ways, my experiences at both United Evangelical Seminary and Life Church were full of mixed messages for women. For example: On the one hand, we *love* that women are part of our seminary, and we want more female faculty. On the other hand, we're going to keep hiring and promoting predominantly male faculty—and these male faculty, however well-intentioned, are not always sensitive to the concerns of female students or aware of how unwelcoming their classrooms might feel.

Or: On the one hand, we *love* that women are a part of our church community, and we want them to participate in our leadership and ministry. On the other hand, when these female leaders see things differently from the way we do, or when they have an opinion we don't like, we're going to assume we're right and they're wrong.

Unfortunately, not only are mixed messages present in faith communities—even egalitarian ones. They're also present in the Bible itself. The books that make up the Bible were written predominantly—perhaps entirely—by men. These were men who, at least in New Testament times, saw Jesus honor women and treat women as equals. They saw God's Spirit descend equally on people of all genders,[6] and they saw the freedom and equality this brought to some of the earliest Christian communities.[7] At the same time, these were also men who embodied the mores of their time and culture. They were humans who internalized the narratives ingrained in them since childhood. They loved Jesus and wanted to follow him— and yet they also sometimes paid a little too much homage to the respectability politics of a harsh and all-consuming Roman Empire.

No doubt it was exceedingly difficult to navigate these things. And no doubt these tensions are behind some of the mixed messages women ended up receiving.

Take Ephesians 5:21-33, for example—a classic staple of Christian wedding fare. In this passage, Paul gives some mixed messages about gender roles in marriage. First, he instructs everyone, regardless of gender, to "submit to one another out of reverence for Christ."[8] Up until this point, Ephesians 5 hasn't particularly been about gender. Paul wants all sorts of people to submit to one another in Christian community—across lines of class, ethnicity, social status, age, gender, and any other walls humans build to try to separate ourselves from one another.

Paul envisions church as a loving, beautiful, messy place where no one is valued more than anyone else, where we all honor one another's needs above our own—which is one of those things that only really works if everyone is doing it. Our reverence for God works itself out in reverence for each person created in God's image and deeply loved by God. We are all part of God's family together. We are all God's children together. God is our leader, and we are a community of equals looking to walk together with God. *Submit to one another out of reverence for Christ.* I like this part.

But then the passage goes on. In the original Greek, v. 21 is part of the same sentence as vv. 22-24. And, while v. 21 may not be gendered, what follows certainly is. Here's my (fairly literal) translation:

> *21Subjecting yourselves to one another in fear of Christ, 22the wives to their own husband as to the lord, 23since a husband is head of the wife as also the Christ is head of the church, himself a savior of the body; 24but as the church is subjected to the Christ, so also the wives to the husbands in everything. 25The husbands: love the wives, just as also the Christ loved the church and handed himself over on its behalf, 26in order that he might sanctify it, after cleansing in the washing of the water with a word, 27in order that he might present to himself the church, glorious, not having blemish or wrinkle or any such things, but in order that it might be holy and blameless. 28So the husbands [also]9 ought to love their own wives as their own bodies. The one who loves his own wife*

loves himself. [29]*For no one ever hated their own flesh but nurtures and cherishes it, just as also the Christ the church,* [30]*since we are members of his body.* [31]*"For this reason a person will leave [the] father and [the] mother and will be joined to their wife, and the two will be (made)* [10] *into one flesh."* [32]*This mystery is great; but I speak to Christ and to the church.* [33]*However, y'all* [11] *also, each one, in this manner let each love their own wife as themselves, and the wife, that she might fear the husband.* [12]

There are a lot of things that could be said, and have been said, about this passage. Parts of it don't seem very nice. But there are ways to explain away some of its harshest-sounding patriarchal aspects.[13]

We could note, for example, that Paul's call to submit in vv. 21-22 is not actually a command form, as many translations would have you think. In Greek, the word translated as "submit" or "be subject" in v. 21 is actually in its participle form, which means that a more literal translation might start off, "being subject to one another..." or "while y'all are submitting yourselves to one another..." or something along those lines. The action is ongoing and assumed, not instructed or commanded.

We could also note that v. 22, in Greek, doesn't actually have a verb. In other words, a literal translation of this phrase would not read "Wives, submit yourselves to your own husbands," but rather just "Wives to your own husbands." Our translations take the verb "submit" from the previous verse and fill it in here. Likewise with v. 24, which also lacks a verb; while the NIV reads, "As the church submits to Christ, so also wives should submit to their husbands in everything," a more literal translation would read, "As the church submits to Christ, so also the wives to the husbands in everything."

The first time Paul actually does use a command form is in v. 25: "Husbands, (y'all) love (your) wives, just as Christ also loved the church and handed himself over on her behalf." Husbands are directly commanded to love their wives, whereas wives are just assumed to submit to their husbands. Maybe Paul isn't trying to control women's actions so much as influence and instruct men to be better and more loving husbands —which, of course, benefits their wives.

Plus, the whole passage is not actually so much about marriage as it is about Christ and the church. Basically, Paul takes the cultural assumptions he shares with most of his readers about marriage and uses these assumptions to say some important things about Christ's relationship with the church. Paul wants to help people better understand that Christ loves the church deeply and sacrificially—just as, in the worldview of Paul's day, a good husband loves his wife. He wants to invite the church to submit to Christ's leadership and follow Christ's example—just as, in the worldview of Paul's day, a good wife submits to her husband. And he wants to help the church understand the profound, intimate unity between Christ and the church—not unlike the profound, intimate unity between two marriage partners.

We can say a lot of things that make this passage sound a little nicer. And there's value in that. At the same time, though, there's no real way of getting around the patriarchy in Paul's words. Even if he is mostly writing about Christ and the church, he's also writing about gender roles in marriage. The passage is full of gendered assumptions that Paul has no interest in challenging.

Paul writes some beautiful stuff about submitting to one another—totally in line with the other beautiful stuff he writes elsewhere about there being no male and female in Christ[14]— and then he writes some patriarchal stuff about wives being subject to their husbands.

So, which is it, Paul? Are we all to submit to one another as equals, in a community focused on being one in Christ? Or are wives to submit to their husbands, in a community focused on enforcing hierarchical gender roles?

It's a mixed message. Both are clearly there. But it's not at all clear what to make of it.

If Ephesians 5:21-33 is an example of a mixed message when it comes to marriage, then the last few chapters of 1 Corinthians are perhaps an example of a mixed message when it comes to women in ministry.

In 1 Corinthians 14:34-5, while giving instructions about prophesying in church meetings, Paul writes, "Women should remain silent in the churches. They are not allowed to speak, but must be in submission, as the law says. If they want to inquire about something, they should ask their own husbands at home; for it is disgraceful for a woman to speak in the church."[15]

This is some harsh stuff. There's disgrace. There's submission. There's silence—the all-too-familiar silencing of women's voices. There's the assumption that women have husbands, and that women center themselves in the home—and that husbands know all the things their wives don't know. (God forbid a husband might find something confusing at church and go home and ask his wife about it!)

I thought of this passage when, one day after maybe the first or second session of my Sexuality and Ethics class in seminary, I was walking back to my apartment, chatting with a male classmate along the way. My classmate told me, to my surprise, that he was planning on dropping the class. Why? Well, because our professor was gay, of course.

We went back and forth about this for a minute:

Male classmate: "Are you going to stay in this class?"

Me: "Yeah, totally. It seems great so far. Why do you ask?"

Male classmate: "Really? You're going to stay? It doesn't bother you that the professor is gay?"

Me: "Ohh...I see. No, it doesn't. Gay relationships don't bother me...and even if they did, our professor told us he's celibate..."

Male classmate: "Really? It doesn't bother you?"

Me: "Yes, really."

Male classmate: "But even though he's celibate, he still identifies as gay!"

After a minute or two of this kind of exchange, my classmate asked me, "Do you talk about these things with your husband?"

At first I wasn't sure what to say. I wasn't sure what Ken had to do with any of this.

I started to reply, "Sure, we talk about these things. Why do you ask?"

And then it hit me. *Oh no*, I thought. *Did I just have 1 Corinthians 14:35 used on me?* "They should ask their own husbands at home..." It was a new experience.

As with many scripture passages, and especially the controversial ones, there are lots of different ways to think about 1 Corinthians 14:34-5.

It's possible, for example, that there was a particular group of women, at this particular time, in this particular church—the one in Corinth—who were speaking up inappropriately, derailing the whole church service by misusing their newfound Christian freedom to talk at inopportune moments or say unhelpful things.

On the other hand, Paul does say, "Women should be silent in the churches"[16]—plural "churches." And the scope of his instruction is broad. Depending on your translation, it may sound like Paul means to speak to "all the congregations of the Lord's people."[17]

As usual, there is some ambiguity here—and perhaps more so in the original Greek text than in many of our English translations. In Greek, the phrase "all the congregations of the Lord's people" could apply either to what comes right before it or what comes right after it. It could be "For God is not a God of disorder but of peace—as in all the congregations of the Lord's people. Women should remain silent in the churches" (NIV). This makes it sound like "women should remain silent" is a separate thought from "all the congregations." Or, it could be "For God is not a God of confusion but of peace. As in all the churches of the saints, the women should keep silent in the churches" (ESV). This is a very different vibe.

It isn't clear whether God is a God of peace in all the churches or if women are to be silent in all the churches.

I also noticed, when translating this passage, that women are encouraged to learn. It's not just that they can ask their husbands specific questions if they really must—as the NIV's "if they want to inquire about something, they should ask their own husbands" implies—but that if they want to learn, they should be able to learn. This word for "learn" comes from the same root as the word translated throughout the New Testament as "disciple"—a learner. If women want to be disciples, they should be able to be disciples.

Plus, the word translated as "ask" here is a strong one. It could also be translated as "demand." I'm picturing these ancient Corinthian Christian women going home after church and saying to their husbands, "The law might tell me to be silent, and all your male cronies might think education is wasted on women. But I want to learn. In fact, I *demand* that you let me learn!" And Paul backs them up. It's not the worst.

It's also possible, as some scholars have suggested, that Paul is quoting from something the Corinthian churchgoers wrote to him so that he can argue against it. In other words, the passage could read something like this, with quotes around the parts that may have come from the Corinthians and not Paul:

> [33]*For God is not a God of disorder but of peace—as in all the congregations of the Lord's people.*
>
> [34]*"Women should remain silent in the churches. They are not allowed to speak, but must be in submission, as the law says.* [35]*If they want to inquire about something, they should ask their own husbands at home; for it is disgraceful for a woman to speak in the church."*
>
> [36]*Or did the word of God originate with you? Or are you the only people it has reached?* [37]*If anyone thinks they are a prophet or otherwise gifted by the Spirit, let them acknowledge that what I am writing to you is the Lord's command.* [38]*But if anyone ignores this, they will themselves be ignored.* [39]*Therefore, my brothers and sisters, be eager to prophesy, and do not forbid speaking in tongues.* [40]*But everything should be done in a fitting and orderly way.*[18]

This might seem like a bit of a stretch. But it does seem possible to read vv. 36-40 in a way that pushes back against vv. 34-5. As in, *You say women shouldn't be speaking in church. But did God's word originate with you? You don't get to just make up rules like that. I want all of you to be eager to prophesy. Do not silence one another. Just make sure you do things in an orderly way.*

We know that there was an ongoing correspondence between Paul and the Corinthian church. And there are plenty of other places in Paul's letters where translators have put quotation marks around some sentences—making an educated guess, without ever being one hundred percent sure—to indicate that these were the congregation's own words that Paul quotes back to them. It may feel jarring to read 1 Corinthians 14:34-5 like this, because we aren't used to it. But it feels natural enough elsewhere. Surely whoever decided where to add quotation marks was not infallible.

So there's some ambiguity to it. Regardless, though, these verses about women being silent in church, and being in submission to their husbands, are pretty harsh.

And yet. Just three chapters prior, Paul writes this: "Every woman who prays or prophesies with her head uncovered dishonors her head—it is the same as having her head shaved."[19] He also writes, "Judge for yourselves: Is it proper for a woman to pray to God with her head uncovered?"[20]

There is a lot going on in 1 Corinthians 11—about long hair, and head coverings, and what all these things meant in that time and culture.[21] Ultimately, though, whatever women were or weren't supposed to be doing with their hair or clothing, it seems clear that women were praying, and women were prophesying. Publicly. During church gatherings. Paul was concerned with the way in which they were doing it, but he wasn't concerned with the fact that they *were* doing it.

It makes sense, then, that in the next chapter—in 1 Corinthians 12—Paul writes that God gives each person spiritual gifts to build up and strengthen the church community. Paul makes no gendered distinctions here. He acknowledges and rejoices in the full range of spiritual gifts given to women—everything from wisdom, to knowledge, to faith, to healing, to miracles, to prophecy, to spiritual discernment, to speaking in tongues and interpreting tongues,[22] to being apostles, prophets, teachers, helpers, or guides.[23]

So, Paul, which one is it? Are women to use their spiritual gifts in public—prophesying and teaching and preaching and the like—just so long as their heads are covered? Or are they to be silent in the churches, going home and asking their husbands any questions they might have?

. . .

I'm not saying there is no reasonable way to reconcile Paul's seemingly contradictory instructions for women. I'm just saying that these things can feel like mixed messages, and for good reason. Especially in faith communities where Paul's letters are taken as a set of literal instructions for today's churches, this can all get really confusing, really fast.

Masculinist interpretations of scripture oversimplify the complexity of these messages. Too often pastors and churches speak of the Bible as if it *only* contains limiting messages for women—clear claims about what women "can" and "can't" do, hierarchical instructions about *what he must be* and *what she must be*. But the real story is more complicated than that. The Bible does contain these messages, but it also contains liberating ones. It contains stories of women leading, preaching, and being all-around spiritual badasses—women filled with God's Spirit and following God's calling in their lives.

We can acknowledge the complexity of scripture, the liberating words alongside the confining ones. This might require a complete overhaul of what we've been taught and what we've practiced. But we can learn to read scripture in more balanced, more nuanced, less masculinist ways. And that might change everything.

18

WHEN THE ANONYMOUS DISCIPLE IS A MAN

*W*hen I took my first preaching class in seminary, one of our main tasks for the quarter was to prepare and preach three sermons. The first two were preached in the classroom; the third could either be preached in the classroom or in an actual, real-life church service—in the wild, if you will.

I had given a boatload of informal sermon-like talks before, mostly to the college group at Faith Bible. But I hadn't really preached a formal sermon. I hadn't thought to ask whether I might preach sometime at Life Church. It seemed a little forward. My preaching class, though, served as a kick in the butt for me to consider that question. So I swallowed my OMG-this-feels-so-presumptuous anxieties and asked Pastor John if I might complete my third assignment at church. He said yes.

John assigned me a Bible passage to preach on, as part of the series he had planned for the summer. The text was Luke 8:1-15—a story Jesus tells about a farmer who scatters seed in four different kinds of soil. Initially, I was less than excited. Anyone who has been going to church for a while has probably heard a million sermons on this parable.

But I studied, and wrestled, and let the passage marinate. I wrote down all my thoughts and questions. I read the rest of the book of Luke up to that point. I did word studies. I read commentaries. All the normal preacher stuff. And through this process I ended up with a couple of ideas that I wanted to focus on in the sermon—ideas I could get excited about and hoped others would too.

First, I was struck by how *weird* this story must have sounded to those who heard it. Jesus' hearers were likely much more familiar with farming than most of us Los Angeles area city dwellers. They would have known that the farmer in the story is *so wasteful*. Doesn't he know that the seed he scatters on the path, the rocks, and among the weeds won't grow well? What does he think he's doing? I wanted to help people feel the strangeness of it all.

The second driving thought, relatedly, had to do with how powerful and amazing the seeds are. Unlike normal seeds, which are limited in quantity, this seed is unlimited. There is a never-ending source of it, and planting it does not deplete its supply. According to Jesus' parable, God's words are like that. God just keeps speaking. If God speaks to one person or group of people in one way, it does not deplete the supply of love from which God is able to speak to another person or group in a different way.

And, unlike normal seeds—which would often bear a crop of maybe fifteen-fold in a good year—this seed, when it hit good soil, bore a crop of up to one hundred-fold. That's more than 6x the normal return on investment, for anyone who's into that sort of thing. The power of God's words to heal, transform, and bear fruit—fruit like love, generosity, kindness, patience, peace, and joy[1]—in our lives and our communities is very strong.

. . .

To explore these kinds of thoughts—and just to keep things interesting and help longtime churchgoers hear a familiar story with fresh ears—I spent a large chunk of the sermon speaking imaginatively from the perspective of a disciple. Not one of the twelve named apostles, but just a random anonymous member of the big, unruly group of people who were following Jesus around from town to town to hear him talk and see him heal.

I gave a little background on what I meant when I used the word "disciple" in this context. I mentioned that the disciples were a group of learners who followed Jesus around, and that they included the twelve (male) apostles but were far from limited to them. These disciples included both men and women. I pointed out that Luke even names a few of Jesus' female disciples in Luke 8:2-3, right before he tells the four soils story: Joanna, Susanna, and Mary Magdalene.

Then I got into the character of an Anonymous Disciple. I talked, in the first person, about what it was like for me to hear Jesus teach. I reflected on some of the reasons I decided to leave my hometown and follow this rabbi around the Judean countryside. I mentioned some of the things I really liked about his teaching so far, and some of the things I found difficult. I shared my struggle to be on this journey with people I really didn't like, including several tax collectors.

Then I went through the parable line by line, talking—still in the Anonymous Disciple persona—about how each part of the story struck me as I heard it. I asked questions about what things might mean. I pointed out the parts I found confusing. I talked about the reactions I saw as I looked around at my compatriots in the motley group of people listening to Jesus, and how these reactions changed as he went on with his story. I talked about how people were paying rapt attention at the beginning, how many began to murmur skeptically by the middle, and how some eventually walked away in disgust while others just sat there looking confused. I talked about how, after the parable was over, most people left but a few came closer to Jesus. I shared why I had been one of the ones who came closer —one of the ones who surrounded Jesus and pressed in on him, asking more questions, trying so hard to understand.

Once I wrapped up the sermon, our usual Q&A time began. Because it was my first time preaching at Life Church, and because people there were nice, I didn't get any particularly hardball questions. There was plenty of positive feedback. It was great.

At one point, a woman raised her hand and shared some thoughtful reflections on the Anonymous Disciple character; as she spoke, I noticed that she referred to the Anonymous Disciple as a "he" several times. I appreciated her reflections, but the pronouns caught me off guard. In my mind, the Anonymous Disciple was a woman. *I'm* a woman, after all. I didn't try to lower my voice or act particularly masculine when I spoke in character. There was nothing particularly gendered, one way or the other, about the words I had spoken—except, perhaps, if you assume that only men knew basic things about farming, which I doubt would have been true. I had even pointed out specifically that Jesus had both male and female disciples.

I almost felt like I was making a feminist statement, of sorts, by speaking so much of the sermon in the voice of a female disciple—that is, an anonymous disciple, who in my mind was female. But, despite all this, some portion of the congregation —including some women in the congregation—heard it as a male voice.

I don't blame the woman who shared these reflections. But I do think it's interesting. In retrospect, I probably shouldn't have been surprised. After all, most of us who have been involved in (male-led) churches for a while have heard *so many* sermons about male Bible characters and hardly any about female Bible characters.[2] As a result, most of us have come to associate important people in the Bible with maleness by default.

Sometimes, as women, we are so accustomed to not seeing ourselves in scripture that even when a female preacher talks about female disciples and then speaks in the voice of an anonymous one of these disciples, we assume that this disciple is a man. Sometimes we've been so conditioned to erase women from the Bible that we don't even see them when they are there.

What does it do to us, when all the stories we hear preached from our pulpits are about men? Men are the protagonists. Men are the apostles. Men are the disciples. Men follow Jesus. Men make adult human choices about how to respond to Jesus. They grow in their understanding of Jesus. They say goofy things that make Jesus rebuke them. They are sent out to do the kinds of things Jesus is doing.

Women do appear in the text of the Bible, but they are often ignored. Their presence is minimized. They hardly take up any space in most sermons. And when Bible women do get some airtime, if you were to hear many (male) preachers talk, these women exist primarily as objects: The subject is the man, and the issue is how he treats a woman. A male preacher might say, *Look how Jesus showed grace toward a prostitute. Wow, isn't he merciful. Let's be merciful too.* Or, he might preach, *See how Jesus took pity on a woman and healed her daughter. We, too, should be agents of healing in our world.* Or, perhaps, *Listen to Jesus talk about how men shouldn't look at women lustfully. We, too, ought to be sexually pure in our thoughts and actions.*

By default, the preacher and hearers are both assumed to

be men. We are taught to identify with Jesus, not with the women in these stories. We are taught to hear Jesus talking *to* men, *about* women.

Don't get me wrong—I'm all for men hearing that they should follow Jesus' example in honoring women. (Remember the dude who "never quite figured out how to treat women"?) The world would be a much better place for everybody if more men actually interacted with women like Jesus did.

But it isn't enough. It assumes a male perspective and uses women as object lessons to teach men how to be more holy. It perpetuates (usually white) men's tendency to see themselves as protagonists of a movie, while the rest of us are accessories, bit actors, assistants, or extras—or, sometimes, in the case of women, distractions and temptations. Villains, really, but minor ones.

Can we learn—in our pulpits and our Bible studies, our small groups and our personal Bible reading—to really see women in scripture? What would it look like to stop ignoring them? And can we learn to see them not as object lessons for men but as full humans—people who learn from and follow Jesus, just like their male counterparts? Can we see them as active participants with Jesus in the kingdom of God? Can we see them in the gospel stories among Jesus' many unnamed disciples—learners who were learning so that one day they could teach?

For that matter, can we talk about the women in scripture who preach and teach? I'm thinking of people like the Samaritan woman at the well, who, after chatting with Jesus, realized Jesus was the Messiah and went back to her hometown to tell everyone about him.[3] I'm thinking of the women who were the first witnesses and preachers of the resurrection.[4] I'm thinking of women like Mary, the sister of Martha, who subverted

gendered expectations of female servitude and stubbornly
chose to sit at the feet of Jesus and listen to him teach.[5] (The
laundry could wait.) And—from the passage I was preaching
on that morning—I'm thinking of women like Mary Magdalene, Joanna, and Susanna, who traveled with Jesus and helped
provide for him out of their own means.[6]

I want to see and honor these female disciples and others
like them—the women who show up, however quietly, in just
about every story about Jesus. They are there. *We* are there.

When we as women don't see the women in these stories,
we have a harder time seeing ourselves in our scriptures. Plus,
when men don't see the women in these stories, they have a
harder time seeing the women in their own lives and communities as an important part of the story of faith. Men need to be
pushed toward seeing women—both in the Bible and in the
present day, because it's all connected—as active agents, gifted
and called, equal partners in community and life and ministry.
Men need to be encouraged to see the women in their lives as
more than passive objects to be treated a certain way, more than
bit actors in a world where the man is clearly always the heroic
protagonist.

Nobody really benefits from a masculinist reading of scripture. But this is the way it's been done—so often, for so long,
with so much outsized attention to men and so little attention
to women. Women need to hear scripture preached in ways
that affirm our presence and importance; men need to hear this
too, lest they miss the strong, equal partners we could be.
People of all genders need to hear and know that women
matter.

This might feel uncomfortable for those men who are
accustomed to only seeing themselves in scripture—men well-
acquainted with the habits of ignoring women. It might feel
like they have something to lose from a more balanced
approach to scripture. But valuing women more does not need

to mean that we value men less. Remember the seeds: God's words are so powerful and abundant that a farmer can strew them carelessly all over a field; likewise, freedom and power and full humanness is not diminished for one group when attained by another. There is more than enough to go around. Abundantly. One hundred-fold.

19

BLESSED ARE YOU

"Blessed are you among women." —Elizabeth[1]

"Surely, from now on all generations will call me blessed."
—Mary[2]

"We must move away from the strategies provided by corporate
feminism that teach us to lean in but not how to actually
support each other...We need to understand that sometimes
the fiercest warriors need care and kindness. We can't be afraid
of their anger or their willingness to shout."
—Mikki Kendall[3]

*a*s we look to demasculinize the ways we read scripture,
we learn to see the women in the Bible—and to see
them as their full selves. And as we do so, there is blessing.
Healing. Freedom. Because the Bible is not *just* full of patriarchal assumptions and mixed messages for women. It's also full
of liberation—if we're looking for it.

One of the (perhaps unexpected) places I see this liberation is in Luke's version of the Christmas story.

In Luke's gospel, things get pretty wild pretty fast. Right from the start, there are angels. There are miraculous pregnancies. There are unlikely-sounding prophecies and people bursting out into spontaneous song like it's a Disney musical. And, while this doesn't always come through strongly in evangelical Christmas narratives, there are two women central to the story: Elizabeth and Mary.

First, an angel appears to Elizabeth's husband Zechariah, telling him that Elizabeth is going to become pregnant and give birth to a son, even though the couple is well past childbearing age.[4] Then, around six months later, that same angel appears to Mary.

Depending on our upbringings, denominations, and experiences, we might have a lot of thoughts about Mary. Theologians and ordinary folks have reflected on Mary over the years with some mix of richness, honor, and oddness. Whatever she might have come to mean to us over two thousand years, though, Mary was a real historical human. This is worth remembering. In her own time and place, in the reality of her own life, Mary was an unmarried teenage girl living in poverty in a small town in the middle of nowhere. And the angel comes to her—not to her fiancé, or father, or any of the men who may have been considered authority figures in her world, but directly to Mary—and says, *You are going to have a son, and you should name him Jesus.* Mary says, *How? I'm a virgin.* The angel says, *Through the Holy Spirit.* And Mary says, *Oh, cool, then. Let's go. Let's do this.*[5] (But actually.)

Can you imagine being Mary here? An angel suddenly appears, out of nowhere, just about giving you a heart attack. The angel tells you not to be afraid, but that doesn't stop your heart from pounding in your chest. Then the angel carries on with this message: You—you, in your small town, in your youth, in your vulnerability and insignificance in the eyes of your world—*you* are going to miraculously give birth to a king, the holy one who will be called the Son of God.[6]

What do you do with this kind of radically life-disrupting news? Who do you talk to? Who might even begin to understand? Where do you go, there in your small hometown, full of people who generally expect pregnancy to work in the usual way?

Mary remembers what the angel told her about her relative Elizabeth. Elizabeth is now six months pregnant, miraculously, after decades of infertility. So, Mary sets off to visit Elizabeth. She grabs a water bottle and a granola bar, types in "Judean hill country" in her Google Maps app, hops in her parents' trusty old Jeep, and heads off toward Elizabeth's place.

Just kidding. Mary's journey to the hill country of Judea was a slow one. It likely lasted around three to five days, depending on where exactly Elizabeth lived. The roads were known to be dangerous, full of robbers. My hope is that she found a caravan she could travel with that would help keep her safe. Regardless, it took courage to go off on her own like that, apart from her family, fiancé, and hometown community.

She must have felt it was necessary. I imagine her thinking, *this is all so wild, and unexpected, and incredible, and terrifying, and wonderful, and complicated. I don't know if anyone will understand. But if anyone could, maybe it's Elizabeth.*

It was the only thing to do.

This is how Luke tells it:

> [39]*In those days Mary set out and went with haste to a Judean town in the hill country, [40]where she entered the house of*

Zechariah and greeted Elizabeth. ⁴¹When Elizabeth heard Mary's
greeting, the child leaped in her womb. And Elizabeth was filled
with the Holy Spirit ⁴²and exclaimed with a loud cry, "Blessed are
you among women, and blessed is the fruit of your womb. ⁴³And
why has this happened to me, that the mother of my Lord comes to
me? ⁴⁴For as soon as I heard the sound of your greeting, the child in
my womb leaped for joy. ⁴⁵And blessed is she who believed that
there would be a fulfillment of what was spoken to her by the
Lord."[7]

Mary arrives safely, enters the house, and greets Elizabeth
with a usual type of greeting. Elizabeth does not give a usual
greeting back. There's no *what's up, girl?? So good to see you!!*
Long time no see! Instead, Elizabeth cries out loudly: *You are*
blessed among women! And the fruit of your womb is blessed too! You
are blessed because you believed that what the Lord said would
happen.

Elizabeth shouts a loud blessing. And little end-of-second-
trimester John the Baptist does a jump inside Elizabeth's
growing belly. She interprets this as a jump for joy, a jump of
exultation. Elizabeth is filled with the Holy Spirit, and she
speaks. This exact language of being "filled with the Holy
Spirit" is only used a few other times in the New Testament. It's
used when the angel tells Zechariah that John the Baptist will
be "filled with the Holy Spirit" even from his mother's womb.[8]
Zechariah is himself then "filled with the Holy Spirit" later on
in this chapter,[9] as he speaks his own prophetic poem a few
verses after Mary's. Much later, the believers at Pentecost in the
book of Acts are "filled with the Holy Spirit,"[10] speaking in
other languages as the Spirit enables them. Peter and Paul are
each described as being "filled with the Holy Spirit" in some
parts of Acts, particularly when they have something especially
bold to say.[11]

Elizabeth joins the ranks of men like John the Baptist,

Zechariah, Peter, Paul. She is filled with the same Spirit. And she, too, speaks boldly. She speaks in a loud and confident voice. In the original Greek text, Luke actually uses three different words to express how intense Elizabeth's voice is: She "exclaims"—meaning that she spoke out, or cried aloud. Her voice is "loud"—or, literally, "great." And it sounds like a "cry," which is a word that can also be translated as "outcry," or "clamor." (Paul uses this same word for *clamor* when he writes to the Ephesian Christians that they should try to stay away from things like anger, malice, brawling, and clamor.[12])

It's a fighting kind of cry—a loud, great, clamor. And, in Elizabeth's case, it's full of the Holy Spirit. It's bold, prophetic, and true—and extremely unladylike. While Zechariah, the priest, is still unable to speak, Elizabeth—also descended from Aaron[13] but not allowed to be a priest because of her gender—speaks loudly. Elizabeth has something to say, and she says it. She has prophecy to speak. She has inexpressible joy to try to express. She doesn't have time to take a step back and make sure her voice is gentle enough, her words are inoffensive enough, and nothing she says is threatening to anyone.

Elizabeth refuses to engage in what Mikki Kendall calls "the tone policing of respectability."[14] I think Elizabeth knows that, as Kendall puts it, "no woman has to be respectable to be valuable."[15] Elizabeth's blessing for Mary is pure unruly holy clamor. And it is important.

Mary and Elizabeth greet one another in the midst of their male-dominated world, but in this scene, there are no men to be found. Zechariah is who knows where. The baby boys John and Jesus have not been born yet. It's just a raw, unfiltered, real, beautiful human interaction between two female relatives, one older, one younger.

Immediately after she receives Elizabeth's clamorous blessing, Mary launches into the beautiful prophetic poem known as the Magnificat. I love the way Kathy Khang connects Elizabeth's blessing with Mary's prophetic poem:

> Elizabeth is unafraid and generous in her word of blessing and exhortation. I imagine that's because she knows what I often have to remind myself: finding and using our voice isn't a zero-sum game where we compete with others. Elizabeth isn't competing. She knows this is a journey for both of them, and she sets the stage for Mary to speak...Elizabeth isn't there just to provide an audience or to be a foil or competitor. She's the one whose presence and words remind Mary who she is and what is to come.[16]

Isn't it beautiful when women can do this for one another? Mary and Elizabeth are learning—to borrow Kendall's words once again—not just to "lean in," but to "actually support each other." They are among the "fiercest warriors" who also "need care and kindness."[17] This care and kindness is what they offer one another, and what they joyfully receive.

Mary, then, sings this song:

> *My soul magnifies the Lord,*
> *[47]and my spirit rejoices in God my Savior,*
> *[48]for he has looked with favor on the lowliness of his servant.*
> *Surely, from now on all generations will call me blessed;*
> *[49]for the Mighty One has done great things for me,*
> *and holy is his name.*
> *[50]His mercy is for those who fear him*
> *from generation to generation.*
> *[51]He has shown strength with his arm;*
> *he has scattered the proud in the thoughts of their hearts.*

> [52]He has brought down the powerful from their thrones,
> and lifted up the lowly;
> [53]he has filled the hungry with good things,
> and sent the rich away empty.
> [54]He has helped his servant Israel,
> in remembrance of his mercy,
> [55]according to the promise he made to our ancestors,
> to Abraham and to his descendants forever.[18]

I think about the popular Christmas song "Mary Did You Know?"[19] And I think about all the things Mary actually did know. The Magnificat makes it clear that Mary knew exactly who her son was.

From the angel Gabriel, Mary knew that her baby Jesus would be called the Son of the Most High and that God would give him the throne of his ancestor David.[20] She knew that Jesus would reign over Jacob's descendants forever, that his kingdom would never end.[21] She knew that Jesus would be holy, called the Son of God.[22]

From her relative Elizabeth, Mary knew that she and her child were blessed.[23] She knew that he would be called Lord.[24] She knew that the baby was a fulfillment of God's miraculous promise.[25]

And, from the depths of her own soul, Mary knew that all generations would call her blessed.[26] She knew that her baby would participate in God's mighty deeds—scattering the proud, bringing rulers down from their thrones, lifting up the humble.[27] She knew that Jesus would fill the hungry with good things and send the rich away empty.[28] She knew that Jesus would embody God's help and mercy, God's remembrance toward God's people.[29]

Mary knew. Maybe not some of the specifics. But she knew the general scheme: the salvation and renewal, the deliverance, the healing, the power, the reversal. When Mary held her sleeping baby boy, she knew exactly who that sweet little face really was.

She knew all these things before there was any actual, messy, glorious, agonizing, bloody, miraculous childbirth. She knew these things before shepherds started randomly showing up to see the baby, bumbling and blustering about angels and messiahs and mangers.[30] She knew these things before the old man Simeon crashed baby Jesus' circumcision and spoke of God's salvation in the sight of all the nations, about light for revelation to the Gentiles and glory to Israel, about the falling and rising of many, about people's thoughts being revealed, about a sword piercing Mary's own soul.[31] She knew these things before the old woman Anna, in her own astute prophetic way, gave thanks to God and spoke of the redemption of Jerusalem.[32]

Mary knew, before any of this. But I'm sure it didn't hurt to hear from the shepherds and Simeon and Anna, anyway. Each odd occurrence—each encounter with a stranger who miraculously knew something about Jesus—served to confirm what Mary already held in her heart, what she had already spoken in the Magnificat. And she treasured it all.[33]

Mary knew—and, even more than just knowing, she spoke these things into being. She sang these hopes like prophecy over Jesus' life. And her words came true.

I love the way Kelley Nikondeha writes about this:

Throughout her life, Mary pondered the God who overshadowed her. She hummed her magnificent song of overturned expectations as her son learned Torah and took on the mantle of rabbi in Galilee. She sang it through tears to console herself as he hung on a cross at Golgotha, when she didn't understand what her world was coming to anymore. And on

Easter Sunday—how full and glorious the song must have sounded then! Maybe by then her friends knew the chorus, and the women sang with her as the resurrection reversed death itself.

I listen to Mary hum as I read the stories about Jesus. I witness her bravery to sing of revolution under the thumb of the Roman Empire. She was brave to believe God's announcement to her, holding fast to the song in the face of years of conflicting messages and even crucifixion. She let the song grow into an anthem as her son grew into the Messiah. That liberation anthem called out the best in her, giving her words to sing, full voiced, even when all evidence proclaimed something quite contrary. She never stopped believing in God's grand reversal.[34]

I love this image of Mary, mother to the young boy Jesus, humming her song over him. It's a song of freedom composed from the depths of Mary's soul—inspired by God's spirit, filled with God's desires. It's a song of reversal of fate, reversal of expectations, and deep, deep joy. It's a song about Jesus, yes—but also, very unashamedly, about Mary herself. *From now on all generations will call me blessed.*

Mary has so much knowing, so much wisdom, to offer. She overflows with it—with what Glennon Doyle might call Knowing with a capital "K."[35] Mary can't contain herself. She has so much to teach us, through the generations—these generations that will call her blessed—about who God is, what God is like, what God does.

Mary sings of a God who sees the people at the bottom of the social order—people who know they need God to *do* something. People like her. And this God does something. This God helps these people. This God does not leave the proud to keep thinking they're better than everyone else, but scatters them. This God does not leave corrupt and selfish rulers—of whom there never seems to be a scarcity—in their thrones, but brings them down.

Mary dreams of a day when all of this will be made so clear, so obvious—a day when her eyes see these things she so deeply believes in. And, in the interim, she sings. She prays. She hopes. She prophesies. She raises Jesus to believe these things about God as much as she does. From her own liberation, Mary raises Jesus to be liberated, and to be a liberator.

In the midst of a stunningly patriarchal world in which women were expected to disappear into the background, Mary and Elizabeth take up space. They take up space in Luke's narrative. They take up space in the story of God's love and redemption in the world. They boldly claim the importance of their voices. They break out of the confines of what is considered respectable behavior. They bless one another, inspire one another, speak life into one another. They are here for themselves and for each other. *Blessed are you.*

I dream of a world where all of this is entirely unremarkable and mundane—where a woman stepping boldly into a priestly role of blessing, as Elizabeth does, is not particularly noteworthy but just the expected way of things.

I dream of a world where opportunities and roles available to women are not so constricted and limited that it often feels like we're all competing with one another for a small slice of that ever-elusive pie—a pie that was never baked for us in the first place.

I dream of a world where women are no longer socialized to just get along. A world where women are no longer told, constantly, in a million different ways: don't make waves, don't be too loud, don't draw attention to yourself, don't stir up trouble, don't make anyone upset; do hold your tongue, do speak gently and quietly, do defer to others, defer to men.

I dream of a world where all women's inspired and holy prophecies, songs, poems, spoken word pieces, essays, paintings, and all other sorts of creative work echo through the ages, so full of truth, in a way that the whole world can hear.

I dream of a world where women's voices are amplified rather than silenced—where hundreds and thousands and billions of ordinary, amazing women like Mary and Elizabeth raise their voices and are heard. A world where women's words are taken seriously, held like holy fire in all the fullness of their prophetic power and goodness. A world where women freely speak words of liberation that send sparks through the souls of everyone who hears them. A world where women's Knowing, women's wisdom, is seen and honored, and no woman is assumed to know less than she does. Mary and Elizabeth help us dream.

20

THOSE PESKY BIBLE WOMEN

When I read Ruth Everhart's book *The #MeToo Reckoning: Facing the Church's Complicity in Sexual Abuse and Misconduct*, I thought: This should be required reading for seminary students. (And all pastors too, for that matter—but that's a little harder to enforce, since no one's assigning them homework.) *The #MeToo Reckoning* was published in 2020, the year after I graduated from seminary, so I guess that's a pretty good excuse for why it wasn't included in my own curriculum. But seminaries now? No excuses.

Seminary angst aside, I came across Everhart's book after I graduated, and it blew my mind. I won't try to do the whole thing justice here. But I will include one part that stood out to me. It has to do with Jesus' parable about a persistent widow who keeps demanding justice for herself. I was familiar with this story, but I'd never heard it talked about quite like this.

Here is the story:

¹And he was speaking a parable to them, for the purpose of (showing) it is necessary (for) them always to pray and not to be weary,

[2]saying, "A certain judge was in a certain city, not fearing God and not respecting humanity. [3]But a widow was in that city and she went to him, saying, 'Vindicate me from my opponent.' [4]And he did not wish to, for a time. But after these things he said within himself, 'Even if I do not fear God nor respect humanity, [5]because, indeed, this widow affords me trouble, I will vindicate her, in order that, going, she might not annoy me into an end.'"

[6]And the Lord said, "(Y'all) hear what the unjust judge says; [7]but should God certainly not make vindication of his chosen ones who cry out to him day and night, and will he have patience at them? [8]I say to y'all that he will make their vindication quickly. However, will the child of humanity, coming, then, find faith on the earth?"[1]

Everhart reflects on this parable in light of systemic issues of sexual abuse (and subsequent cover-ups) in churches:

We aren't told the nature of the widow's legal trouble, or even if she's in the right. Jesus does, however, address the widow's decorum. Does she pursue her cause like a 'good girl'? Does she choose her words carefully and deliver them in a modulated tone during office hours? Not at all. The widow is annoying. She shows up at all hours of the day and night and bangs on her opponent's door...

Her *opponent*. When Jesus uses that word, it suggests that women can *have* opponents. Fancy that. Jesus doesn't suggest that the widow lower her expectations or lower her voice. Jesus doesn't suggest she come back in the morning after she's pulled herself together and can talk nicely. Apparently, her actions are nice enough for Jesus. Pounding on the door of the unjust judge is fine.[2]

Apparently, her actions are nice enough for Jesus. I like that.

Later on, reflecting more personally on her own experience of sexual assault and her subsequent pursuit of justice, Everhart writes:

> The parable of the persistent, pestering widow comforted me as I went through the legal process. This parable offers encouragement to all who pursue justice, even those using methods that are socially unacceptable. The gospel truth is that the Mighty One sides with the vulnerable who disrupt power. Bringing embarrassment is a reasonable thing to do, even if the guilty party is powerful.
>
> It's tempting to leave the pursuit of justice to others—let someone else persist and speak truth to power. It feels uncomfortable to be vocal, especially if we grew up with the message that women should be quiet and submissive. This parable sends a different, empowering message. Jesus lifts every vulnerable person from the margins and encourages her to seek her day in court.[3]

Amen to all of this.

This is the kind of thing that helps me think about what it looks like to be a woman in the church today. I feel the pull of wanting to come across as a "good girl," as Everhart calls it, choosing words carefully and speaking in gentle tones, doing everything possible not to be seen as annoying. I'm uncomfortable having opponents. I'm uncomfortable operating in ways that might be seen as socially unacceptable. I feel the temptation to sit back and let someone else speak up.

I need this parable. I need this kind of reflection on it. I need *women's* reflections on it. And I need the particular reflections of women who have had to pursue justice in this way—women who have been sustained and encouraged by this story while walking a difficult road.

.   .   .

It turns out that the persistent widow is not alone. The Bible is full of women who took the actions they could take—doing what they could do, in the contexts they were in, in times and cultures and communities that placed more limitations on women than I've ever experienced. I wish things were different. I wish these women had been totally free to express their gifts and their full humanity with every fiber of their being. They weren't. And yet, they were amazing and inspiring nonetheless. We can look to them as we think about our own lives in our own sexist contexts.

When I think of brave Bible women, I think of the women in the Exodus story. I think about the Hebrew midwives Shiphrah and Puah, during the time of their people's enslavement in Egypt. They defied Pharaoh's orders and refused to kill the baby boys they helped deliver. They even lied to Pharaoh's face about it—which took some guts, to put it mildly.[4]

I think about Miriam, as a child, bravely hiding her baby brother Moses in the reeds along the river, risking everything for the chance of his survival. Then, just as brave and also incredibly clever, she made an arrangement with Pharaoh's daughter such that Miriam's mom ended up nursing her own son—and getting paid for it.[5] Miriam went on to become, in her own right, a powerful prophet and leader, songwriter and minister. Her song, as recorded in Exodus 15, is short, but her words hold power. Certainly the women of her community thought so as they followed her, playing tambourines and dancing.[6]

I think about Pharaoh's daughter, who found the helpless Hebrew baby abandoned in the reeds—in the little basket his mom so lovingly wove for him, strand by strand, weeping and hoping against hope that God might intervene. Pharaoh's daughter broke ranks with her family's privilege and (abuse of) power, subverted her own father's orders, and became an answer to Moses' family's longshot prayers.

Kelley Nikondeha explores all this and more in her book *Defiant: What the Women of Exodus Teach Us about Freedom*. For Nikondeha, these women of Exodus "demonstrate the power to defy death from any side of the river. They show that the resistance is not limited to one tribe or one segment of the wider sisterhood but is open to any woman willing to enter the fray and work for freedom."[7] There is a place for everyone who seeks justice. As a materially comfortable white woman, this looks different for me than for my sisters of color or sisters facing financial hardship. Often my place involves taking a step back, making room, following the lead of those who have experienced injustices I haven't experienced and thus better know how to push back. But there is still a place. This is good news.

When I think of Bible women who lived lives of courage and conviction, I think, too, of the women in the very earliest New Testament-times churches. In a more patriarchal world than I can easily imagine, many of them still managed to do a hell of a lot of speaking, leading, teaching, and ministering.

I think of Junia, named by Paul as "outstanding among the apostles."[8] I wish I knew more about who exactly she was and what she did, such that Paul—yes, Paul, with all his mixed messages about women—held her in such high regard. Regardless of the details, Junia was considered an apostle—and not just an apostle, but a truly outstanding one. The word translated as "outstanding" here could also mean "eminent," "notable," "marked," or "illustrious." Junia was an eminent apostle; she was illustrious among the apostles. This is high enough praise, apparently, that later (male) Bible translators felt the need to turn Junia's female name into the male name Junias. But Junia was a woman—and a badass woman at that. I bet Paul didn't want *her* to shut up in church. And I bet she wouldn't have, even if he had wanted her to.

I also think of Priscilla, a Jewish woman who met Paul in Corinth after she and her husband Aquila moved there fleeing persecution in Rome. There's a fun story in the book of Acts where a new convert named Apollos is super excited about God and knows a lot about the scriptures but still has much to learn about Jesus. Apollos is one of those naturally confident people (what would that be like?) who feels like he can go ahead and "speak boldly in the synagogue"[9] even though there is so much he doesn't actually know.

Priscilla and Aquila hear him speak and think, *oh no...this guy speaks so passionately and persuasively, but he doesn't actually know a thing about Jesus!*[10] So, they invite him to their home and "[explain] to him the way of God more adequately."[11] After Apollos spends some time learning important stuff from Priscilla and Aquila, he gets sent off to preach elsewhere—this time with the blessing of the community.[12] Now that Priscilla and Aquila have taught him, everyone is excited to hear Apollos preach. They're no longer groaning inwardly at all the things he clearly doesn't know.

Basically, Priscilla and Aquila are a wife-husband power couple, leading and teaching together, functioning in effect as Apollos' seminary professors—teaching him so that he can go and teach others. Priscilla was the kind of awesome female professor I wished I'd had more of in seminary two thousand years later.

This is by no means an exhaustive list of badass Bible women. It's just a few snapshots from different parts of the biblical story —snapshots of women's courage and giftedness as they lived lives of bold faith within the confines of their world.

These are the things I think about—the things I want to think about—as I figure out how to live in this world. These are the things I long for faith communities to think about together. As a woman, I need churches to reflect on these things. If we want to build new kinds of churches and a new kind of world together, we need to learn to read the Bible in new ways. There is so much to deprogram. There is so much we're missing. There is so much to learn to see differently.

At the church I'm a part of now, we often talk about repentance as changing one's mind. This isn't just something our pastors made up. It comes directly from the Greek word translated as repentance in the New Testament: *metanoia*. The *meta* part has to do with change, and the *noia* part has to do with the mind—understanding, perception, thinking.

It turns out that it's good to change our minds. It's holy to change our minds. Repentance doesn't just mean recognizing something we're doing that might be classified as "sin," asking for forgiveness, and trying not to do that thing anymore. It means being willing to do a one-eighty on any of our ways of thinking—and our ways of viewing the world, our ways of engaging with ourselves and our communities and our planet —that don't line up with love, justice, and goodness for all people.

Many of us have dwelled too long in faith communities that tend to read scripture in a male-centered, male-dominated way. It's (long past) time to change these habits.

I'm learning to ask, when I read the Bible: Where are the women? Who are they, and what are they doing? Where are women absent, and what do we make of that? Are they really absent from the scene, or are they just not mentioned directly in the text—and, if they are present but not mentioned, where might they be, and what might they be doing?

I'm seeking out pastors, scholars, and other writers—female pastors, scholars, and writers from a diversity of backgrounds— who can help me see things differently. I'm trying to deprogram my mind from the masculinist readings of scripture we get so often—the ones where people automatically assume that the Anonymous Disciple is a man. I'm trying to reprogram myself to see the women in scripture and not skim over them.

I need to know that women are more than bit players in God's story. We need to know this, together.

EXPANDING THEOLOGY

21

BOOKSHELF MATH

*W*hen everything shut down in March 2020 due to the COVID-19 pandemic, it took me a few days to realize that our local library had closed, too. It eventually opened back up in the summer, and I'm pretty sure I was their number one curbside pick-up patron for the next several months. But in those early days of the pandemic, I had no idea if or when the library would open again. What was I to read?

In retrospect, I should have thought ahead and checked out ALL THE BOOKS while things were still closing down slowly and sporadically rather than suddenly and completely. But before I knew it, plans were canceled, local friends and family were inaccessible, and there was nowhere to go and nothing to do except hang out at home, take walks around the neighborhood, figure out how to use Zoom, and, ideally, read a lot—except for one little issue. No more access to limitless free books. Yikes. Watching the entire Battlestar Galactica series with Ken could only take me so far.[1]

Then I looked around and remembered that I own a few books. This is something I re-realize every time I move—so many book boxes!—but tend to forget in-between.

It occurred to me that I might not be the only person bummed out that the library had closed. I wondered if others at my church might feel the same way. I figured some of them probably had books in their homes, too; it seemed possible that I might have a book someone else would want to read, and vice versa. What if we made a shared Google doc, I wondered, as a sort of church-wide lending library, where people could add the books they're willing to lend out, and anyone who wants to borrow a book could contact its owner and work out a plan to pick it up?

I thought it seemed like a reasonable idea. I got as far as chronicling all my books—except for some books I dislike enough that I wouldn't really want anyone else to read them, and others I haven't actually read—in a spreadsheet.

When I made the list, I was aware that it skewed pretty white and male. I was a little bummed about this. I worried about what people at my multiethnic, progressive-leaning church would think about my collection, how they might judge me because of it. I also hoped that some of them might have more diverse collections and could help me diversify. But I also figured, a good book is a good book. White dudes have written some good books, and people might want to read some of them.

So, I made a list of 143 books that I would be happy to lend out. The lending library never actually happened, but I've been thinking about this list. It offers a snapshot of the thinkers and theologians who shaped my sense of God and faith up until that time—both in my evangelical church life in my twenties, and in my time in seminary. It got me thinking about just how white-dominated and male-dominated all of this was.

In seminary, the syllabi were often full of white men. In some courses, for the last book of the quarter, we would be offered a choice among a handful of books not written by white men. In a way that might be comical if it weren't so tragic, the choices often went something like this: a (usually male) Black author, a (usually male) Latino author, a (usually male) Asian or Asian American author, and a (usually white) female author.

How much does that totally suck? For one thing, it erases women of color's voices entirely. (And, as I've learned in my own reading after graduating from seminary, there are *so many* women of color writing brilliant and important things, so please don't tell me they're too hard to find.[2]) It also means that all of us seminary students were asked to choose whether we wanted to learn from one woman or from one person of color. There wasn't room on the reading list for both.

As I was thinking about my spreadsheet of books, I wondered what it might look like to put some numbers to them—to explore, numerically, just how white and male these books skew. So I did a little math.

First, to keep the list faith-specific, I took out the novels, as well as nonfiction books that don't expressly deal with themes of Christian religion, theology, or spirituality. I kept any book that was assigned reading for a seminary class, even if the book itself was not explicitly religious.[3] I then added back a few books I'd initially figured were too densely academic for most people's taste, especially amidst the anxiety of the early days of the pandemic. (In those days I found myself with a shorter-than-usual attention span, better suited to *A Game of Thrones* than the minutiae of different modes of biblical interpretation). I also removed authors who are difficult to categorize racially because they lived before the era of our modern racial categories.[4]

All in all, I ended up with 129 books and a total of 145 authors or editors.[5] For the books with multiple authors or editors, I identified the race and gender of each individually.

Where I had multiple books by the same author, I counted this author multiple times.[6]

So here's the breakdown. Of these 145 authors, 114 (79%) are male. 116 (80%) are white. On the flip side, only 31 authors (21%) are female, and 29 authors (20%) are people of color.

Taking race and gender together, 95 of these authors (66%) are white men. Twenty-one (15%) are white women, 19 (13%) are men of color, and 10 (7%) are women of color.[7]

Clearly, my collection of books was heavy on the Y chromosomes and light on the melanin. Even more so than I would have thought from just looking at it, without doing the math.

By the time I was in seminary, I was somewhat aware of the whiteness and maleness of the Christian books I tended to read. This bothered me, but I didn't know what to do about it. I didn't know that I could advocate for reading lists to be changed.[8] Even if I had known, I wouldn't have known which scholars to advocate for, or how to find them. (Now—several years and a lot of research later—I know many authors whose work definitely should have been on some of those seminary reading lists. But at the time, I had no idea.)

I didn't want my theology to be shaped only by white men. Within the confines of seminary curricula, I intentionally sought out female voices and voices of color; I tried to sign up for classes taught by female professors and professors of color where possible,[9] as well as classes whose topics were relevant to race and gender.[10] If I hadn't come into seminary with these areas of interest already in mind, I'm sure my reading lists could have trended even whiter and even more male.

My list was also skewed by the fact that I excluded any books I dislike enough that I wouldn't really want someone else to read them. I got rid of a lot of books in that category when I moved away from Southern California. (When I put these

books in a box labeled "free" outside my door in student housing, one or two conservative students seemed delighted to see
them and a bit incredulous that I was giving them away.) But I
still have a few, and they didn't make it onto my lending library
list. These tend to be the most conservative books I have, and I
have no doubt that their authors are overwhelmingly white
men. If a book made it onto my list, that means I don't hate it—
which means that, when I read it, I didn't recognize enough
racism or sexism to make me think, *I really don't want to lend this
to someone in my church community.*

All of these things together—the egregious numbers,
combined with the ways this list could have been even more
white-male skewed—are kind of terrifying. I went to a seminary that, in theory, is committed to both gender and racial
equity. Within the (limited) elective options I had as an MDiv
student, I specifically sought out opportunities to learn about
race and gender and to learn from women and people of color.
And within my collection of books, I excluded the ones that
pissed me off with their blatant racism or sexism. I still ended
up with 79% male authors, 80% white authors, and only 7%
female authors of color. These were the "experts" who filled my
bookshelves.

Certain white men get to be "experts" on anything and
everything, really: pastoral ministry, spiritual practice, theology,
church history, ethics, biblical studies, preaching, and whatever
else they like. They get to write books with definitive-sounding
titles, like *Pastor: The Theology and Practice of Ordained Ministry*
(William Willimon), or *Old Testament Ethics for the People of God*
(Christopher Wright), or *The Gospel in a Pluralist Society* (Lesslie
Newbigin—who was a man, just to be clear). Meanwhile, books
by white women often pertain specifically to gender—*Birthing
the Sermon: Women Preachers on the Creative Process* (ed. Jana

Childers), for example, or *Women and Early Christianity: A Reappraisal* (Susanne Heine). Books by men of color often pertain specifically to race, like *Martin & Malcolm & America: A Dream or a Nightmare* (James Cone), or *Racial Conflict and Healing: An Asian American Perspective* (Andrew Sung Park). And books by women of color often pertain specifically to both race and gender, like *Ella Baker and the Black Freedom Movement: A Radical Democratic Vision* (Barbara Ransby) or *Women, Race, and Class* (Angela Davis). This is not true in every case. But there is definitely a pattern.[11]

The generic "textbook" kinds of texts—on biblical interpretation, theology, ethics, pastoral ministry, and more, at least in my experience at United Evangelical—are almost always written by white men. These white men feel—and are—authorized to speak on behalf of the academy, and on behalf of Christians, churches, theologians, and biblical scholars in general. The books I was exposed to that were written by people of color and by women, in contrast, were much less likely to be general textbooks, much more likely to deal specifically with race and/or gender.

Don't get me wrong—I'm glad people are writing about race and gender-specific things, and I'm glad that the people writing about these things are those who can write from experience. That's a huge step up from men trying to write about women in the pulpit, or white people trying to write about (and often distorting) Dr. King's vision for the U.S. I just wish white men were not considered the default "experts" on everything.

Maybe this is a little more detail than you needed. But I offer these reflections—which feel more like confessions, really—in case they're helpful as you think about your own bookshelves, or favorite podcasts, or streaming series, or movies, or magazines, or websites, or sermons and preachers. Who wrote these books? Who hosts these podcasts, writes and directs these series and movies, edits these magazines, creates and edits content for these websites, preaches these sermons? Whose perspectives do we inundate ourselves with?

If your bookshelves look very different from mine, that's awesome. If not, let's get in there and do some work—whether that means buying more books by women writers and writers of color (and especially women writers of color), or checking out more of these books from the library, or listening to different podcasts, or watching different movies. The point is not to consume more, but to consume differently, and to be shaped differently. Our literal bookshelves may or may not change. But our hearts and minds need to.

As Kathy Khang exhorts us:

> Commit to reading books by authors of color, particularly theologians and Christian leaders of color...Commit to reading books by authors who have a different viewpoint on issues than you do or come from a different racial, ethnic, or socioeconomic experience than you do...If you are a man, listen to women preach. If you are a woman, listen to women preach.[12] And don't limit your consumption to Western voices. There is an entire world out there.[13]

White male voices are the ones that have dominated and still dominate the Western Christian tradition. And, regardless of our own race and gender, most of us who have been a part of this tradition have been deeply influenced by this domination, this diseased lopsidedness. We have grown in strange and twisted ways because of it. We have developed spiritually in dangerous and violent ways because of it. We have been poisoned by it, really. And one of the antidotes—perhaps the most important antidote—is to reexamine the voices we listen to, reexamine the books we read, reexamine whom we consider "experts" on various topics and why.

I did a little experiment in Lent 2021. With Ash Wednesday approaching, I pondered whether there was anything I wanted to give up. In past years I've given up things like chocolate, meat, or Facebook. (I'm not sure which was the most difficult of those three). In other years I've tried to add something, like a daily practice of prayer or journaling.

In early 2021, I realized I had been reading a lot—and, for some time, I had been specifically seeking out books written by women. I was *feeling* the male-dominated-ness of my church experiences and seminary education, and of the Christian world in general. I found it deeply refreshing and healing to take a months-long hiatus from male authors. By the beginning of Lent, though, I had begun to feel the lack of female authors of color in my reading.

Now, I love my white woman authors. Since I graduated from seminary and started seeking out female faith writers, I've absolutely loved books by Rachel Held Evans, Sarah Bessey, Nadia Bolz-Weber, Jen Hatmaker, Barbara Brown Taylor, and more.[14] Each of these women is so brilliant in her own way, and each has ministered to my soul deeply. I have felt seen, known, and healed in these women's work—especially after feeling so unseen and so alienated by a lot of the male authors I read in seminary, authors who write from a set of male privileges I will never have.

I have no regrets about reading any of these white woman-authored books. I think we all need some wise mentors in our lives who occupy a social location similar to our own. For those of us who aren't white men, it can take some intention to find this. That's what it took for me, anyway. And I'm glad I did so.

At the same time, I miss out on so much if I'm not also

intentionally seeking out the voices of women of color. And so, for Lent, I decided to continue my hiatus from male authors while adding a simultaneous hiatus from white authors. Basically, I fasted from white authors for Lent.[15]

It was a good practice. I've tried to hold onto it, in a modified form, far beyond the season of Lent—not totally divesting from white female authors, but continuing to actively seek out female authors of color. And seeking to do so in balance with white authors—not just one or two authors of color here and there as an afterthought, as if they aren't really essential.

I have been learning from amazing women I might have overlooked if I kept looking only for "female authors in general"—who, because the U.S. has been soaked in white supremacy from the start, and because I am a white woman who often moves in white-dominated spaces, tend to skew white. I've absolutely loved books by Mikki Kendall, Kathy Khang, Brittney Cooper, Ijeoma Oluo, Robin Wall Kimmerer, Kelley Nikondeha, and more.[16] I have enjoyed these authors, appreciated their brilliance, and felt challenged by many of them in ways I am not always challenged by my white women authors.

This is what I want, and it's what I need. It's what I need as I learn how to operate as part of God's multiethnic kinship network in a way that does not over-privilege me in my whiteness any more than I want it to over-privilege men in their maleness.

Race and gender are only two of many axes along which we carry privilege or marginalization in our bodies. It's also worth thinking about the people who shape our worldviews in terms of sexual/gender identity, ability or disability, socioeconomic status, age, and global location, just to name a few. I've focused on gender and race here because it's somewhere to start, and it's something I've needed to think about.

If you're white, or male, or both, diversifying your book-shelves (or podcasts, TV shows, etc.) might feel like choosing to stretch and challenge yourself. That's a good thing. We all need that. If you're a woman, or a person of color, or both, it might feel like coming home—finding books that feel like home, that make you feel seen and centered and known. That, too, is a very good thing. It's important, and you deserve it.

In the world I dream of, white men are no more likely than anyone else to be listened to as "experts" on anything—includ-ing, or perhaps especially, the things of God, faith, and theol-ogy. In the meanwhile, until we get there, we can choose to reexamine whom we (consciously or subconsciously) consider an "expert," and on what. We can diversify the hell out of the thinkers we listen to and learn from.

Women of color often experience a whole host of factors that keep their voices from being heard in our white-male-dominated world. We—people of all races and genders—can choose to listen. Both the world and the church desperately need to hear the insights, critiques, guidance, wisdom, love, anguish, frustration, and general brilliance pouring out from the lips and pens and keyboards of women of color. I think more of the world is starting to listen—and more of the church too.

We can choose to center the voices of women and people of color rather than pushing them to the margins. We can be willing to listen and learn, open to expanding our hearts and minds, knowing that we need this desperately. This is the kind of shift I want to be a part of. It's the kind of shift we all need.

22

HER EYE IS ON THE SPARROW

I had never heard anything quite like it. Certainly not in an evangelical context. But there I was, at the seminary chapel service—you know, the one time per week when you put down your books and stop trying to sound smart in your essays and try to remember that all of this actually means something in real life—as the inordinately talented chapel musicians led a ragtag crowd of students, staff, and professors in musical worship.

And then. One of the singers, Megan Moody, led us in a rendition of the century-old gospel hymn "His Eye is On the Sparrow"—with a few changes. Megan had re-written the lyrics, changing masculine pronouns to feminine ones. *Her Eye is On the Sparrow.*

These are the lyrics Megan wrote:

> *Why should I feel discouraged?*
> *Why should the shadows come?*
> *Why should my heart be lonely*
> *and long for heav'n and home?*

The Holy Spirit is steadfast,
For bold and vibrant is She;
Her eye is on the sparrow
and I know She watches me.

"Let not your heart be hardened,"
Her guiding voice I hear,
And leaning on Her shoulders,
I lose my doubt and fears.

Though by the path She leadeth,
But one step I may see.
Her eye is on the sparrow,
and I know She watches me.

Whenever I am weary,
Whenever clouds arise,
When songs give place to sighing,
When hope within me dies;

In grace I find Her calling,
From woe She sets me free;
Her eye is on the sparrow,
And I know She watches me.

And the chorus:

I sing because I'm broken.
I sing because I'm free.
For Her eye is on the sparrow,
And I know She watches me. [1]

I wish you could hear what I heard that Wednesday morning.

Hearing these feminine pronouns applied to the Holy Spirit did something to me. It was a visceral, gut-level revelation: God is like *me*, as much as God is like any man. The God who watches over me is not a patriarchal authority figure waiting for me to screw up so he can judge and punish—or, alternatively, a benevolent paternalistic being protecting me from the real world in an infantilizing way. God is more complex and beautiful than that. God is *she* as much as God is *he*.

It has taken me a while to become more comfortable with this. It is still taking me a while to become completely comfortable with this.

I fully believe, as most Christians do, that the invisible spirit-God who watches over us is not really male or female, at least not in the way humans are. Thus, if we're going to use masculine pronouns when speaking of God, we might as well use feminine ones too. Neither is really more or less accurate than the other. It's all an approximation, a way of trying to put words to the indescribable *I am who I am*,[2] the God whom no words can adequately capture.

At the same time, most of us who have spent time in evangelical contexts are just so used to hearing God talked about like God is male. And so, feminine God-talk tends to strike us as jarring. It's a controversial thing. The use of feminine pronouns, feminine images, and other kinds of feminine language for God is fraught with all sorts of angst. It tends to provoke disproportionately negative reactions.

For a long time, I wasn't sure how to feel about it.

But in seminary I learned that theologians, both male and female, have been using feminine language to describe God for pretty much all of (Western) Christian history. I had no idea. I assumed that feminine language for God must have been a pretty recent thing—something liberal churches started doing

in light of second-wave or third-wave feminism. But it actually
has a very, very long history.

This history isn't something most evangelical churches talk
about. It isn't something theology or church history classes tend
to focus on. It's often treated as incidental to the development
of the important parts of Christian thought. Or, perhaps, as if
(male) professors and pastors are a little embarrassed by it.
(After all, it takes a brave man to talk about how mother Christ
gives us her breast to suckle.)

Or perhaps these professors and pastors anticipate their
students' and parishioners' negative knee-jerk reactions—as if
describing the Christian God in feminine terms is the first step
down a steep slippery slope that inevitably leads to worshiping
the whole pantheon of Greek and Roman goddesses. Maybe
Christian leaders just don't want to have to deal with all of that
—to expose and confront their parishioners' deep-seated
patriarchy.[3]

I'd like to share a few things I learned in seminary that have
stuck with me.[4] I learned that Clement of Alexandria, who
lived around 150-215 CE, wrote of God's "care-soothing breast,"
and of Christ as breast milk: "For such is the nourishing
substance of milk swelling out from breasts of love...the milk of
Christ, instilling into you spiritual nutriment."[5] Clement refers
to God as father often, and he tends to reserve the language of
mother for the church and for human women. And yet he also
writes of God's "breasts of love" that swell with milk. That
sounds pretty darn motherly to me.

Breastfeeding turns out to be a popular theme. Irenaeus,
who lived around 130-202 CE, also wrote of God as a breastfeeding mother. For Irenaeus, the process of salvation is like
being suckled by the body of Christ. (If you ever wondered

whether eating Jesus' body in Communion has a bit of a canni-
balistic vibe, perhaps this is a better way to understand the
metaphor—it's less like eating a human sacrifice and more like
being nourished by Christ's breast milk.)

Augustine, then, who lived from 354 to 430 CE, wrote that
the church "[drinks] at the fountain of the Lord's breast."[6] And
Bernard of Clairvaux (1090-1153 CE) wrote this: "If you feel the
sting of temptation, suck not so much the wounds as the
breasts of the Crucified. He will be your mother, and you will
be his son."

Suck the breasts of the Crucified. Christ will be your
mother. Drink at the fountain of the Lord's breast. These are all
the words of male theologians, spanning the first millennium
or so of church history. So many breasts. So much suckling.
Cue so much discomfort from most of the men—and from
people in general—in any given modern-day evangelical
church. But such has God been depicted by theologians over
the years. Such has Christ been pictured: a generously,
graciously, joyfully breastfeeding mother.

If we're willing to see it, there is so much life in that image.
There is so much beauty, so much grace. God pours life-giving
nourishment into us, strengthening us and helping us grow—
like a woman who has just become a mother, with all the inten-
sity and intimacy of her relationship with her newborn.

For the female theologian and mystic Julian of Norwich, then,
who lived from around 1343 to 1416 CE, the idea of Christ as
mother—and feminine language for God in general—was
nothing new. Julian took this rich theological history and ran
with it.

In her work *Showings*, Julian paints a picture of the Trini-
tarian God as Father, Mother, and Lord. Julian writes, "The

almighty truth of the Trinity is our Father: for he made us and keeps us in him; and the deep wisdom of the Trinity is our Mother, in whom we are all enclosed; the high goodness of the Trinity is our Lord, and in him we are enclosed, and he in us." The deep wisdom of the Trinity is our Mother. We are all enclosed in God, just as we would be in a mother's loving, comforting arms. And God isn't only a gentle, caring Mother. She is also a wise one. God is like a woman full of deep wisdom —the kind that comes from her experience, from the depth of her soul, from her many years, from her struggle and her work toward liberation.

Julian later writes of Jesus: "Our Savior is our true Mother in whom we be endlessly borne, and never shall [we] come out of him." Julian calls Jesus "our Mother, Brother, and Savior." For her, Christ is both our "Mother in nature...in whom we are grounded and rooted" and our "Mother in mercy" who "reforms us and restores us, and, by virtue of his passion and his death and his rising, unites us to our substance." We know we are connected closely to Jesus because Jesus is the Mother who births us.

For Julian, motherly and otherwise feminine imagery for Jesus helps us be grounded and rooted in Christ. It helps us have a sense of unity and wholeness, in ourselves and in God. "The mother may give her child suck of her milk," Julian writes, "but our precious Mother Jesus feeds us with himself, and does it, full courteously and full tenderly, with the Blessed Sacrament that is precious food of my life; and with all the sweet Sacraments he fully sustains us, mercifully and graciously."

Here, too, is breastfeeding—and family, and rootedness, and groundedness, and mercy, and sacrament, and restoration, and reformation, and unity, and tenderness, and sweetness, and sustenance, and graciousness. This is a taste from the deep well of feminine God-talk. This is some of the fruit of thinking of God not just as a father but also as a mother.

So there's your brief tour of historical theologians writing about breasts and otherwise using feminine imagery to speak of God. Really, though—as I slowly came to realize while learning these things—all these theologians were just following the lead of the Bible.

In the Hebrew scriptures, in Genesis, we read that male and female were made in God's image.[7] This is something Christian theologians have debated about a lot over the years. Are women *really* created in God's image, just like men are? (In other words: How can we use Genesis to justify keeping women in an inferior social status?[8]) But the Genesis creation story is clear. Yes, women are created in God's image. And that means that God is as feminine as God is masculine. God is not really male or female—and yet, there is something about God that is reflected and refracted in human women just as much as in human men.

Several of the Hebrew prophets use feminine imagery to help people wrap their minds around who God is and what God is doing. The prophet Isaiah, for example, imagines God as a woman in labor, birthing something new—and also as a nursing mother, who can't help but show compassion to her child.[9] The prophet Hosea writes that God is "like those who lift infants to their cheeks," "[bending] down to them and [feeding] them."[10] That sounds pretty mother-like to me.

A couple chapters later, Hosea likens God to a mother bear— "like a bear robbed of her cubs."[11] This mama-bear God is not nice to those who do the robbing. We get some violent language here: some tearing open, some devouring, some mangling. Motherhood is not always gentle, meek, and mild. I imagine God being full of righteous feminine rage—the kind that fills a mother if her children are being harmed, strengthening and emboldening her to tear apart whatever is harming them. God tears apart unjust laws and systems, inequity and abuse of all sorts. That's how passionate God is about defending people who are vulnerable.

In the New Testament, then, Jesus picks up this prophetic thread of feminine imagery and applies it to himself, likening himself to a mother hen: "How often have I desired to gather your children together as a hen gathers her brood under her wings, and you were not willing!"[12] Apparently Jesus did not share any qualms we might have about referring to God in the feminine. He used motherly imagery to describe himself, to articulate the depth of his lament over the city and over the people who rejected him and his ways of peace.

Jesus also uses feminine imagery for God in the parable of the woman looking (and looking and looking!) for her lost coin.[13] Luke 15 contains three stories: the lost sheep, the lost coin, and the lost child (also known as the Prodigal Son). In each story, someone is looking for what is lost and eventually finds it. If the shepherd in the first story and the father in the third story each in some way represents God, then so too does the woman in the second story. God is like a woman searching and searching for her lost coin. When she finds it, she calls her friends together to rejoice with her, and there is joy. God searches. God finds. God rejoices in community. Like a woman.

The image of God as woman is also implied in the metaphor of being "born again." Evangelicals love this "born again" language. But do we think about who is doing the birthing?[14] Nicodemus asks Jesus, "Can one enter a second time into the mother's womb and be born?"[15] And Jesus answers—if you can call it an answer—"Very truly, I tell you, no one can enter the kingdom of God without being born of water and Spirit. What is born of the flesh is flesh, and what is born of the Spirit is spirit."[16] Jesus pictures the Holy Spirit as a

mother. Spirit gives birth to spirit. That's feminine language for
God if I ever heard it.

When women are free to theologize, preach, write, lead, and
dream about who God is and what the church could be, we
tend to think about these kinds of things.

Kelley Nikondeha, for example, imagines God as a midwife.
Nikondeha reflects on the courageous Hebrew midwives
Shiphrah and Puah[17]: "These women demonstrate deliverance
not as warriors on the battlefield but as midwives at the
birthing stool, bringing life into a dangerous world...This is
another gift from Shiphrah and Puah—the ability to see God
with feminine hands in the work of shalom and salvation."[18]
God with feminine hands. God, doing the work of life when the
powers-that-be commanded death. God, the midwife whose
skilled hands bring peace and justice into our world.

Sarah Bessey connects feminine God-talk with self-care.
After a car accident left her in chronic pain, Bessey had to learn
to take care of herself in new ways. And, in so doing, she found
herself seeing God in new ways. Bessey writes, "Perhaps self-
care is simply joining with God to care for ourselves as a
mother would care for us...I discovered God's metaphor as a
wise, capable, strong, patient, kind, no-nonsense, deeply loving
mother."[19] Kind of like Hosea's mama bear. But also like Isaiah's
tenderly nursing mother. And also like Jesus' mother hen who
wants to gather her children under her wing.

Bessey goes on to reflect, "This has been the question God
has given to me as a practice of spiritual discernment during
my life with chronic pain: How would God like to mother me
today? If God was a strong, patient, wise, kind, no-nonsense,
deeply loving mother, what would She want for me today?"[20] I
like that question: How would God like to mother me today?
What would a wise, caring parent, who wants the best for me,

say to me today? What would she want me to do, or not do? What would she want me to say yes to, or no?

Parents of any gender can be, as Bessey puts it, "wise, capable, strong, patient, kind, no-nonsense, [and] deeply loving."[21] But if we picture God only as a father, I think we're missing something. We're missing the nuance of imagining the ways these attributes take shape in a mother's arms. We're missing another dimension—and an equally important one, not just a secondary or trivial one—of who God is and how God relates to us.

Sue Monk Kidd wrote a whole book on these sorts of things. It's called *The Dance of the Dissident Daughter: A Woman's Journey from Christian Tradition to the Sacred Feminine*. At one point, Kidd reflects:

> I noted that the lack of a divine female image supported an imbalance in our consciousness that diminished our wholeness as persons. The feminine goes underground in our psyches just as it does in our God. When this happens we exclude, overlook, and undervalue the feminine within ourselves and in the world around us.
>
> Not only that, but as long as we have a divine Father who is able to create without a divine Mother, women's creative acts are viewed as superfluous or secondary. And as long as the feminine is missing in the Divine, men would continue to experience entitlement and women would be prey to self-doubt and disempowerment. It was that simple.
>
> Internalizing the Divine Feminine provides women with the healing affirmation that they are persons in their own right, that they can make choices, that they are worthy and entitled and do not need permission. The internalization of

the Sacred Feminine tells us our gender is a valuable and marvelous thing to be.[22]

As Kidd observes, how we speak of God—which reflects how we think about God—has everything to do with who is considered valuable in our world, and who is considered worthless. Exclusively male language for God plays into a more general devaluation of the feminine, and of everything and everyone deemed feminine. It contributes to women's disempowerment. On the flip side, speaking about God in a more balanced way affirms women in our full humanity—worthy and good, just as God made us.

This is important for individual women's flourishing. It's also important for the flourishing of our communities and our world more broadly. It has implications for how power operates. It influences the extent to which women are esteemed and free—or degraded and repressed—in our societies.

We need to know God as Father, and God as Mother, and God as all the many other metaphors we find in scripture and experience in our lives. When we exclude feminine language about God from our worship services, prayers, and conversations, we miss out on the richness these metaphors can bring.

Feminine God-talk is all over the Bible, and it's all over many centuries of Christian theological reflection. The Christian tradition holds rich resources that point toward more balanced ways of thinking about God. We aren't always aware of these resources, and sometimes we aren't open to them. But I'd love to see more faith communities recover this legacy today. I want to hear and speak language that helps me remember that women are God's image-bearers, fully.

I want my theology to be expanded by non-male voices reflecting on a non-male God. We need to know God as birthing mother, nursing mother, mama bear, mother hen. We need to know Christ as the one who nourishes us with love from her own body. We need to know God as a midwife, God as a no-nonsense mother. We need to know that her eye is on the sparrow. Our sense of our value as women—and our communities' sense of our value as women—depends on it.

23

BRIGHTLY SHINING GOD

Brightly shining God—
  God of the prophets who spoke truth to power—
  shine your face on us.

You make meaning and beauty out of ordinary things.
  We come fully alive in your light.

Let your brightness touch our daily work,
  our time with friends and family and community,
  our interactions with strangers,
  our Zoom calls, our meals,
  our walks outside, our time spent alone.

Infuse our lives and communities with your love;
  leave nothing and no one untouched and unchanged.

Help us see your light that shines, candle-like,
  in the darkness of injustice,
  and has not been overcome by it.

Help us be truth-tellers who live in your light.

Brightly shining God,
    shine your face on us.

I wrote this prayer for a worship service at my current church. The scripture passage for the morning was a story often known as the transfiguration, found in Luke 9:28-36. In this story, Jesus takes three of his besties up on a mountain to pray, and soon enough Jesus' face randomly starts shining and his clothes turn bright white like an angel's. The old school (that is, long-dead) prophets Moses and Elijah appear and start casually chit-chatting with Jesus like all of this is totally normal. After a minute, a cloud envelops everyone, and a voice from the cloud says, "This is my son, my chosen one; listen to him."[1] (If I heard that, I think I just might start listening.)

Tasked with writing a brief pastoral prayer based loosely on this story, I thought about how I wanted to address God. This feels more complicated than it used to—which may go hand in hand with the kind of church service where prayers are written ahead of time rather than spoken spontaneously during the worship service. You have more time to think about things. There are pros and cons to both approaches, but one thing I like about sitting down during the week to write a prayer for Sunday morning is that this practice tends to increase the thoughtfulness of these prayers. We have to think about how to address God, and about so many other things.

It wouldn't be terribly difficult here to poke fun at the kinds of spontaneous prayers you tend to hear in evangelical churches. (*Father God, we just pray, just, like, that you'd hear us, God, and hear what's on our hearts, Lord Jesus, and just come, and, just, be with us, God, just be with our hearts, Lord God, Jesus, Father, we just love you, Father God, amen God.*) But that would probably be in bad taste—after all, if a prayer is sincere, I don't think God cares how many "just"s and "like"s are in it. [2] And it would also be hypocritical, because I can't say I haven't prayed these kinds of prayers myself, plenty of times.

But I have enjoyed the chance to give my prayers a little more thought beforehand. It helps me reexamine the words that might come out of my mouth spontaneously. Do they line up with what I believe about God, what I want to believe about God? What kind of a God is conveyed through my prayers? And does this God that I speak of come off as masculine, feminine, both, or neither? These questions are especially important when prayers are spoken in front of a faith community as part of a worship service—that is, when a community is invited to pray together, affirming the words crafted by one person on behalf of the whole.

These things matter in personal prayer, too. If I'm praying on my own, it might seem like whatever I say or imply about God sticks with me and doesn't hurt anyone else. But how I see God impacts how I relate to others and our world. It impacts the communities I'm a part of.

Words spoken in prayer matter, and words spoken in church services matter. I appreciate Mihee Kim-Kort's reflections on this as a female pastor. Kim-Kort writes:

> Like the clergy robe, [the pulpit] represented a space that could be occupied only by certain bodies, that is, usually white, male or masculine-presenting bodies. Power, authority, and legitimate calling were rooted in this very specific, narrow way, and despite my own ordination status, I struggled with the demons that whispered doubt about my ability or calling. It wasn't just the robe or the pulpit, but the words and the language of the liturgy, the songs, prayers, and references all around us, all the time. People still defaulted to the

male and masculine without thinking when it came to
speaking about God.[3]

The words spoken in church services mattered to Kim-Kort.
They caused her to feel unwelcome in the pulpit, even in a
denomination that affirms female pastors. The default,
unthinking masculinity of people's God-talk was detrimental to
her sense of confidence and belonging in her role. She had
jumped through all the hoops you have to jump through to get
ordained (and the hoops are many), bravely breaking into a
leadership space traditionally occupied by men—only to find
that the reality of occupying this space as a woman is still a
difficult one. And one of the things that makes it harder is
people's tendency to speak as if God were a man.

How is a woman supposed to serve as a representative of
God—an image of what God is like and what God is about, and
a leader of God's people—when all the language used in
church services implies that God is male, so God's representa-
tives probably should be male, too?

In seminary I first learned of the long Christian tradition of
speaking of God with feminine imagery. (Remember all those
breasts?) In post-seminary life, I've been exploring how this
works itself out in our faith communities, pragmatically speaking. How can we expand our communal theology by incorpo-
rating some of the church's long-standing, beautiful, feminine
God-images into our worship services—and other aspects of
our faith communities—today?

This can be a fraught thing. One of my seminary professors
suggested that perhaps the best way to do it is sneakily, such
that people don't consciously notice. I'm not convinced this is
always possible. My sense is that people who have been going
to church for any length of time are often so primed to expect

masculine language for God that any feminine language at all strikes them as jarring. It might be futile to try to sneak it in.

On the other hand, there's also a lot of room for creativity here. We don't always have to straight-up refer to God as Mother—as valid, beautiful, and biblical as this is. There are also other ways to speak of God, other ways to speak to God. As I write liturgy—and as I pray in general—I've been exploring ways of addressing God that may not sound explicitly feminine, but that don't exactly sound masculine, either.

These are some of the ways I've addressed God in pastoral prayer, along with the scripture passages they were inspired by:

- God of liberation—from Jesus' words about releasing the captives and letting the oppressed go free (Luke 4:18-19).
- God of abundance—from the massive haul of fish (Luke 5:1-11).
- God of Sabbath rest—from Jesus picking grain and healing on the Sabbath (Luke 6:1-11).
- Healing God—from Jesus healing a centurion's very sick son and then bringing a widow's son back from the dead (Luke 7:1-17).
- Brightly shining God (as in the prayer at the beginning of this chapter)—from Jesus' transfiguration (Luke 9:28-36).
- Vinegrower God—from Jesus' image of himself as a vine who gives life and nourishment to the branches who are connected to him (John 15:1-8).
- Loving God—from Jesus' instructions to love one another (John 15:9-17).
- Trinity God—from Jesus' prayer for his followers to be made one, as he and his Father are one (John 17:6-19).

These are just a few ideas, based on a few scripture passages. I hope it helps give a sense, though, of how something like this could be done with lots of different passages. We can ask ourselves: What impression do we get of God in this text? What images or metaphors does the passage invite us to consider? Is God a shepherd,[4] or a friend, or a guide, or a source of hope? What does this scripture mean to us about how God operates in our lives and communities? Is God revealed as one who brings peace, or gives life, or defends the vulnerable, or challenges us, or comforts us, or encourages us, or reveals truth to us?

Any of these roles and characteristics can be used to address God in prayer. And none is, or needs to be, particularly gender-specific.

When uprisings for racial justice gained a new level of national attention in late spring and early summer 2020, my pastor, Lina Thompson, said something I hadn't heard before, but that made so much sense. She said, *the Holy Spirit is the Spirit who brings justice.*

Sometimes we wonder where the Holy Spirit is, what the Holy Spirit is doing, and how we might discern such a thing. Lina's insight into the Holy Spirit as the bringer of justice helps with this discernment. I fully believe, for example, that God's Spirit was in those 2020 protests. I fully believe that God's Spirit stands alongside—and dwells within—people and communities who march in the streets, make noise, cause a disturbance, and make policy demands in support of the dignity and value of Black life.

I've been pondering this idea of the Holy Spirit as justice-bringer alongside the idea of God being as feminine as God is masculine—and what this all might mean in our lives, our communities, our world. I'm still pondering. In the process, I wrote this poem:

Kitchen in the Clouds

In her kitchen in the clouds
she cooks a feast,
mise en place,
she takes cutting boards

and places on them
every form of dominance,
chops heaping bowls of
white supremacy, of

patriarchy, homophobia,
chef's knife in hand,
decisive, she chops
loudly and does not hold back.

With expert touch she cuts
police brutality, slices
corrupt healthcare systems,
then takes racist rhetoric

and throws it on the fire
where it will burn and burn
and burn. She takes it all
and fries it up, destroyed,

burned up, turned into
something new,
unrecognizable:

She serves justice on a platter.

Her touch is power,
all the power to all the people,
her stove's sparks illumine truth,
invite all to draw near:

She takes and throws
upon the open flame
indifference to Black life,
callousness toward immigrants,

sticks skewers through misogyny
and grills it up.
She soaks love like beans
for hours until it swells

and softens and is ripe to eat.
Then she sets the table
for her feast, no seats
of honor, all are equals,

so much room for all
who hunger for a place
of many mountains fallen down.

In her kitchen in the clouds
she stops and hovers,
waiting, unsure who will come
to share in what she cooks,

the table set,
the feast all served.
The guests begin

to straggle in:

the weary, haggard,
lonely, scarred,
the prophets and the protesters,
the ones contending

for a better world
and not content,
the desperate ones,
the angry ones,

the migrants and the refugees,
the lovers and the fighters,
the ones imprisoned and detained,
the ones cut down before their time.

For all who stomach
what she cooks,
this meal is peace at long,
long last.

This is who the brightly shining God is. This is what the God of liberation does. This is what the God of abundance longs for. God is Father, yes, but also so much more.

I long for more expansive theologies that encompass more of this vastness. Patriarchal God-talk has dominated our church services, prayers, and liturgies—really, our hearts and minds, as individuals and as communities of faith—for too long. Patriarchal voices have dominated our seminaries and pulpits for too long. In the midst of this, I believe God is inviting us to radically open up our view of who God is and what God is doing. I believe we can learn to speak to and about God in new ways. I want us to know, more deeply and fully, the Holy Spirit who moves toward all sorts of justice.

Fortunately—because these things can be hard, so hard—I fully believe that God is in the process of cooking up something new. And she is good at it.

UNERASING HISTORY

24

BROTHER SEYMOUR AND HIS
SISTERS

*D*epending on what kind of church tradition you've been steeped in, if any, you may be quite familiar with the Azusa Street Revival. Or you may never have heard of it in your life. I was the type who had never heard of it—until one day, during my sophomore year of college, when I was praying.

That might sound odd, because it *was* odd.

I was living in Stanford's African / African American focus dorm, called Ujamaa. The dorm served as a center of Black community on campus. It also served, for non-Black residents like me, as a space to learn about and engage with Black histories and experiences. Before college I could probably count on one hand all the Black people I knew personally—and three of them were members of the same family. So living in Ujamaa was eye-opening. I went to as many talks and discussions as possible, and I learned so much. I still remember a Black dorm-mate commenting on the look on my face when I first learned that Irish people like my own ancestors had not always been considered white—that they contended for, and eventually achieved, assimilation into the racial construct of whiteness. (A construct that has not been at all consistent over the course of U.S. history.) It's possible my jaw actually dropped.

It was in this context—living in Ujamaa and learning a ton about race—that I was praying in my dorm room one day by myself, kneeling at the edge of my bed, when suddenly I saw two words appear, as clearly as if they were written on the inside of my eyelids. *Brother Seymour*. They appeared out of nowhere and then disappeared quickly.

This was not a normal experience for me. But it was kind of cool. I was surprised and intrigued. I had no idea what the words *Brother Seymour* meant, or who he was, or if he was an actual person at all. The words were completely unfamiliar to me, as far as I could tell. So I got up, went over to my desk where my laptop was sitting—I wouldn't own a smartphone for another three years—and typed "Brother Seymour" into the Google search bar.

Somewhat to my surprise, a Wikipedia page came up. I learned that there really was a person named William Seymour, whom a lot of people called Brother Seymour. He was a Black pastor, back in the early 1900s, and the leader of the Azusa Street Revival—a years-long multiracial movement centered on Azusa Street in Los Angeles, where people came to worship and encounter God in some intense ways, often involving miraculous gifts like speaking in tongues. The revival is often credited as the beginning of modern-day Pente-costalism.

I've thought about William Seymour quite a bit, on and off, in the many years since. At first, I was mostly interested in Seymour's role in early Pentecostalism. I wasn't raised with any of that charismatic stuff.[1] Supernatural things weren't wholly unspoken-of in the Presbyterian church I grew up in, but they also weren't emphasized.

When I got to college, I met people who believed in all sorts of charismatic manifestations of the Holy Spirit that I hadn't been exposed to before. For the first time, I knew people who spoke in tongues. I knew people who were ready and excited to pray for physical healing, expectant that God might well cure someone on the spot. I met people who received "words of knowledge" from God for other people—something they would not normally have known, like a little prophecy about another person's life.

This was all new to me and very exciting. And so, when I saw the words *Brother Seymour* and then learned that he helped spark a revival of charismatic faith that had a vast impact around the world, I figured it might be an invitation from God to dig more into this charismatic stuff.

Among other things, I started occasionally visiting "Miracles Church" (not its real name)—an international hub of all things charismatic, located just a four-hour drive from where I lived. Miracles Church offered three different services every weekend—totally different music and preaching, not just the same service at different times—so it was easy to spend a long weekend there with friends as a sort of inexpensive spiritual retreat. I visited every year or two from around 2009 to 2015.[2]

In the pre-Trump era, when I was less aware of political things, I found my Miracles visits fun and inspiring. I loved spending time in a church so different from the one I attended regularly. I loved that people really believed in a God who moves supernaturally on a regular basis. I loved the music, and I loved that there was often a good hour of it in each church service.[3]

One time, a lady standing and singing next to me turned to me in the middle of the worship music set, pointed to the ceiling, and exclaimed, "There it is! The Glory Cloud is here!"[4] I looked up and saw maybe some dust particles pushed off the rafters by the sheer decibel level of the praise band. But if she saw a glory cloud, that was okay by me.

On one trip to Miracles in my early twenties, I wandered into the church's bookstore, looked around a bit, and noticed that—amidst lots and lots of books written by Miracles pastors—one shelf offered an assortment of books about William Seymour. I picked one, a biography, and brought it to the cash register, where a friendly employee shivered a bit when he touched the book and said he felt like this book would be life-changing for me. (At the time, I was excited to hear that. Later, I would wonder if Miracles bookstore employees said this to everyone about every book they buy.) The employee told me that William Seymour used to put a bucket over his head and just sit there in front of the congregation during the sermon time, waiting until he felt the Holy Spirit speak. I was intrigued.

At some point, I realized that a charismatic, put-a-bucket-over-your-head relationship with the Holy Spirit wasn't the only interesting thing about William Seymour's life. It was also incredible that Seymour, as a Black man in Los Angeles in the early 1900s, gathered and led a fully multiethnic church.

Did I mention that this was over a hundred years ago?

Seymour pastored in a time when newspaper headlines said things about his ministry like "Whites and Blacks Mix in a Religious Frenzy," "Crazed Girls in the Arms of Black Men," and "Women With Men Embrace."[5] (The horror!) It was deeply scandalous for people of different races to gather together and do the things people normally do in churches, like sing together, pray for one another, or greet each other with a hug. This was considered especially shocking and anxiety-inducing when these people were a mix of men and women. The craze! The frenzy.

Seymour himself was the son of enslaved parents, and he

had grown up in the South during a time when Black people were theoretically free from enslavement but in practice subject to Jim Crow segregation and other forms of racial violence at every turn.[6] He experienced plenty of racism in his own church background, including a stint at a white Bible school where Seymour was forced to sit outside in the hallway when he wanted to take classes there.

In some sense, Seymour took his own painful and demeaning experiences of racism and turned them around into a beautiful vision of equality and racial justice that came to life at Azusa Street. His leadership team included both Black and white people, and many Latino people were active in the revival as well. Under Brother Seymour's leadership, the revival embraced people of all races as siblings in faith—equal in the sight of God and therefore in the community of faith, even if not anywhere else.

Eventually, in seminary—maybe ten years or so after first seeing Seymour's name in prayer—I started to think more about the women of Azusa Street. I got to write a twenty-page research paper on a topic of my choice for my Women in Church History and Theology class, and when I sat down to think about what I might want to research, I thought of the Azusa Street Revival. I had a vague memory of reading that women were an important part of the movement. I had a general sense that there may have been some women in leadership, but I knew nothing of the details. So, after running the topic by my professor, I got to work.

I spent a few weeks reading everything I could find in the seminary library about Azusa Street, about women in the early Pentecostal movement, about Black prophetic preaching, about William Seymour and his leadership. I read a wild (and probably not totally credible) eyewitness account of the early days of the revival.[7] I read a compilation of *The Apostolic Faith* news-papers produced by the mission over several years. I read a book of William Seymour's sermons.

The research was fascinating. I learned that in the first decade of the twentieth century—long before any major denominations began ordaining women[8]—William Seymour put together a leadership team that was half women. Six out of twelve. Women did everything that men did in the movement, at least in its early days, and the movement flourished for it. Men and women of all races led side by side as equals.

I learned about white women like Clara Lum and Black women like Jennie Evans Moore Seymour, both of whom were a part of that initial twelve-person leadership team. *The Apostolic Faith* newspaper, which served as one of my primary research sources? It was put together, edited, published, circulated, and likely in large parts written by Clara Lum. That book of William Seymour's sermons? It was likely compiled from Lum's sermon notes. Lum built the newspaper mailing list that reached up to fifty thousand recipients,[9] and when she moved to Oregon in 1908 and took those mailing lists with her, the Azusa Street Mission never quite fully recovered.[10]

Jennie Evans Moore Seymour ministered in her own right at Azusa Street before she married William Seymour in 1908. She was an evangelist and a gifted musical worship leader in the revival, and her leadership roles only continued to grow once she and William married.[11] She led the mission alongside William for twelve years[12]—preaching, filling in as pastor when he was traveling, and sometimes traveling as an evangelist herself. After William died, Jennie served as the mission's sole pastor.[13]

As I researched, I wondered: How was the Azusa Street Revival able to become such a place of freedom and empowerment for women, over and against all of the prevailing gender norms of its day, both inside and outside churches?

. . .

I learned a few things.

I learned that gender equality in the revival was tied to a particular understanding of what ministry is and where its authority comes from. For Seymour and his team, spiritual authority came from the direct empowerment of the Holy Spirit, not from human authority figures, church boards, or denominational structures. In one of my favorite Seymour quotes, he preached, "The first thing in every assembly is to see that He, the Holy Ghost, is installed as the chairman. The reason why we have so many dried up missions and churches today, is because they have not the Holy Ghost as the chairman. They have some man in His place."[14] I'm not at all convinced that the Holy Ghost is a "He." But I very much appreciate the sentiment. We need the Holy Spirit as our leader, not "some man in His place."

I learned about the revival's rejection of all forms of favoritism, breaking down societal hierarchies based on race, class, and gender, and affirming a radical vision of the equality of all people before God. And I learned that the Azusa leaders expected Jesus to return imminently. This motivated them to adopt a mindset where every possible minister is needed urgently—no time to worry about "qualifications" (including gender) that other churches deemed necessary.

I also learned more about Seymour himself: his character, background, and leadership style, and some of the things—such as his own experience of racism as a Black man—that led him to lift up the leadership of other people who had likewise been assumed unable to lead. As I read Seymour's sermons, I was struck by the ways he didn't gloss over women in scripture or treat them as object lessons for male behavioral improvement.

Seymour spoke of the Samaritan woman at the well,[15] for

example, not as a shameful slut with a few too many men in her life, but as a "child of God" whose "heart was so filled with love that she felt she could take in a whole lost world." That's beautiful. In Seymour's words, when the Samaritan woman ran back to tell her village about Jesus, she "ran away with a well of salvation." Seymour spoke of this woman as a powerful evangelist with a passion worth emulating; she was someone with "something to tell."[16]

Seymour also preached about Rebekah,[17] speaking of her as "the type of a sanctified soul."[18] He honored Rebekah as a woman who "wore her jewels" and "did not put them aside, or into her pocket"—just as we, too, are called to allow the "abiding anointing in our hearts" to "[shine] forth upon our faces."[19] She was an example of shining faith for us to follow, of God's anointing for the world to see.

Just as Seymour saw these Bible women as gifted and anointed leaders and preachers, likewise with the women in his world. He saw women as gifted partners in the gospel and treated them as equals. This mindset opened doors for women and allowed the movement as a whole to flourish.

As I learned these things, I thought: If Seymour could preach this way about women at the beginning of the twentieth century, surely male preachers in the twenty-first century are plumb out of excuses.

From Brother Seymour, and from women like Clara Lum and Jennie Evans Moore Seymour who ministered alongside him, I learned that a leader fully supportive of women in ministry— someone who really practices what many pastors will happily preach about, like everyone's equality before God and everyone's gifting from the Holy Spirit—can make all the difference. Historical role models like Seymour help me dream of what could be. They inspire me not to settle for anything less than full equality. They help me see that there is something urgently, grossly wrong with sermons that keep casting the Samaritan woman as a whore,[20] for example, or other biblical women like Rebekah as inconsequential sidekicks. They help me lose patience—in a good way—with arguments that we can't change too much, too fast.

It took a seminary research project to expose me to the women-affirming history of the Azusa Street Revival, even after being aware of and interested in William Seymour for many years. Our stories of Azusa Street often gloss over women's roles in the revival. But they were there. And their leadership was central to the movement.

How many other stories do we tell of Christian history that forget, downplay, or erase women in this way? How can we even know, when we haven't been taught these things? Reclaiming women's humanity in church means wrestling with this reality. It means recovering these stories, telling a fuller and more honest version of history. It means looking back at history to remind ourselves of what has been and what could still be. And it means refusing to accept arguments for gradual change when urgency is needed, for minuscule incremental changes when radical changes have been made in the past and could be made again.

Apparently it was possible, in 1906, to build the kind of community that really does treat people of all races and all genders as equals. Surely it is more than possible today.

25

DREAMING THROUGH TWO THOUSAND YEARS

*T*he dream of full, real, *felt* equality for women turns out to be a very, very old dream. And it is a dream that has actually been realized, to some extent, at some points in history. I was surprised to learn this. The history of women in church is much more complex than I had assumed. Azusa Street wasn't the only place where women experienced moments of equality, of being treated like full humans in church. And it wasn't the first. It turns out that for all two thousand years of Christian history women have been fighting for—and sometimes achieving—freedom to lead and minister as God calls. (Usually followed by, you guessed it, aggressive pushback from men in power.)

I didn't learn this until seminary. Probably because evangelical churches tend to ignore history in general, and because they especially tend to ignore, downplay, and erase women's contributions in particular. But what I've learned about historical women in the Christian tradition has made me think. These women have inspired me. And they have changed things for me.

I would like to share some of their stories with you.

. . .

We can start very close to Christianity's beginnings. Sometime between 110 and 113 CE, Pliny the Younger, who was governor of the Roman province Bithynia and Pontus,[1] exchanged letters with Roman Emperor Trajan. (Because having pen pals has always been fun.) Pliny wrote the emperor to discuss his concerns about the troublesome Christian community in his province.[2] These pesky Christians were engaging in all sorts of worrisome, antisocial behavior. For example, they refused to burn incense to the statues of all the gods, including Caesar. Since many Romans believed that the prosperity of their cities was tied to keeping all the deities happy, failure to sacrifice to any deity was a big deal. Governor Pliny and Emperor Trajan wrote back and forth about what methods of punishment were legal or necessary to keep the Christians in line.

In his letter, Pliny mentions two female slaves. In a casual, offhand way, he refers to these two women as ministers in the church. Personally, he has no particular respect for these women. In fact, he tells Trajan that their status as enslaved people justifies him torturing them to find out what exactly was going on in their anxiety-inducingly radical social movement— to learn exactly how seditious these Christians were, how dangerous to the fabric of the empire.

These women were treated especially poorly by the state because of their status as enslaved people. But they were leaders in the second century church. Pliny's words suggest that women—all kinds of women, from all socioeconomic statuses —were ministers at this time, and no one seemed to think twice about it. Women of the lowest social class, with the least amount of power and privilege in their world—a world in which they were considered nobodies, fit to be tortured without remorse by the empire's agents of "law and order"—existed in the church as everyone else's equal, not disqualified from leadership in any way.

These women were valued ministers. They were the people you wanted to get to if you were looking for information about the whole movement. They were women of courage and character who risked torture and death to minister in the ways God gifted and called. And, in the context of their faith community, they were free to do so. In the early second century.

In the second and third centuries, a type of Christian literature known as the Apocryphal Acts became quite popular. The Apocryphal Acts are basically ancient fan fiction—stories about what some of Jesus' apostles may (or may not) have done with the rest of their lives after the events recorded in the Bible.[3]

The Acts of the Apostles—that is, the book of Acts in the New Testament—is fairly male-dominated.[4] But the Apocryphal Acts are often much more female-centered, much less afraid to feature women. It's possible that women wrote at least some of them—that they were by women, for women.

In these stories, women are often the ones who take initiative, the ones who give up everything for their faith. They're the ones who lead exemplary lives full of intense devotion to Christ. While other early Christian writings—the ones written by men, for men—often cast women as objects of sexual temptation, the Apocryphal Acts highlight women who live ascetic lives of singleness, giving up marriage for their devotion to God. As Elizabeth Clark writes, women in the Apocryphal Acts "[rejected] traditional social and domestic values for the sake of Christianity, understood as rigidly ascetic discipline."[5] That's badass.

Don't get me wrong—I'm all for (egalitarian) marriage for women who want to get married. I don't want sexual objectification and ascetic celibate discipline to be the only two options for women. But there's something striking about the women in these second- and third-century stories and the way they pushed back against the dominant models of marriage and family life of their time. It's something to think about—perhaps especially the next time you hear modern-day evangelicals talk about "family values," and the importance of the nuclear family, and how we have to fight back against anything that might be a threat to the "traditional" family (you know, the kind with one husband, one wife, and 2.5 children, which is clearly what all Christians everywhere at all times should aspire to).

Apparently, Christian women of the second and third century thought differently. As Clark puts it, "By no means are the women of the Apocryphal Acts the docile housewives commended in 1 Timothy"; rather, "These determined women are willing to risk social disapproval and life itself to uphold their faith."[6]

For example, take the *Acts of Paul and Thecla*.[7] Thecla is a young unmarried woman, and she has a suitor named Thamyris. Unfortunately for Thamyris, Thecla has ears and eyes only for the apostle Paul—but in a very chaste kind of way. She just really loves to hear Paul preach. She goes and listens to Paul for days on end. Thamyris doesn't love this, so he teams up with Thecla's mother, Theocleia, to try to convince Thecla to stop "behaving like a mad person" (in Theocleia's words) and instead to "turn to" her fiancé (in Thamyris' words). But Thecla "did not turn away, but paid rapt attention to Paul's message."[8]

Later, Thecla is about to be burned to death by the governor —who, by the way, "wept and was astounded at the power in her"[9]—when God sends an enormous storm cloud "full of rain and hail"[10] that puts out the fire, saves Thecla, and kills several other people in the process.

Thecla then runs afoul of the governor again, after a man named Alexander "[falls] in love with her" and "embrace[s] her on the street."[11] His "embrace" is unwanted, and Thecla fights back: "Seizing Alexander, she ripped his mantle, removed the wreath from his head, and made him a scandal."[12] Thecla, one; street harasser, zero. Unfortunately, Alexander then takes Thecla to the governor, who—because apparently victims of sexual assault have been treated poorly by the legal system for a long, long time—sentences Thecla to be thrown to the wild beasts.

Even here, though, there is a note of resistance. The women of the community hear the governor's judgment and are "panic-stricken." They "[shout] at the platform, 'An evil judgment, an unholy judgment!'"[13] This is remarkable stuff—this collective of second-century women, gathering together and raising their voices to protest injustice. Their voices may not have made a difference in Thecla's fate—she was still thrown to the beasts—but perhaps they made a difference to the real women who read a story like this. Perhaps they gave women courage and permission to speak up against injustice in their own world.

But Thecla's story does not end here. When she gets thrown to the wild beasts, God protects her from them, in a dramatic, gory, and drawn-out narrative. On top of that, during her ordeal with the beasts, Thecla decides to baptize herself—even though her beloved teacher Paul had told her to wait. Apparently, as devoted as she was to Paul and his teaching, Thecla was not afraid to take matters into her own hands when the occasion called for it. To be fair, she assumes she is about to be eaten by vicious seals in the watery pit that she dubs a baptismal font as she throws herself into it. But the fact remains that she baptizes herself. And that's badass. When Thecla jumps into the water, the poor seals, "seeing the light of a flash of fire, [float] dead."[14]

One more Thecla highlight: She makes man-style clothing for herself. Thecla "gird[s] herself and sew[s] her mantle into a garment in the fashion of men."[15] So much for modern-day conservative takes on what is or isn't fitting attire for a woman of God.

In the *Acts of Paul and Thecla*—which is really about Thecla much more than Paul—Thecla assertively, creatively, and counter-culturally makes a place for herself in the family of God. She lives a life radically different from what everyone around her expects. She refuses to be who society thinks she should be. And this carries a high price.

Then and now, the powers-that-be do not treat women who step out of line kindly. And yet, Christian women keep doing it anyway—since at least the second century. Thecla's story may be fictional, but her story surely says something powerful about real women around the time of its writing. It speaks of their boldness, their struggles, their courage, their faithfulness.

In 412 CE, the early church father Jerome penned a letter eulogizing a Roman widow named Marcella. We learn from this letter that Marcella, after being widowed, was presented with a financially attractive marriage proposal by an "illustrious" older man named Cerealis; she replied, "If I wished to marry rather than to dedicate myself to perpetual chastity, I would seek a husband, not an inheritance."[16] Boom. Valuing men for more than their net worth—and husbands as equal life partners rather than financial providers—since the patristic era.

Later on, Marcella continued her badassery by becoming perhaps the first Roman noblewoman to pursue a monastic life.[17] Eventually, after some years, other women began to join her.[18] Jerome refers to Marcella casually as the "teacher" of these younger women,[19] acknowledging that she did an excellent job of training others to live a faithful Christian monastic lifestyle.

Marcella and Jerome's friendship began at Marcella's initiative, while Jerome was visiting Rome. According to Jerome, Marcella "never came without asking something about scripture, nor did she immediately accept my explanation as satisfactory, but she proposed questions from the opposite viewpoint, not for the sake of being contentious, but so that by asking, she might learn solutions for points she perceived could be raised in objection."[20] In other words, Marcella was frickin' smart. And she was not afraid to show her intelligence to Jerome. She wasn't intimidated into silence by this famous, powerful man. She wanted to learn from the best. And yet she didn't mindlessly believe whatever he said.

It strikes me that this is our work as women: to learn from women, from men, from nonbinary people, from people like us and people different from us—and, at the same time, to take everything with a grain of salt, to filter everything through our own intelligence and wisdom and experience. And, especially, to take with a grain of salt everything taught by people in power, particularly by people who have been in power a long time. Marcella asked Jerome all her brilliant questions and then examined his answers from her own perspective to determine what she believed. This is how we search for truth and perhaps find it.

After Jerome left Rome, other people started coming to Marcella for wisdom, just as Marcella used to come to Jerome. "If an argument arose about some evidence from Scripture," Jerome writes, "the question was pursued with [Marcella] as the judge."[21] Marcella taught both men and women with authority, and with Jerome's approval and appreciation. She judged and led wisely.

At one point in his eulogy, Jerome gets all self-conscious and starts worrying about what other men might think if they read his letter. It's fascinating. He writes, "An unbelieving reader might perhaps laugh at me for laboring so long over the praises of the ladies."[22] I read this and thought, *labor away,*

Jerome. Praise those ladies. Jerome defends himself from antici-
pated sexist criticism by looking to the women of the New
Testament, including "the holy women who were companions
of our Lord and Savior" who "ministered to him from their own
substance,"[23] as well as Mary Magdalene, who "was first worthy
to see Christ rising, even before the apostles."[24] Jerome insists,
"We judge moral excellences not by people's sex, but by their
quality of spirit."[25]

This is what we still need today. We need men, and all
people, to follow in Jerome's footsteps, not judging and margin-
alizing human beings by gender—or by race, or sexuality, or
any other aspect of identity—but seeing and honoring their
"quality of spirit." I'm all about those "praises of the ladies." I'm
all about lifting up Mary Magdalene, and the women who
ministered to Jesus, and the many brilliant Marcellas of
Jerome's age and ours. If Jerome could do it over sixteen
hundred years ago, surely we could do it now.

Hildegard of Bingen (1098-1179 CE) was, among many other
things, a female preacher in the medieval era. In one preaching
class in seminary, my professor, Dr. Lisa Lamb, began each
session by talking about a preaching hero from history. One
day, she put up a slide with a picture of Hildegard and a few
bullet points about her. One bullet point simply read, "tithed."
So, when Dr. Lamb asked if anyone knew anything about
Hildegard, and no one said anything for a few seconds, I help-
fully chimed in, "I think she tithed." I thought Hildegard must
have been really good at giving ten percent of her money to the
church.

Dr. Lamb had to explain that, actually, Hildegard *was*
tithed. Her family sent her away to a cloistered convent
because they had ten kids and wanted to give one to the
church—and because Hildegard's spiritual visions freaked

them out and made them worry she would be accused of witchcraft.

I learned from Dr. Lamb that despite these sorts of difficulties, Hildegard created an amazing life for herself. She did everything from preaching to composing music to writing books about medicinal herbs to designing plumbing systems. Clearly, she was brilliant. And while she may not have freely chosen the cloistered life, she ended up becoming the head of her convent, serving as a minister to the other women there— caring for them spiritually, exercising faithful and loving leadership, and preaching bold prophetic sermons. She also ventured out of the convent on multiple preaching tours, even into her sixties and seventies.

As the story has it, when Hildegard was first considered for a higher position in her monastic community, there was a male monk who opposed her leadership—because, of course, she was a woman. This monk developed a tumor on his tongue and became mute. He took this as a sign that he had been wrong to impose his sexist views on the abbey. When he communicated his remorse and change of heart, his tongue was healed.[26] It seems that God supported Hildegard's leadership. And eventually the men around her did, too.

Over time, as Hildegard shared her spiritual visions with others, these visions came to the attention of the pope. The pope sent a commission to listen to Hildegard and try to determine whether her visions were legitimate. This is one of those things that kind of sucks, because he didn't believe her in the first place, but is also kind of awesome, because he was the pope. He was the person who was supposed to speak for God, basically, and he was open to spiritual direction from a woman. After hearing back from the commission, the pope declared Hildegard a prophetess, a "light not to be hidden under a bushel." Thus, Hildegard became a sort of de facto advisor to the pope. Casual.

If a pope in the twelfth century could listen to a woman's prophetic voice, surely modern-day men in power can learn to listen to women's critiques of patriarchy—including women of color's critiques of white supremacist patriarchy, queer women's critiques of heteropatriarchy, etc.—in our churches today.

Hildegard was just one of many Christians of her time, both men and women, who are often known as "mystics." Christian mysticism was a movement that placed a strong emphasis on a personal experience of oneness with God.[27] Several mystic writers in late medieval Europe are considered influential enough to have made their way into our church history classes. Mystic-type ideas neither originated with nor ended with these people. But it still seems like an interesting time—and a time, perhaps, when women were pushing back against the patriarchal stuff happening in the Catholic church.

Then, in 1215, a bunch of bishops got together in the Fourth Lateran Council and decided, among other things, to severely limit women's roles in the church. They prohibited women's ordination.[28] Not too long after, in the mid to late 1200s, Thomas Aquinas (you know, the "humane thinker") wrote his *Summa Theologica*, making all sorts of sexist arguments to justify this prohibition.

So, you've got the church cracking down on women's religious leadership roles. And yet, you've also got women mystics like Hildegard (and Julian of Norwich, mentioned in Chapter 22) who are visioning, thinking, praying, writing, preaching, and generally influencing the course of Christianity.

In some sense, perhaps, mysticism was a sort of late medieval protest movement. It affirmed the divine spark in both men and women.[29] At a time when theological education was limited to men, mysticism eschewed formal education as

the main way of knowing God,[30] in favor of things like medita-
tion, prayer, and personal piety. These are democratizing
things, equalizing things—things anyone can engage in, regardless of gender, education level, or formal title in the church.
The religious establishment felt so threatened by these things
that they condemned many mystics, women and men alike, as
heretics. The struggle is real, and longstanding. And the backlash is often vicious.

Another moment of equality for women came in the 1600s with
the early Quaker movement. Quakers emphasized the Inner
Light within each person as a guide to truth and faith. Their
communities downplayed formal qualifications, did away with
ordination, and affirmed women as preachers and prophets.[31]
They believed that Christ's Spirit had led them to a consensus
that women were equal to men and could be sent out as
Quaker preachers, evangelists, and counselors, ministering and
leading just as men did.[32]

Quaker societies financially supported female preachers
who traveled around the colonies spreading Quakerism. These
Quaker women relied on the Inner Light as "a source of
strength and power" as they embarked on difficult journeys,
often experiencing rejection and persecution from local
authorities.[33] Female traveling preachers carried certificates
affirming that they had their husbands' permission to do so.
(Typical.) Not so typical, though: Male traveling preachers likewise carried similar certificates from their wives.

Quaker women also enjoyed something approximating
egalitarian marriage. Wedding vows were re-written in Quaker
communities to convey a mutual commitment between two
equal spouses.[34] (And here I thought I was being a rebel by
using egalitarian language in my own wedding ceremony in
our conservative church in 2016.)

The picture was not entirely rosy. Quaker women missionaries faced severe persecution, sometimes to the point of execution. Quakers in general were often hated and regarded with great suspicion by prominent members of other Christian groups. As women led alongside men, they were subject to hatred and persecution alongside men. In Boston, for example, both men and women were hanged on Boston Common in a group execution as punishment for their Quaker ministry there.

Within Quaker communities, men's attitudes toward women could be a mixed bag. There is evidence that men and women sometimes had separate meetings. On the one hand, this gave women all sorts of opportunities to lead and minister among fellow women; on the other hand, it afforded fewer opportunities to lead mixed groups.[35] And, as often happens in groups that start out with some awesome egalitarian ideals, many Quakers moved away from these ideals as time went on.

But still, this was 1600s England, and 1600s colonialist America. In a milieu of European Christian denominations and traditions establishing themselves in the colonies, Quakerism offered an alternative marked by equality. It offered women freedom to use their gifts. Quaker women were encouraged to follow their own intuitions, to trust their own sense of God speaking to them, to engage in community fully and freely in ways that were generally penalized elsewhere. At its best, this applied to Black and white women alike—especially in the Quaker movement's earliest days, when its opposition to chattel slavery was strong.

The Quaker movement, or at least many strands of it, created communities of equals across gender and racial identities. All this, four hundred years ago.

. . .

In 1666, one of these early Quaker female preachers, Margaret Fell, wrote an essay called *Women's Speaking Justified*.[36] My mind was blown when I read it. Language quirks and style aside, Fell's essay could have been written today. Unfortunately, women's speaking in church still needs to be justified. But Fell did a brilliant job of it four centuries ago.[37]

Fell draws our attention to the creation account in Genesis 1, noting, "Here God joins [man and woman] together in his own Image, and makes no such distinctions and differences as men do."[38] She points out that God creates and blesses both male and female, together, to be fruitful. And God gives both of them, together, all of the good gifts of the natural world.

Later on, Fell reflects on Jesus: "Jesus owned the Love and Grace that appeared in Women...and by what is recorded in the Scriptures, he received as much love, kindness, compassion, and tender dealing towards him from Women, as he did from any others."[39] Jesus was glad to receive women's ministry, Fell argues; given this, why shouldn't we be just as glad?

She then moves on to the resurrection, remarking on the male apostles' slowness to believe the women who were its first witnesses. "Mark this," she writes, "you that despise and oppose the Message of the Lord God that he sends by Women; what had become of the Redemption of the whole Body of Man-kind, if they had not believed the Message that the Lord Jesus sent by these Women, of and concerning his Resurrection?"[40] What would have become of Christianity, Fell asks, without those early women preachers—without their faithfulness to tell what they saw, even though the male disciples had to see for themselves before believing them? The male disciples weren't there at the tomb, but the women "sat watching, and waiting, and weeping about the Sepulchre...and so were ready to carry his Message."[41]

This kind of theological and biblical reflection is still happening today. Many of Fell's arguments felt so familiar to me when I read them in 2017. I had no idea a brilliant female preacher spelled them out in the 1600s. If I am tempted to assume that time naturally brings progress, Fell's essay reminds me that sometimes we've been going around in the same circles for centuries.

Jarena Lee was an African American woman from New Jersey who had an intense conversion experience as a young woman in 1804.[42] Looking for a church to help her live out her newfound faith, she tried a white Methodist church pastored by an Englishman, but she had a strong sense that "this is not the people for you."[43]

Lee then went to an African Methodist Episcopal church and heard Bishop Richard Allen speak. During the church service, Lee felt that God gave her a powerful experience of forgiving another person, and she was so moved by this experience that she "did leap to [her] feet," "though hundreds were present,"[44] and started spontaneously preaching. "For a few moments," Lee writes, "I had power to exhort sinners, and to tell of the wonders and of the goodness of him who had clothed me with *his* salvation."[45] Bishop Allen was receptive, in that moment, to Lee's inspired preaching.

Four or five years after this initial experience of spontaneous preaching, Lee received a strong sense that she was to "go preach the Gospel." She replied, "No one will believe me"— to which God said again, "Preach the Gospel; I will put words in your mouth, and will turn your enemies to become your friends."[46]

So, Lee went to Bishop Allen and told him that God had called her to preach the Gospel. Allen replied that the denomination did not allow women preachers. Lee writes with lament that, upon hearing this, "That holy energy which burned within me as a fire, began to be smothered." She reflects:

As unseemly as it may appear nowadays for a woman to preach, it should be remembered that nothing is impossible with God. And why should it be thought impossible, heterodox, or improper for a woman to preach, seeing the Saviour died for the woman as well as the man? If the man may preach, because the Saviour died for him, why not the woman, seeing he died for her also? Is he not a whole Saviour, instead of a half one, as those who hold it wrong for a woman to preach, would seem to make it appear?[47]

A whole savior, indeed. With this conviction, but without the formal authority of the church, Lee went off on preaching tours of her own. She writes, "In my wanderings...I have frequently found families who told me that they had not for several years been to a meeting, and yet, while listening to hear what God would say by his poor coloured female instrument, have believed with trembling, tears rolling down their cheeks."[48] Lee traveled where other preachers had not gone, and she found that her preaching was highly effective.

Lee's perseverance and courage in pursuing her call to preach is striking. She did what she felt God wanted her to do, without formal church recognition, or financial support, or anything else. All this, in the early 1800s.

These are not the only remarkable stories—not the only remarkable women—in (Western) church history. And I don't want to tell stories only about remarkable women. I want ordinary, unremarkable women to be free to live and love and serve and lead as God calls us. No limitations imposed by patriarchal churches. No hesitations stemming from internalized sexism. No uncertainty about what's appropriate or good or godly.

Proponents of churchy patriarchy often act like feminism is a new thing. As I learned more about Christian history in seminary, I realized that nothing could be further from the truth. It was like slowly finding pieces to a puzzle I didn't know existed. Christian history is not nearly as simple as it often comes across in the male-dominated ways it is taught. As historian Beth Allison Barr writes, "Women's leadership has been forgotten, because women's stories throughout history have been covered up, neglected, or retold to recast women as less significant than they really were."[49]

This realization was infuriating. So often we only get part of the story, and we don't even know enough to know that that's what we're getting. How could we? And often the part that we do get makes it sound like the church has always operated in one male-dominated way—with the strong implication that this is the way things should continue to be, since it's the way things have always been.

Learning a fuller history has helped me stop believing the lie that we are the first or second (or even the fifth or sixth) generation of women to find ourselves struggling for equality— and sometimes, in some ways, succeeding. Feminism did not begin with the #MeToo movement and other twenty-first century feminist work, as important as that all is. It did not begin with second-wave feminism in the 1960s and 70s, as important as that was. It did not begin with the battle for women's suffrage or any other aspect of first-wave feminism back in the nineteenth and early twentieth centuries.

We are not the first women to long to lead and minister freely. Ordinary women throughout church history have pushed for their rights to be acknowledged, for their full humanity to be recognized, for their liberty to lead and heal and write and teach and offer their gifts fully. And there have been moments of breakthrough, moments of freedom. These moments give us glimpses of what has really been, and what could still be.

Enslaved women were leading churches in the second

century. Women were writing and reading stories of faithfulness and martyrdom centered on their own experiences in the second and third centuries. Marcella was teaching in the fifth century. Hildegard was advising the pope in the twelfth century. Quaker women were traveling as preachers, commissioned and blessed by their churches, in the seventeenth century. Margaret Fell was arguing from the Bible in 1666 that women should be preaching. Jarena Lee was bravely pursuing her call and using her preaching gifts in the early 1800s.

Courageous women have been pushing back against patriarchal church rules—the kind that try to tell us what we "can" or "can't" do—since long before the era of modern-day feminism. As we struggle in our own contexts, we join this history. We can draw on the strength of such a great cloud of witnesses[50] over two thousand years. We can find our place historically in a tradition whose attitude toward women has been more of a sine wave of cycles than a linear, up-and-to-the-right trajectory of progress.

As we do so, we find ourselves looking ahead into the unknown—a path toward freedom that is possible but far from inevitable, the future of Christian women not at all guaranteed —and, in so doing, we find our own power to shape that unknown.[51]

RECLAIMING AGENCY

26

LET IT BE DONE FOR YOU

I had the opportunity to give a brief sermon on the phrase *Your kingdom come, your will be done,*[1] and it got me thinking about women and will. This is definitely the shortest passage I've ever preached on—just seven words in English, eight in Greek. It was part of a sermon series on the biblical text known as the Lord's Prayer—going through it line by line over the course of several weeks. We got to (or had to?) slow down and take time to sit with each of the phrases Jesus teaches his followers to pray.

This is the prayer, located right in the middle of a long series of Jesus' teachings known as the Sermon on the Mount:

Our Father in heaven, hallowed be your name,
your kingdom come, your will be done, on earth as it is in heaven.
Give us today our daily bread.
And forgive us our debts, as we also have forgiven our debtors.
And lead us not into temptation, but deliver us from the evil one.[2]

As I was preparing for the sermon, I took a closer look at those eight Greek words. *Your kingdom come, your will be done.* A more literal translation might read: *Let it come, your kingdom; let it happen, your will.*

I got interested in the two key nouns here: *kingdom* and *will.* I learned that, among many possible meanings of the Greek word translated as *kingdom*, one is "royal power." *Let your royal power come.* I like this. I think it opens up some important questions: How do we see power operating in our world today? How do we see Jesus using power in the gospels? In what ways are these two things—Jesus' use of power, and the uses of power we see around us—radically different? And what do we do with all of this?

Then, I looked up the noun translated as *will,* as well as its closely related verb form: *I will* (or *she wills,* etc.), in the sense of *I wish,* or *I want,* or *I desire.* The verb is much more common than the noun; throughout the book of Matthew, all sorts of people *will* all sorts of different things.

One particular instance stood out to me. The verse is Matthew 15:28, and the passage is an uncomfortable one. Jesus interacts with an unnamed Canaanite woman; as he does so, he comes across as a little stand-off-ish, to put it mildly—or even racist and sexist, to put it more harshly.

Here's the passage:

²¹*Leaving that place, Jesus withdrew to the region of Tyre and Sidon.* ²²*A Canaanite woman from that vicinity came to him, crying out, "Lord, Son of David, have mercy on me! My daughter is demon-possessed and suffering terribly."*

²³*Jesus did not answer a word. So his disciples came to him and urged him, "Send her away, for she keeps crying out after us."*

²⁴*He answered, "I was sent only to the lost sheep of Israel."*

²⁵*The woman came and knelt before him. "Lord, help me!" she said.*

*26*He replied, "It is not right to take the children's bread and toss it to the dogs."

27"Yes it is, Lord," she said. "Even the dogs eat the crumbs that fall from their master's table."

*28*Then Jesus said to her, "Woman, you have great faith! Your request is granted." And her daughter was healed at that moment.*3*

Jesus' words in v. 28, translated more literally, read something like this: *Oh woman, great, your faith; let it happen for you as you will.*

Let it happen for you as you will. Jesus' words to the Canaanite woman here are remarkably similar to Jesus' words to God in the Lord's Prayer: *Let it happen, your will.* The phrase is not exactly the same, but the resemblance is striking. The *let it happen* part is exactly the same. And the *as you will* part—where the "you" is the woman—is basically another way of saying *your will*—where the "you" is God. It's just a matter of verb versus noun. Same basic idea, same root.

As far as I can tell, this is the only place in the whole book of Matthew where Jesus says something to a human being that is so similar to what he says to God in prayer.

In other passages, Jesus asks other people what they want. He asks the mother of James and John, for example, *what do you will?*[4] At another point, he asks two blind men, *what do y'all will that I should do for y'all?*[5]

Jesus also speaks, sometimes, about what he himself wants. For instance, when Jesus laments over Jerusalem, he says, *how often I willed to gather your children together, the way a hen gathers her chicks together under the wings, and y'all did not will.*[6] (The relevant verb is used twice in this phrase: Jesus *wanted* to gather people, but people did not *want* this.)

The word for *will* comes up again when Jesus prays to God in anguish in the Garden of Gethsemane, soon before his death: *My father, if it is possible, let this cup pass away from me;*

however, not as I will but as you.[7] Jesus articulates both his desire for the cup of suffering to be taken from him and his desire to be faithful to God, regardless, until the end.

But nowhere else in the gospel of Matthew does Jesus say anything to a human being that sounds remotely like *let it be done, your will*—nowhere but his conversation with the Canaanite woman.

C.S. Lewis wrote, in *The Great Divorce*: "There are only two kinds of people in the end: those who say to God, 'Thy will be done,' and those to whom God says, in the end, 'Thy will be done.' All that are in Hell, choose it."

I've enjoyed Lewis' writings as much as the next Christian who likes to ~~overthink~~ think deeply about things, but his oft-quoted line about "Thy will be done" strikes me as a bit of a false dichotomy. Where does the Canaanite woman fit into this? Jesus says to her, *let it be done for you as you will*—which is basically another way of saying "Thy will be done." But, in this case, it's a good thing. Jesus holds her up as a shining example of faith. He remarks on her great faith, and then he heals her daughter—which is what she wanted so desperately that she was willing to publicly humble herself before a man from an ethnic group that thought of her ethnic group as "dogs"[8] and wasn't afraid to say so. And, apparently, what she wanted was what God wanted, too.

This unnamed Canaanite woman—whom the disciples wanted to send away, and whom Jesus first ignores and then insults—is the only person in the whole book of Matthew to whom Jesus ends up saying, basically, *you are so in tune with God's will that I want you to have exactly what you want. You want all the right things. I have nothing to teach or correct you on, and everything to praise you for. You go, girl. Right on. Let it be done for you as you will.*

. . .

Many of us have been taught to see God's will as something generally set against our own wills, as if these two things are always in conflict. It's as if Jesus actually meant to teach his followers to pray not just *your kingdom come, your will be done,* but rather, *your kingdom come, not my kingdom,* and *your will be done, not my will.* Women especially are often church-socialized to see things this way—to see our own wills as fundamentally flawed and untrustworthy, in need of being subordinated and subsumed by God's will.[9] (And God's will sometimes tends to look an awful lot like the will of men in power.)

I want to dream together of a better way. This better way involves getting more in touch with the deepest desires of our souls—courageously, honestly, freely. It involves acknowledging and honoring the variety of emotions we experience, the variety of things we find ourselves drawn toward and wanting. Not all our desires are good. But a lot of them are. A lot of them involve wanting to see people thrive, friendships thrive, families thrive, communities thrive. We long for meaningful work, for connection, for health, for justice.

I think the way forward involves learning not to assume that our desires—just by virtue of being human, and especially by virtue of being a woman—do not line up with God's desires. It involves learning not to assume that the *your will be done* part of the Lord's Prayer is always opposed to our own will. It involves embracing our own agency, our capacity to act boldly on our own good desires, our ability to approach and ask of God like the Canaanite woman approached and asked of Jesus.

Sometimes *God, your will be done, not mine* rolls off our lips more easily than *God, this is what I want. This is what I need.* It sounds holier. And it's how many of us were taught to think—

that our own wills don't matter. But they do. The Canaanite woman's will mattered to Jesus. Our wills matter to God too.

The goal is not to hide or efface our wills, but to seek that our wills would line up more and more closely with God's will. I want to believe, and to see other women believe—really believe, in the core of our souls, in a way that no person or institution can take away from us—that God doesn't actually want us to be less demanding, or strong-willed, or stubborn, or needy, or ambitious. (Remember the persistent widow?) I want us to know, really know, that God sees the good and beautiful desires within us, and that God affirms those desires.

Jesus' words in the Garden of Gethsemane—*not my will be done, but yours*—are certainly one way to talk about God's will. But they aren't the only way. Jesus spoke these words in a very particular circumstance. Sometimes God does invite us into things that would never have naturally fallen among our own desires for ourselves. But this is not true for everyone, and not all the time. We are not constantly in the Garden of Gethsemane contemplating our own imminent deaths. And we are certainly not Jesus.

Sometimes we may become aware that God wants something different from what we want. But other times—lots and lots of other times—the desires we find in the depths of our souls are good. They are sacred. We do violence to ourselves and to the divine spark within us when we ignore, downplay, deny, or try to purge ourselves of these desires, assuming they aren't from God.

I want our faith to embolden us to move toward the good things we desire—to get after these things with a sense of urgency, a sense of holy agency, a sense of confidence that God is with us as we do so.

And I want us to offer our friends, daughters, mothers, sisters, and all the other women in our lives this blessing: The desires of your soul are not bad. They are not things to be ashamed of. They are precious to Jesus. Jesus sees the things you want that line up with what God wants—the things that line up with justice and goodness and peace and mercy—and says, *yes, and amen. Let it be done for you as you will.*

27

I LEFT A CHURCH

or some reason, the title of this chapter plays in my head to the tune of the 2008 Katy Perry song *I Kissed a Girl*. "I left a church..." So that's a little embarrassing. But I thought you should know.

After about a year and a half at Life Church, it became clear to me that it was time to leave. There had been a series of smaller disappointments that slowly snowballed over time, gaining momentum as they rolled along. And then there was the incident where I felt that Pastor John refused to take two young women's very valid safety concerns seriously. I ended up getting to the point where, while something within me still dared to believe that church could be inspiring and life-giving, I knew this one just wasn't—not now, not for me.

By the end, I found myself praying, *God, why? I just needed a place to rest and recharge after all the other churchy things that have been difficult and painful over the last few years. But this has just been one more round of difficult and painful. Why?*

I don't think we always, or even often, get the answer(s) to that question. But I wonder if, for me, in this particular situation, some part of the "why?" was this: I needed to know—really know—that I had the power to leave.

I needed to know that I had agency. I needed to know that I did not have to stay in a situation that I felt was not good for me. I could jump off a ship that I felt to be burning and sinking beneath me. I could swim away and see whether the unknown open waters might hold an island somewhere that would actually offer health and sustenance. Nothing good would come from stubbornly refusing to jump.

I think it's safe to say I'm not the flighty type when it comes to churches. I spent the first eighteen years of my life attending the church where I was baptized as an infant. Then I moved to California for college, quickly found Faith Bible Church, and stayed there for eleven years, only leaving when I moved away for seminary. That covers the first twenty-nine years of my life: two churches, one in the Seattle area and one in the Bay Area.

But I left a church, for the first time, at age thirty-one—*left* left, as opposed to finding a new church when you move to a new city. And I didn't exactly *like* it. But it was a new experience for me, and a surprisingly empowering and healthy one. I have no regrets about leaving. Ken and I spent a lovely month or so —our last month in Southern California—at a local Mennonite church, content to sit in the back and breathe a breath of fresh air.

The experience of leaving Life Church made me think about what it means to leave a church. It made me think about what it means to have the power to leave. Sometimes we don't have much power to change the things that need to be changed. But, if nothing else, we do have the power to leave.[1]

In that sense, effecting change in churches is easier than, say, effecting change in the U.S. as a whole. Even if a church doesn't care at all about the negative experiences people are having,[2] most churches care—a lot—about how many butts are in their pews (or chairs, or whatever). If people start leaving in significant numbers, church leaders take notice. They freak out about it. They may or may not come to the right conclusions about what needs to change, but you know they're forming committees and talking in pastors' meetings and fretting and hand-wringing and strategizing and (hopefully) doing some soul-searching and pray-ing. They're troubled, and they're trying to figure out what to do.

Sometimes, for churches that are initially unwilling to change, a significantly sized exodus might open leaders' eyes a little bit. It might open up new conversations that will be good for the church in the long run, even if losing members is painful in the moment.

Those of us who experience frustration, pain, disappoint-ment, anger, or disillusionment with our churches can help this process by meeting with church leaders and being open about our experiences, our concerns, and why we're walking away. We can vote with our feet, refusing to stay in a situation that isn't good for us, or that isn't good for those we love. And we can let this be known.

Nothing about this is easy. These conversations are hard. Leaving is hard. We may feel trapped by relational loyalties or by a sense of guilt or obligation. We may experience (valid) anxieties and fears: What will others think of us if we leave? Where will we find our sense of community and belonging? We may even wonder if we will be disappointing God.

But I think God desires community to be life-giving for us, not soul-draining. Church may be at times difficult, painful, messy, and costly—but it should also be a place of grace, connection, growth, freedom, and joyful belonging. Sometimes a church is not, or is no longer, this kind of place for us. And it might be time to go.

It might be time to quit cold turkey, or to take a step back and think about things, or to visit other churches to see what they're like. It might be time to speak frankly with church leaders about our concerns, fully accepting the risk that these leaders may not respond well—the risk that these conversations may reveal things we're not sure we wanted to know, things that might make it necessary to leave for good.

I think of the time one of my (white male) seminary professors was talking to our class about the practical aspects of getting a job at a church. He told us, "If you had to leave a previous job because of a theological disagreement, but your coworkers and supervisors there would still speak well of you, that's a really powerful reference to have."

I heard that, and I thought about Faith Bible, where I was no longer able to work once I became openly LGBTQ+ affirming. Would my colleagues and supervisors there speak well of me? For the most part, I think so. There are some things I would do differently if I could do it all again, but, in general, I think I did the best I could to speak kindly, treat people well, articulate our differences in a respectful way, and not burn bridges unnecessarily.

And so, when my professor said that, my first thought was *oh good, that makes a lot of sense. I think I have that going for me.*

As I think about it now, though, I'm struck by the sheer amount of privilege wrapped up in his words—wrapped up in this idea that you can speak up about the things that are important to you, and people will still like and respect you. Even if they disagree, and even if those disagreements are so serious that you end up having to leave the church. I've come to realize that speaking up about stuff, and how people react to the person speaking up, is quite gendered. It depends a great deal on the identity of the person who is speaking up.

As a woman, if I express an unpopular opinion, I will often

immediately be placed in a category described using words like divisive, arrogant, abrupt, aggressive, harsh; a man can express the exact same opinion, using the same words, tone, and body language, and come across as strong, intelligent, a free-thinker, assertive, courageous. As a woman, any emotion I might show while trying to speak up about things I care about can and will be interpreted as weakness, irrationality. (Remember how *it's hard to talk about money*?) It will be used as a reason not to listen to me, a reason to assume that my words aren't also logical and well thought out.

This is all racialized as well. If I were a Black woman, for example, I would have to deal with people's stereotypes and fears of the "angry Black woman" trope. People tend to respond to critique or disagreement from a woman of color even more poorly than from a white woman.

It's a form of white male privilege to be able to speak your mind and have others still respect you while also thinking you're dead wrong. Many of us don't have that privilege. The relationships I was able to maintain at Faith Bible were, to some extent, dependent on my choice to hold back, to only rarely express the entirety of what I was thinking and feeling, to keep things pleasant, to choke down my anger and be polite. Sure, I didn't burn bridges—but at what cost?

At Life Church, I tried to have some of the conversations I had been afraid of having at Faith Bible. In theory, it should have gone better; after all, this was a church that believed that men and women are equals and that neither gender is better suited to lead. It turns out that conversations about disagreements are still hard. Especially when one person has institutional power as a pastor and the other doesn't; especially when that person with institutional power is a man and the other isn't. Long story short: I tried, and it didn't go great. But I think it was worth it to try.

I think it's worth speaking up when we find ourselves in

disagreement with church leaders about something deeply important to us. I think it's especially worth speaking up when we experience marginalization in our churches because of who we are or what we believe.

This isn't easy. There are risks involved. Sometimes we're not in a position to choose to take those risks. But sometimes we are. In these cases, I want to learn how to have the hard conversations that need to be had. And I want to see more and more women do the same. I want us to do this with eyes wide open—not caught off guard by the kinds of responses we might get, not terribly surprised if we burn some bridges just by being honest. Perhaps if a church is the kind of place where voicing dissenting opinions burns bridges, we didn't need those bridges anyway.

People often say that there is no perfect church. (And, as the joke goes, if you do find the perfect church, don't join it, because you'll ruin it!) I think this is true but not necessarily helpful. Of course there is no perfect church. But there are churches that are mostly healthy, and there are churches that are pretty darn unhealthy.

There are churches whose flaws and failures are things you can work through as a community, maybe even look back and laugh about from the other side.

Then there are churches whose flaws and failures might be fine for someone else but are too triggering and traumatic for you, such that you are not able to engage in that community in a healthy way, even if someone else could. This doesn't mean there's anything wrong with you. It just means that different people respond differently to the same things. It's good to be aware of how we're responding—to pay attention to what our body, brain, and intuition are saying to us, and to honor these things. Maybe sometimes you need to leave but it's okay for others to stay.

And then there are those churches whose dysfunctions are profound and unfixable—usually because people in power are not willing to fix them, and there is no meaningful account-ability for these people in power. (In many religious organiza-tions, the deep pockets of certain donors play a huge role here too.) These churches' diseases are so fatal, their entrenched structures so oppressive, that you need to get the hell out and take as many people with you as possible.

Sure, there's no perfect church. But not all churches' imper-fections are equal. And not all churches' flaws call for the same response.

Sometimes people feel a sense of calling to stay and try to change things. Sometimes people want to work from within a community to undo the structures and attitudes that oppress them or oppress others. I admire these people and honor what they're doing. I also wonder, though, if this is more of a special calling than a reasonable default. Often, trying to stay is too much, too stressful, too soul-crushing—and that is okay. It doesn't mean we failed. It doesn't mean we didn't try hard enough. It doesn't mean we weren't strong enough or faithful enough. It just means it's time to leave.

I long for more people—especially women, especially people of color, especially LGBTQ+ people, and anyone else who has been marginalized in their church communities—to feel a deep sense of freedom: freedom to stay and engage when called to, and freedom to leave when not. I long for us to feel and own our agency to vote with our feet.

I long for greater freedom to separate our sense of ourselves and our rightness with God from the guilt and shame others may heap on us if we leave. After all, if these others would rather shame us than listen to our stories and trust our wisdom about what makes for our flourishing, then they are not *for* us.

And, as much as we might love them and cherish the good times we have shared, we owe them, as the apostle would say, nothing except love.[3] We don't owe them our presence at their gatherings. We don't owe them our approval of their practices and teachings. We don't owe them our silence in the face of things that hurt us or hurt others. We don't owe them our church membership. We don't owe them our participation in the systems that oppress us or oppress others. We owe them only the continued offer of friendship and goodwill—to the extent that they would embrace it, and to the extent that the friendship would be a genuinely healthy one. But we do not owe them our willingness to stay.

There are probably plenty of people who are too quick to leave a church, jetting at the first offense rather than staying for the work of reconciliation. But I think there are also plenty of people who are too slow to leave. And when we stay too long in churches that are not healthy for us—where we are not growing and thriving as we could be—we are complicit in the dysfunctions and oppressions of these churches.

I think of a story Linda Kay Klein tells in her book *Pure: Inside the Evangelical Movement that Shamed a Generation of Young Women and How I Broke Free*. A woman told Klein that she had stayed for many years in a church that didn't fully embrace women in leadership. Then, one day, this woman and her husband were holding their newborn daughter, and they looked at one another and said, "Are we willing to have our daughter taught the things that we were taught?" The woman was struck in that moment with this thought: "If I can't accept that for her...why do I accept it for me?"[4]

I, too, wouldn't want my hypothetical daughter—or anyone else's daughter—to grow up in a church where she is not encouraged to follow whatever dreams God places in her heart.

And I wouldn't want my hypothetical son to be shaped by a church that sees women as less than his equals. Yet I stayed in just that kind of church, as a young woman, for eleven years.

There were lots of reasons why I stayed so long, and some of them were good reasons. Everyone's journey is different and takes different amounts of time. I want to look back on that time in my life with a hell of a lot of grace for my younger self. At the same time, though, these things are worth thinking about. Especially for women who are still in environments like that—in places where perhaps a part of you wants to get out, and another part of you wants to stay; where perhaps a part of you wants to believe it isn't that bad, or is afraid of leaving.

My hope and prayer, for all of us, is for vision, strength, courage, and faith. May we have clear vision with which to see our own churches—perhaps to see them through the eyes of a parent looking at her newborn daughter and wondering whether she wants her daughter to grow up there. May we have strength to look long and hard for communities that are healthy for us. May we have courage to build these kinds of communities together. May we have faith to believe this is possible.

28

Y'ALL, BE ANGRY

Y'all, be angry, and do not sin;
let the sun not set on y'all's rage,
but do not give a place to the devil.[1] —Paul[2]

"I grew up hearing that church was the place where you could
come with everything—all your baggage. Yet it often felt as if
we still needed to check certain bags at the threshold…The
unspoken message was 'Don't bring your sadness, doubts,
criticism, hopelessness, angst, frustrations (unless it's about the
coffee or homeless people on the corner), and certainly not
your anger.'" —Mihee Kim-Kort[3]

*a*s you may have noticed, there are some things I'm
angry about. I'm an angry woman. I'm an angry Christian woman. I want to figure out how to build something new,
but I also want to tear stuff down—so much stuff. And I think
that's okay. We can't really build new things without tearing
some old things down—if not in the world in general, then at

least in our own minds and souls and relationships and communities. And tearing things down often involves getting frickin' angry about some of those things that need to be torn down.

I want to go back to the Bible here, because I've seen scripture verses wielded like big clumsy carrots and sticks to try to get us to all just play nice, and I don't think that's right. Everyone playing nice only perpetuates the status quo. It's a way of pretending everything is okay when it isn't. And I don't think that's really what scripture is about.

Don't get me wrong—I'm all for being kind. But also, increasingly, I'm all for getting angry.

I've most often heard Ephesians 4:26 translated as "In your anger do not sin" (NIV). (Does that sound familiar? I feel like it's something pastors like to quote.) I was surprised to realize, when I came to this verse in its original Greek, that it actually says something more like "Be angry and do not sin." This is all in the second person plural, so one might say: "Y'all, be angry, and y'all, do not sin," or "Y'all, be angry, and do not sin."[4]

Y'all, be angry!

This is what Paul wants to tell the church in Ephesus. And I find it kind of comforting. Because there are so many things to be angry about. There are the things that impact me directly, like many of the faces of the hydra-monster patriarchy. And there are also the things that impact me less directly. I'm not Black, but I'm angry that police kill Black people and get away with it. I'm not materially poor, but I'm angry that we aren't doing enough about climate change, the effects of which are felt most acutely (for now) among people living in poverty.

Anger is a totally reasonable response to these kinds of things. It's a healthy response. It means we care. It means we're acknowledging what's wrong in our world.

Anger is a normal part of the range of human emotions. And it turns out that the Bible is not nearly as uncomfortable with anger as many Christians are—or as many faith communities and church leaders are.

Y'all be angry, and do not sin; let the sun not set on y'all's rage.[5]

I like that Paul uses an imperative (command) form to tell his peeps in Ephesus, communally and collectively, to be angry. I also like—and here I imagine Paul wouldn't be averse to adding "as much as possible, as far as it depends on you"[6]— that he wants these angry people not to find themselves *still* angry at the end of the day.

What exactly *let the sun not set on y'all's rage* means is not totally clear. But I think it means something more—or something different—from what we might be tempted to think, or what we might have been told: to just forgive and let go.

It seems connected to what Paul writes a few verses later: "Get rid of all bitterness, rage and anger, brawling and slander, along with every form of malice"[7]—or, more literally translated, "All bitterness and rage and anger and brawling and slander, let it be taken away from y'all, with all malice." *Let it be taken away from y'all.* I like how, in this literal translation, the passive voice makes the removal of bitterness and brawling feel more like a prayer than a command. As in, *God, I don't know if I can just "get rid" of these things so easily. But would you let them be taken away from me?*

It also seems a bit ambiguous where all this rage and slander and such is coming from. Are we praying to get rid of our own malice, or others' malice? I wonder if, as much as we want to be rid of these things in our own beings, we're also praying for these things to be removed from others, such that we are no longer their target. *God, I don't want to be the object of others' brawling and slander. Let it be taken from me, please.*

Really, it's a communal thing. We are all rid of these things together—or we're all impacted by them together. Either they are taken from us collectively—or we're all torn apart by them, prevented from being a healthy community.

I think Paul wants the Ephesian faith community to learn how to be angry without destroying themselves in the process —that is, how to be angry without giving in to the kind of bitterness that takes root, and grows, and finds expression in things like brawling and slander, and tears apart communities. Paul wants them to be angry, but not to hold onto malice.

I'm reminded of Willie Jennings'[8] words: *"I felt the struggle, the old struggle to keep the anger from touching hatred. My faith— no, Jesus himself—was the wall that kept the anger safe from hatred. Anger yes, hatred no, because if anger touched hatred, I would be poisoned by death himself and become trapped in an addiction that few have been able to escape."*[9] I like how Jennings puts this, and I think Paul would agree. Paul might say: Anger, yes; hatred, no. Indignation, yes; bitterness, no. Rage, yes; malice, no.

This is all easier said than done. But I think Paul writes these things because he wants the church community to learn how to be angry without self-destructing. He wants to see people learn to support one another, speak truthfully, heal wounds, and thrive together—anger and all.

I don't think we can do this without finding meaningful ways to express the anger that we hold. I don't think we can do this without actively and urgently seeking out ways to try to right the wrongs that cause us to be angry.

Not only is this the right thing to do, but it is also a more effective way of "letting the sun not set on our rage" than trying to just let go and move on. When things evoke deep anger in us, is it really possible to simply set them aside and go to sleep? Can we really just let it go—all in one day? When we try to do this, we often end up suppressing our anger—which is unhealthy for us, and it's not great for the people around us either. Our repressed anger tends to burst out in harmful ways.

Perhaps we are not meant to just try to stop feeling angry by the end of the day, but, instead, to not let another day go by without doing something with our anger—something healing, right, and good. Maybe we're not meant to judge our emotions but to honor them, to listen to them, to attend to them as a guide. Maybe we're meant to let our anger move us to action, motivate us to exercise our agency.

I think of Audre Lorde's words in *The Uses of Anger: Women Responding to Racism*: "Every woman has a well-stocked arsenal of anger potentially useful against those oppressions, personal and institutional, which brought that anger into being. Focused with precision it can become a powerful source of energy serving progress and change."[10] Anger can be useful. There is power in it, power that can be used for good.

I think of a story about Jesus, recorded in Mark 3:1-6. Jesus wanted to heal a man's withered hand, but the religious leaders didn't care about the dude and his hand. They just cared about what it would look like if they let Jesus heal on the Sabbath. They were waiting for Jesus to do something that looked bad, something they could accuse him of. And Jesus got angry at them.[11] Then, immediately, Jesus asked the man to stretch out his hand; the man did, and Jesus healed him.

In other words, Jesus got angry, and then he moved urgently to do something good with that anger—something healing and liberating for the man, and, at the same time, something that messed with the worldview of the powers-that-be. So much so that these powerful people went away wanting to kill Jesus.[12]

This is what "let the sun not set on y'all's rage" looked like for Jesus in that moment.

I wonder what it looks like for us and for our communities. Maybe it looks like joining or organizing protests. Maybe it looks like getting angry about something racist, sexist, or other-wise harmful that we witness at work, or at church, or in other settings—and not letting the sun set before we take appropriate action in response. We might speak out in the moment, if possi-ble. We might seek out the person affected by what happened, express validation and affirmation, and ask what we can do to be supportive and help make things right—or at least a bit better. We might speak with the person who made a racist or sexist comment. We might bring the matter to HR, or otherwise make a fuss about it. These are just a few examples.

Christians sometimes speak about anger as if it's a bad thing—as if the goal is to try to get rid of our anger, maybe through prayer or journaling or singing a lot of soothing worship songs. Mihee Kim-Kort is spot-on in articulating the vibe we often get in church: "Don't bring your sadness, doubts, criticism, hope-lessness, angst, frustrations (unless it's about the coffee or homeless people on the corner), and certainly not your anger."[13]

As women, especially, we're often expected not to be angry. Men laugh at our anger; they're afraid of our anger; they dismiss our anger—as Dr. Jones did when he brushed off my concerns with "it's hard to talk about money in church." In our cultural gendered scripts, anger is coded as masculine. It's one of the few emotions men get to express. (This is a problem, too.) And it's decidedly unfeminine—just like Elizabeth's loud prophetic clamor.

I don't want to be contained within these culturally imposed expectations. I *am* not contained within these cultur-ally imposed expectations.

I don't really want to be less angry. Instead, I want to be angry in ways that align more closely with God's anger. I want to get more angry about the things God gets angry about—

things like inequity, needless suffering, dishonesty, greed, racism, mistreatment of immigrants, misogyny, abuse of power, sexual abuse, spiritual abuse—and to figure out what to do with this anger. And I want to let go of the other kinds of things I might get angry about—things that are less about justice and more about my own ego, convenience, or preferences. (Like that church coffee.)

I want to see what happens in our faith communities and in our world when women acknowledge our anger and use it for good. I want to see what happens when we connect our anger with our agency and let it move us toward justice. People might not respond positively to this. But it might be exactly what our communities need. It might help us take whatever steps we need to take toward justice and love for all people. I want to see us take those steps—before the sun sets, preferably.

REIMAGINING
AUTHORITY

29

OH, SO THAT'S A HERESY

While I was studying at United Evangelical, I met a friend of a friend, let's call her Kate, who was also in seminary but at a different school. I got to talking with Kate about seminary stuff. I was curious which classes she liked best, and she asked me the same. I mentioned being fascinated by church history, and Kate's eyes lit up.

"Yeah," I said, "so interesting, right? There's just so much I didn't know—like all the drama and squabbles in the early years that influenced so much about the Christian tradition."

Kate replied enthusiastically, "Yeah! SO interesting. I'm fascinated by how those early church councils declared different theologies to be heresies, and how we still see threads of some of those heresies in our churches today. I was learning about them, and it was like, ohhh, so *that's* a heresy. And *that's* a heresy. Wow. Good to know!"

I don't exactly disagree. Plenty of theologies deemed heretical long ago do have their ways of sneaking into modern-day churches, in everything from sermons to worship songs to aesthetically attuned Instagram quotes. It really is fascinating. And it's good to notice and think about these things.

At the same time, though, something about what Kate said didn't quite sit right with me. As I thought about it more, I realized that for me, a different kind of thread ran through what I had been learning about church history and how I was responding to it. The kind of thread you can tug at and find yourself tumbling down a long (but important) rabbit hole.

This thread involved some nagging questions. How, exactly, were historical decisions about orthodoxy and heresy made? We learn about church councils in our history classes—what they were called, when they happened, what was debated, and what was decided. But often we don't learn how they were structured, or who was or wasn't invited—and why. Often we don't ask whose voices were heard and whose voices were ignored.

These councils were made up of men—prominent, educated, powerful churchy men. Just like many decision-making bodies in our churches and denominations today. I couldn't help but wonder how the composition of these councils impacted the kinds of perspectives they were able to see, the kinds of experiences they took seriously, the kinds of decisions they made. What do we do with the fact that women's voices were never heard at these decision-making tables? Was I really supposed to believe that these powerful men—many of whom wrote mind-blowingly sexist things about women—were acting with women's best interests in mind? Would some decisions have been different if women had been involved in the process? If so, which decisions, and how?

The people who participated in these councils were human. Humans tend to make some good decisions and some bad decisions. We can be incredibly wise and discerning one moment, and equally obtuse and misguided the next. It isn't always easy for us to know which aspects of our thinking are good, loving, and just, and which are narrow-minded and self-serving. We are imperfect, and power among us operates imperfectly. This was true throughout church history. And it's true in the present day, as churches continue to wrestle with their policies and positions on the controversial issues of our time.

The longer I spent in seminary, the more I started taking churchy declarations of orthodoxy and heresy with a large grain of salt. Homogenous councils of people in the present day —particularly powerful, wealthy people—rarely make the best and most-informed decisions. Why would we assume that these same sorts of councils in church history were always right about everything—and that it's our responsibility today to cling to their decisions at all costs?

As I contemplated church history in my classes, I thought often of my own experience of (slowly) becoming LGBTQ+ affirming while working in college ministry for Faith Bible Church. I thought about some of the church leaders' responses. No one explicitly used the word "heretic," as far as I can recall. But the sentiment was similar, as were the power dynamics.

Some church leaders expressed concern that I was "leading students into sin" by being unwilling to teach them that gay relationships were against the will of God. That was a bummer. But what I found most disheartening about the ensuing conversations was not just that we had different opinions about what is or isn't "sin." The worst part, for me, was that many of the church leaders seemed unwilling to acknowledge that Christians could legitimately come to a conclusion different from theirs.

Maybe that's my straight privilege talking. Maybe I should have been just as deeply bothered by these leaders' non-affirming views as I was by their apparent unwillingness to consider the possibility that they could be wrong. But this is where I was at.

I get that it's complicated. I get that change is hard. I get that the "traditionalist" view, in which the Bible prohibits same-sex relationships, is a deeply held belief for many people. It's what many of us have been taught from a young age. It's an important part of many evangelicals' identity, as people of faith who desire to operate in radically different ways from mainstream U.S. culture. There are lots of reasons why churches and church leaders aren't ready to consider changing their minds about LGBTQ+ sexuality.

But none of this means that LGBTQ+ affirmation is heresy. It just means that LGBTQ+ affirmation is different from the views of the people currently in power at a lot of evangelical churches.

People with power tend to assume that their position is the orthodox one. But when asked how they know this, sometimes all they can offer is circular reasoning: Well, all our church leaders currently hold this position; therefore, this is what our church believes; therefore, this is what everyone at our church *should* believe; therefore, this belief must be orthodoxy; therefore, this is the position people must hold in order to become leaders; thus, all our church leaders currently hold this position.

Learning about church history in seminary, I wondered: Were those councils back in the early church so very different? There must have been some degree of groupthink. *This is what makes sense to the majority of us; therefore, it must be true, and the minority view must be heresy.* This is often how orthodoxy gets established, and how it gets passed down from generation to generation.

And yet, sometimes things considered orthodox in one

generation are seen as quite wrong in the next generation. Jen Hatmaker puts it this way as she reflects on now-venerated justice seekers like Dr. King and Gandhi: "The Bible has been used to justify human rights abuses since its canonization, including every injustice these freedom fighters opposed. It was 'right' until it clearly wasn't. Hindsight is clear on the arc of moral justice, but the present day is not."[1] Questions of orthodoxy versus heresy, or right versus wrong, or good theology versus bad theology, are not always as clear as they may seem.

Perhaps an important part of our freedom as women is the freedom to reexamine orthodoxy and heresy. We are free to rethink, when necessary, what we have been told about God and the Bible and the world and churches and people and everything, and how these things are determined. We are free to question views and policies handed down to us, especially those handed down by decision-making bodies that did not necessarily represent us or have our best interests in mind.

Ultimately, male-dominated church councils and elder boards and denominational leadership committees do not get to decide who is "in" or "out" of the Christian tradition. The Christian tradition is and always has been full of glorious diversity in every way, including diversity of thought and theology. People of faith can be united in love for God and in a mutual desire to see, hear, and learn from one another. We can be united in ways that don't diminish our differences or erase them. We can resist the temptation to cling to whatever power we might have by calling others "heretics" and casting them out.

Full equality may still be a far-off dream. In the meanwhile, though, we can reexamine our notions of authority. We can consider whose perspectives are valued when it comes time to make important decisions on behalf of a community. "Nothing about us without us," as many activists have said. If the decision impacts women, where are the women at the decision-making table? What do they have to say? If the decision impacts LGBTQ+ people, where are the LGBTQ+ people? Likewise with people with disabilities. Likewise with people of color—and people from the specific communities of color most impacted by the decisions being made.

I'd love to see people and churches move, together, from squelching dissenting voices to embracing them; from rejecting minority viewpoints as heresy to wondering whether they might be prophetic; from assuming God is aligned with the views of the powerful to considering what the powerful might be getting wrong; from thinking we're right about everything to admitting there's always room for growth. We can move away from using orthodoxy as a control mechanism that tries to put limits around the kinds of thoughts people can think and the kinds of questions they can ask. We can move toward honoring divergent perspectives, eager to learn from them. And where there are homogenous groups of leaders, perhaps these leaders could become more willing to admit that they don't always know everything—that they could be like eleven of the twelve jurors in the classic play *Twelve Angry Men*, completely convinced about something, and completely wrong.

In the meanwhile, I'd love to see more and more women acknowledge and reject our tendencies to think that church leaders, especially male church leaders, are the only ones who can read and interpret scripture. As Sarah Bessey writes, theology is a game where "everyone gets to play"; it's something that "belongs just as much to the rest of us...as it does to the great scholars."[2] This might feel threatening to existing leadership structures. But it doesn't need to be. It doesn't have to be scary. It can be exciting. It can open doors to new possibilities, new kinds of conversations about what church could look like and what God might be doing in our midst.

The Christian tradition is and always has been wildly diverse. There are so many different ways to know and follow Jesus. Just because people in power believe something doesn't make it true.

In seminary I learned that it's okay—that it's good—to reexamine the things handed down to us. This is part of what it means to be a faithful and engaged Christian, and part of what it means to be part of a community of faithful and engaged Christians.

It's what the whole biblical book of Deuteronomy is about: On the cusp of entering the promised land, a new generation remembers and reinterprets the laws given to Moses many years before. It's what the Protestant Reformers in the 1500s knew when they came up with the motto *ecclesia reformata, semper reformanda*: The reformed church is always reforming. Each generation is tasked with the exciting, humbling, and maybe a little terrifying job of figuring out how to live faithfully as Christians in the new times we find ourselves in—how to hold on to what is good in what we've been given, and how to let go of what no longer serves us well.

As we reexamine all these things, together, we just might find ourselves moving toward a faith and a world that works better for all of us: all genders, all races, all sexualities, all socioeconomic classes, all abilities, all people.

30

PLEASE WELCOME YOUR NEW RULING ELDERS

*B*ack at Faith Bible Church, every now and then I got to witness the formal introduction of a new elder to the church community. (Not terribly often, because elders at that church were appointed for life, like Supreme Court Justices.) On the occasions when this did happen, I don't think I ever felt particularly emotional about it.

Not so when I first attended an ordination service for new elders at my current church—let's call it Peace Presbyterian Church, or Peace Pres for short. When the church staff emailed out pictures and brief bios of each new elder in anticipation of the service, I felt a rush of excitement and joy. This surprised me.

And when we met in person in the summer of 2020—outdoors and socially distant, of course—to ordain these new elders, I may have gotten a single little (wo)manly tear in my eye. It was an amazing thing, to see these six (masked) people standing in front of our congregation to be welcomed and prayed for—five out of the six of them, women; four, women of color.

. . .

There's Susan, a Japanese American woman, retired after a long career in higher education, who loves mentoring and encouraging young adults. On her first Sunday at Peace Pres, in 2016, she went away saying, "I felt seen by God today." How beautiful is that? And how painfully poignant that this wasn't a given for her—that after all her years in churches, and especially in churches whose leadership is dominated by white men, the feeling of being seen was remarkable, surprising, uncommon.

There's Theari, a young woman of Khmer refugee descent who works as a university academic advisor. She has strong roots in her Khmer identity and in the White Center neighborhood she grew up in in Seattle. Theari is, in her own words, constantly working for "social justice and decolonization of our spirituality and our faith." I'm so here for that.

There's Sili, a Samoan woman who has been doing development work in communities of color for over thirty years. Her passion for and experience with antiracist work runs deep. She has led our church in conversations about what justice looks like and how we work for it—conversations about how to root out our internalized white supremacist ways of being, and how to move from charity (which looks nice while maintaining existing power dynamics and never really changing anything) to solidarity (where we recognize that our flourishing is tied together and we learn to live as equals in a new kind of community).

There's Megan, a young woman of Japanese and Filipina descent. She is an elementary school teacher passionate about engaging with her students—mostly students of color—in a way that promotes their liberation rather than subjugation. She has worked her butt off during the pandemic to keep her students engaged and to show up for them in meaningful ways even when everything went online.

There's Marcy, the lone white woman. She's a lifelong

educator who now works for the state education department, supporting new teachers. She has helped lead our church's "white caucus" meetings—a space for white people to process race-related stuff so that people of color don't always have to listen to the sheer endless exhaustion of our every "new" revelation.

There's also Dave, the lone white man. He's awesome too, but this book isn't about him.

One of the things I liked best about the ordination service was that no one felt the need to harp on the gender or race of the new elders.[1] There was no self-congratulatory "Look at us! Look at how diverse we are. We must really be doing something right, unlike all those other churches." There was no "Look how progressive and forward minded we are! Aren't we awesome?" And, best of all, no "Aren't we such good, benevolent people for giving these women of color a leadership opportunity they might not have elsewhere? Look how generous we are. Look how lucky they are to be here." (No wonder women and people of color often struggle with "imposter syndrome." How could we not, when we're constantly being told that we're lucky to be here, that we don't really belong—that we're just a nice token, not to be taken seriously?)

There was none of that nonsense. There was only, as it should be: "Each of these people is amazing! We are so, so blessed and fortunate that they've chosen to serve the church in this way. We're so excited about the mind and heart and experience each of them brings. We're excited about the ways their collective wisdom can work together for the good of the church and our broader community. We can't wait to see their gifts in operation as they lead us."

And that's exactly how I felt. Having been at the church for less than a year—and about half that time online due to the pandemic—I didn't know most of these new elders very well. But I knew all of them a little, or at least had seen them speak in church at different times. I knew enough to know they would be amazing. Seeing them take up these leadership roles gave me hope.

I think of Austin Channing Brown's words in *I'm Still Here: Black Dignity in a World Made for Whiteness*:

> Rare is the ministry praying that they would be worthy of the giftedness of Black minds and hearts...we, too, are fully capable, immensely talented, and uniquely gifted. We are not tokens. We are valuable in the fullness of our humanity. We are not perfect, but we are here, able to contribute something special, beautiful, lasting to the companies and ministries to which we belong.[2]

Amen. I've been sitting with this.

If I may extend Channing Brown's words about Black giftedness to other women of color: I don't know if our church is worthy. But I am grateful. We have been gifted with the leadership of amazing, faithful, talented people, and I know we're better for it. So much better.

Christian leadership is often dominated by white, straight (or straight-passing), upper-middle class, able-bodied men between the ages of thirty-five and seventy. When this is the case, not only are women, people of color, and many other kinds of people held back from using our gifts fully, but the church as a whole is impoverished too. The church needs all our gifts.

I think the ways in which women are (or aren't) respected as leaders in a community says a lot about the ways in which women are (or aren't) respected generally as human beings in that community. I love that our church is the kind of place that seeks to see and appreciate each of these women as fully human, gifted, beloved children of God, and as valued community leaders. I love that melanin-poor skin and a Y chromosome are not regarded as qualifications for leadership.

I wish it felt odd to write about this—to get emotional about it, or to be as deeply moved as I was. I wish this were all entirely unremarkable.

I long for the day when it feels totally ordinary to welcome a diverse group of elders, many or most of whom are female or nonbinary, and for every person in the congregation to look at them and think: I trust these people to lead. I am so thankful for their wisdom and gifts. Our church would be missing so much if they were not here. I would be missing so much in my own spiritual life if any one of them were not a valued part of this community, free to use their gifts. My liberation truly is bound up with theirs. It is good—not just for them but also for me—that they are free.

When Ken and I were quite new at Peace Pres, we sat down next to a couple of strangers at a church fundraising event. They were a husband and wife, closer to our parents' age than ours. In an attempt to make casual conversation, I asked, "So, what brought you to Peace Pres?" The wife replied instantly: "Desperation."

I was surprised by her vulnerable honesty with a stranger. And I also completely understood. So many of us have found ourselves on the underside of poorly-used power in churches. We need to find faith communities where we are seen and empowered. This is an act of desperation, an act of survival.

I keep hearing similar things from people I meet at Peace Pres. *We came here after our last church fell apart,* says one couple. Another person shares, *I wanted to be part of a church that was actively doing good things in its local community, partnering with local leaders to strengthen the community; my former church gave money to these kinds of things but didn't really engage beyond that.* Another: *After going to male-led churches all these years, I told myself, our next church will have a female pastor.*

Many of us are desperate to feel a sense of belonging in a community that we trust will not fall apart when tensions inevitably emerge. We are desperate to be part of faith communities that matter in our neighborhoods and cities. We're done with programs that try to help the poor while always thinking the rich know best—not truly listening, standing in solidarity, or trying to build healthy communities of equals. We are desperate for different kinds of leadership. We're done giving so frickin' much authority to the tall white dude with the deep commanding voice who preaches as if his words come straight from God.

We're desperate for new ways of being.

I'm not always sure what these new ways look like. But I know that, to find them, we desperately need to take steps—preferably gigantic, walking-on-the-moon-type steps, and quickly— toward honoring women, and especially women of color, as leaders in our communities. I know we need to take seriously the questions Ijeoma Oluo asks: "What does it look like to respect qualified women of color as thought leaders instead of waiting to turn to them in dire times as saviors? What does it look like to recognize that the ideas we have to help our communities might just benefit all communities? What does it look like to recognize that we are more than warriors, more than survivors—we are innovators and leaders?"[3]

Sometimes when we become aware of the messes our white dude leaders have gotten us into, we reflexively turn to these very same white dude leaders to get us out. We turn to them—

because we've always turned to them—to show us a new way. It's what we know how to do. But often they don't have a new way. Often all they have are old ways, repackaged to look a little better.

We need more than this. We need something truly new. And we need different people to lead us there. We need people who have seen the things that people who have lived on the underside of unjust systems can see better than anyone else— and who, because of this, know better than anyone else how we might build something new.

I want to see women, and especially women of color, respected as thought leaders, as Oluo writes. I want to see them recognized for their ideas—ideas that can help us all build a better world. I want to see them regarded, rightly, as innovators and leaders. Not just begrudgingly permitted to have a wee little bit of (something approximating) authority in some very particular (tightly controlled) circumstances. Not just hesitatingly, inchingly, resentfully made a little bit of room for. Not just touted as tokens of diversity. But, instead, fully respected, fully encouraged, fully affirmed, fully loved.

This is what I caught a glimpse of while my church's new elders were being ordained. And it's how we might begin to move forward together toward something new.

31

MAYBE DO WASTE YOUR LIFE

*W*hen I was in college, John Piper's 2003 book *Don't Waste Your Life* was all the rage among some of my Christian friends. I think someone lent me a copy once, but I never actually read the thing. At the time, admitting that might have felt like a confession; these days, though, I don't regret it. I don't really feel like I missed out on anything good.

In case you aren't familiar with the book, here's a brief back-cover excerpt, just to give a quick sense of what you might expect to find within its pages:

> I will tell you what a tragedy is. I will show you how to waste your life. Consider this story from the February 1998 Reader's Digest: A couple "took early retirement from their jobs in the Northeast five years ago when he was 59 and she was 51. Now they live in Punta Gorda, Florida, where they cruise on their 30-foot trawler, play softball and collect shells..." Picture them before Christ at the great day of judgment: "Look, Lord. See my shells." That is a tragedy.[1]

Apparently, I needed John Piper to tell me what a tragedy is. And it definitely involves softball and seashells. Not war, or famine, or poverty, or gun violence, or sexual violence, or racism, or the climate crisis, or anything like that. Good thing Piper is here to tell us what kind of lives we should be living, and God forbid there might be any kind of nuance to it—any room for different people's ideas of what makes a meaningful life, or space for all of us to explore these crucial questions together and perhaps learn from one another.

There's plenty to critique here. (And there are some witty critical reviews at *goodreads.com*.) And yet. Even though I never read the book, there was something about the idea of *not wasting your life* that was appealing to me, for a time.

I got into Stanford, as most students at colleges with obscenely low admissions rates do, by being all about productivity, efficiency, and measurable forms of success. That's how you get the proverbial chubby letter in the mail. You do all the homework, study all the time, ace all the tests, and work hard at ten thousand extracurricular activities. You make the most of every moment, building up your resume to be as impressive as possible to the mysterious but all-powerful admissions ~~gods~~ officers.[2]

This didn't end up being a particularly fulfilling way of life for me. By the time I got to college, I was ready for something new. I was ready for a new worldview, a new set of priorities. I realized that the things I had spent so much time worrying about in high school—grades, SAT scores, performance in sports and music, and, of course, various crushes and dating relationships—were not really what I wanted my life to be about at its core.

I believed in God, but I hadn't been very involved with my church's youth group in high school. (Too many cool kids. And, well, I was co-president of the math club.) I hadn't been involved in the Christian club at my high school either, because I felt vaguely embarrassed by the thought of it, and because the timing conflicted with math club, anyway. But when I started college, I was ready for something different. I really wanted to get involved in a Christian community, to grow in faith alongside like-minded friends.

In other words, I was prime recruitment material for Jesus Followers (again, not its real name)—the campus fellowship group I joined as a freshman and ended up working for a few years later. I was burned out on one way of life—focused on my own achievements and success, on being validated by the kinds of systems that get you into a place like Stanford—and ready for a new one. And I believed in Jesus, so it was natural to seek out Christian communities in my pursuit of a better way to live.

At first, this worked great. Jesus Followers' leaders were great at capitalizing on this sort of dissatisfaction with worldly success. They spoke compellingly about the emptiness of achievement and the endless vacuum we get sucked into when we live for the affirmation of others. They invited us into a different way, a way of following Jesus rather than pleasing people—of being great in the kingdom of God rather than by the fickle, arbitrary, unfulfilling standards of the world. I embraced it all, wholeheartedly.

Did serving the kingdom of God mean taking a Sabbath day of rest every week? Count me in. Don't count on me to get homework done on Sundays.

Did succeeding in God's eyes mean giving up personal housing preferences to live with fellow Jesus Followers students so we could host Bible studies in our dorms together? Count me in. I didn't need my own room, anyway.

Did being great for Jesus mean spending fifteen hours a week being a Jesus Followers student leader? Count me in. That's much more important than exploring other interests, or studying abroad, or shadowing or interning to learn about potential career paths.

The *don't waste your life* ethos, I felt, was strong. Do, do, do. Go, go, go. Take every moment captive for the kingdom of God. Throw yourself wholeheartedly into God's plans and purposes —which, of course, neatly coincide with Jesus Followers' plans and purposes. Time spent watching Netflix is something to confess as sin. Time spent with friends, playing board games or whatever, is okay, maybe—if it's building relationships among Christian friends to encourage each other in Christ, or building relationships with non-Christian friends in order to spark curiosity about Jesus.

Creating or appreciating art—what's the point? Sports— sure, it's good to be healthy, I guess...but are you evangelizing to your teammates? That's the real reason you're there.

It's all about productivity—for the Gospel. It's all about making the most of every moment—for God's glory. It's all about efficiency and single-mindedness in building the kingdom of God.

I remember the moment, a couple years after graduating from college, when I was on a retreat with the young adults' group from my church, sitting alone near the river in the Yosemite Valley, staring up at the ridiculous grandness of the rocks rising vertically on all sides. I found my gaze drawn to a waterfall rushing down one of the cliffs, high up and far off in the distance.

A thought occurred to me: Sometimes God makes things just because they're beautiful.

Suspend any skepticism for a second. If you feel the urge to say, *Well, actually, the waterfall is a very important part of the watershed system, and serves a very important purpose*, etc., I'm sure you're right. And yet, this is the thought I had. And it was meaningful to me.

In that moment, staring at the waterfall, I saw pure beauty, simple and glorious. No particular objectives or agendas. No frantic rush to evangelize and lead and strategize for the kingdom. Just heavens and Earth declaring the glory of God[3]—in their own perfect timing, in their own perfect way, not measuring their worth by the number of people they convert or the size of their Bible study group or the number of hours they spend doing stuff for God. Content just being what they are— being enough, and being beautiful.

That waterfall, in all its self-renewing, awe-striking beauty, helped me see that there is more to life than a *don't waste your life* mindset of efficiency and measurable production. More to life—and more to God. Perhaps God wasn't quite as obsessed with Christianized productivity as I was.

Eventually I realized that I had just traded one form of unhealthy and meaningless ladder-climbing for another. I had traded the worldly success ladder for the religious success ladder, the Stanford ladder for the Jesus Followers ladder. I had not actually traded a life of restless, unfulfilled striving for a life of peace and trust in God; instead, I had traded one form of striving for a different one. The sanctioned activities—and the measurements and rewards (and shames and punishments)— were very different, but the underlying system was not all that different after all.

It took me a while to be able to name this. It is taking me longer still to figure out how to unlearn it, how to engage with faith differently—how to live life as a deeply committed person of faith in a way that doesn't make Christianity just another thing to achieve at, compete at, be successful at, seek others' affirmation in. Maybe this will be a life-long journey: to learn the lesson of the waterfall.

Whatever this journey might entail, I know it involves learning to rest. It involves learning to honor my body and soul and heart and mind, the whole and beloved person God made me to be. I know it involves learning to interact with other people in healthier ways, ways that honor the whole and beloved people God made them to be.

I'm no longer interested in a mindset where the goal of every interfaith relationship is conversion to Christianity. What kind of a friendship is that, if I'm trying to change something fundamental about my friend? I want to learn to honor each person's incredible, complex being—created in the image of God, loved by God exactly as they are. I believe God wants people to become more freely and fully themselves—and I want that, too. I don't think God wants people to be molded into whatever shape I think they should take, or whatever shape some pastor or church thinks they should take.

I think of a story from the life of Jesus. Jesus and his disciples are chilling at a dinner party, when a woman crashes the party, breaks open a jar of really expensive ointment, and pours it all over Jesus' head, right there at the table, anointing him. Jesus' disciples say, *what a waste!* But Jesus says, *she has done a good and beautiful thing to me.*[4]

For Jesus, life was not all about efficiency, productivity, doing as much as possible all the time. If it were, Jesus would have taken the expensive oil, sold it, and done something productive with the money, as his disciples thought he should have. For Jesus, it was enough just to spend time with the people he loved and who loved him—with his disciples, and with the woman who crashed their party. It was enough to simply embrace the few and unlikely people who came to him to express their devotion—and to honor the gifts they chose to bring.

Really, Jesus "wasted" his life. He spent his time on Earth teaching and healing limited numbers of people, in small towns, in the middle of nowhere. He kept wandering off by himself to pray. (I could totally see him collecting seashells—and then maybe telling a story or two about it.) He would move on from a town just when everyone wanted him to stay. He would say things that drove people away just when he was starting to get popular. He spent time with the kinds of people whom important people see as a waste. Eventually he died, too young, as a failed revolutionary, never having married or had kids or written a book or become a leader in the official religious hierarchy.

I think about Jesus—and I think about all the people, made wonderfully in God's image, who for all sorts of reasons aren't able to "succeed" in a life of Christianized productivity. I think about people with disabilities that keep them from being able to work, or from being very efficient in their work. I think about elderly people, in their retirement—no longer working, often no longer able to move as quickly or do as many things as they once did. I think about people who are physically sick, or emotionally sick, or depressed, who might need more time and margin in their lives.

I think of stay-at-home parents, investing all their time into one or two or five little humans who won't remember much of it and don't appreciate most of it. That's a far cry from a life spent influencing tens or hundreds or thousands of people through speaking at conferences, or leading the church youth group, or climbing the corporate ladder, or preaching, or starting a nonprofit or ministry organization. But it's no less important.

I think, too, of the artists. I think of people who see seashells on the beach, and flowers growing up through concrete, and robins searching for worms in the field, and other little wonders, and stop and stare in awe. I think of people who create: beautiful things, important things, expressive things, inspiring things, sobering things; things they might never be able to sell; things that aren't explicitly "Christian" but that say something true; exquisite things that enrich our lives and our world.

I fully believe that God sees and loves people who do not operate at maximum productivity in terms of numbers and results. I fully believe that God does not see their lives as a waste. I fully believe that God does not see my time and my life as a waste when I "fail" to spend every second of it on churchy pursuits. It's okay to watch Netflix sometimes—and to do so just because I enjoy the way people use their gifts to tell stories with humor and wit and honesty and beauty, all of which are sacred. It's okay—it's good—just to enjoy the company of the people I watch these shows with, not trying to convert them or push them toward a higher level of spirituality, but simply caring for and accepting them exactly as they are, and letting them do the same for me.

While I was working in college ministry, it slowly dawned on me that what I wanted for the students I served did not always line up with what I thought I should be pursuing in my own life. I expected myself not to "waste" a moment on not-explic- itly-Christian endeavors—but then when I heard students being similarly hard on themselves, I would encourage them to rest, recharge, and take care of themselves. I would tell them that their well-being is important, that it's good to be attentive to what their bodies and intuitions are telling them. I tried to make space for them to become more wholly the unique and wonderful people God made them to be. I encouraged them to pursue their academic and extracurricular interests and see where they might find God in these things. I tried to help them not feel guilty for not spending more time on churchy stuff.

These are all things I wanted for the students I worked with, and for people I cared about in general. For myself though, it was different. I didn't take enough time off. I didn't make enough space to rest and recharge in ways that were restorative for my soul. I didn't prioritize my own well-being. I distrusted my own feelings and intuitions. I lived as if "becoming the unique and wonderful person God made you to be" was for other people but not for me. I tried to be the kind of person I thought a churchy leader should be—which, as it tends to do, involved hiding and suppressing parts of who I actually am. I stunted my own academic and other interests to spend all my time on churchy stuff. Some of these things might sound noble, and a lot of it was what Christian leaders had encouraged—but none of it was good.

For a while, I wondered if I was sometimes too indulgent with students. I wondered if I was doing them a disservice by failing to call them to the difficult life of following Jesus, a life of sacrifice. Now, I think I was just doing for them what you do for someone you love. And this was good. It was good for them; it also helped me see, in time, that I needed to learn to love myself as well. I needed to learn to tell myself the same things I would have told any of them: It's good to be who you are. You are loved and accepted and treasured exactly as you are. As you know God more, you know yourself more, and vice versa. It's good to rest. You do not need to do more, run faster, work harder to please God. If you are being fully you, and loving God and loving people as well as you can, you are not wasting your life.

While the *don't waste your life* mindset is toxic in general, it is uniquely toxic for women. In complementarian settings, women are often basically told something like this: Don't waste your life on anything less than the gospel—preaching it, writing about it, speaking it, teaching it, evangelizing, doing church stuff, leading church programs. There is nothing better you could be doing. Everything else is less important. Oh, but you're a woman? Well, then. You shouldn't be preaching the gospel, or writing about it authoritatively, or speaking about it in a way that doesn't parrot everything your (male) pastor has already said, or teaching anyone but kids, or evangelizing to mixed-gender groups, or leading church programs other than maybe hospitality or visitation. Women should generally stay home and clean and cook and take care of children, because that is their duty, their God-given role in a Christian household.

If you're a woman, you're told the best possible things a human could be doing, and then you're told you aren't supposed to be doing them. That everything you *are* doing— your work, parenting, housework, yardwork, volunteering, creating, caregiving, friendship-building, or anything else—is a lesser pursuit. You are a lesser Christian for it. Your life is more of a waste. Your life is less valuable than the lives of people— that is, of men—who are pursuing better, more spiritual things. You, as a woman, are less capable and clearly less spiritually-minded.

Basically, *don't waste your life* is only for dudes. (Dudes privileged with the financial security to be able to make a lot of choices about how to spend their time.) Women *are* wasting their lives, just by the (God-ordained) nature of things. But that's okay, because women didn't really matter in their own right, anyway. We're just here to support our husbands' lofty callings.

Really, on a societal level, the mindset that prioritizes measurable productivity above all else is exactly the kind of diseased thinking that has lurked behind patriarchal white supremacist U.S. life and law and culture from the start.

It's the imperialist mindset: We have guns and big ships, so it is our right to conquer and steal and enslave, all the while pretending we are culturally superior. We have fancier agricultural machinery, so clearly we're better at farming—even if our ways of farming deplete fields of nutrients and fill the groundwater with dangerous chemicals, favoring a quick dollar over the holistic long-term well-being of people, plants, animals, and land.

It's the toxic patriarchal mindset: Men are, on average, bigger, taller, and stronger than women, able to produce more physical labor more efficiently. Therefore, they must be more valuable, more important, better able to lead.

These are some of the bigger things wrapped up in a Christianized *don't waste your life* mindset. There are so many layers to the rottenness of it all.

I dream of a collective detox—a total reimagining of all of this. I think we need to reexamine, at a deep and fundamental level, what we value and why. It isn't good enough to trade a ruthless, soulless system of competition and achievement in the realm of work and wealth for an equally ruthless, soulless system of competition and achievement in the realm of church and religion.

We desperately need new ways of being together. Ways of being that honor women. Ways of being that honor different cultures' views of the world. Ways of being that honor people with disabilities, that honor stay-at-home parents, that honor artists, that honor all forms of work. Ways of being that honor the land and the animals and the seashells—and the people who take time to appreciate and care for them all.

The patriarchal white supremacist drive toward (some skewed vision of) productivity ends up harming everyone. I think God invites us to live in a very different way. I think God invites us to waste our lives—as the woman at the dinner party wasted her anointing oil on Jesus. I think God invites us to value the people our world and our churches tend not to value: the soft-spoken ones, the slow-moving and inefficient ones, the ones who don't make much money, the ones with humble-sounding job titles, the ones whose work totally sucks and doesn't pay enough. I think God invites us to value the people who are often marginalized in our society and churches: women, people of color, LGBTQ+ people, people with disabilities. Relentless efficiency in the pursuit of doing as much churchy stuff as possible tends to trample over all these people. And it maims the soul of the one pursuing it.

I believe we can do better. I want to be part of that "better." I want to learn to honor the waterfall, to honor the seashells and the seashell collectors. I want to "waste" my life in healthy, restorative, sustaining ways. I want to be part of communities that are learning together to "waste" our lives together, sacredly, beautifully.

32

LEARN FROM THE WILDFLOWERS

When I first started growing vegetables from seed, I was surprised by how *long* everything took. Even the plants that were supposed to grow quickly. I guess quick is relative when it comes to the natural world. Waiting two or three months for lettuce to mature felt like forever. And when it finally came time to harvest a small handful of butternut squashes in the fall, it felt like I had been caring for those plants for most of my life. (In reality, it had taken maybe six months.)

I have only been vegetable gardening in earnest for a few years now, but my expectations have changed dramatically. Instead of giving up on carrot seeds when they don't germinate in a few days—*why can't you be more like the arugula who sprouted a week ago??*—I have learned to accept that they might take a couple weeks to come up, and that their journey will be a long one. And that, at the end of it all, I might have some lovely carrots, and some funky-looking ones, and some stunted chubby ones, and some that just never really grew. I'm happy to have any carrots at all, whenever they're ready.

There are a lot of things I can do to help plants grow well, and I'm slowly learning these things. In the end, though, even if I do everything right—good soil, ideal timing, consistent water, plenty of compost—I can't really control how they grow. Fertilizer can only speed the process so much—and if you give too much fertilizer, that's not good either. Likewise with watering. All my human interventions in these plants' lives only have so much impact. And everything happens slowly.

I don't know a ton about plant biology; I had zero interest in that part of my high school biology classes, and I don't remember it being covered in the one biology class I took in college when I still thought I was a pre-med. I'm interested in learning more now, though, and I have learned a little—mostly stuff that's practical for gardening. I've learned, for example, that each tomato flower has everything it needs for its own pollination—so you can help the plant make fruit by giving it a little tickle so that the different parts of each flower mix. Squash plants, on the other hand, make separate male and female flowers—so you can help the plant make fruit by hand-pollinating the female flowers (the ones that have a little baby fruit at the end) with pollen from the male ones.

Regardless, I have the feeling that no matter how much I might learn about plant biology, it will still be something of a mystery. I really am just like the farmer from Jesus' parable who "does not know how" the seeds grow.[1] I have no idea. It will always be something of a miracle that the monster kale plant outside my window came from a tiny seed I planted a year ago. Every time a seed sprouts, it is both botany and mystery; every time a new leaf unfurls, it is both biology and miracle. I see no contradiction here. Only a mindset that tries to separate human reason from all else—and place it above all else—would see this as a problem.

. . .

At some points, especially early on, I felt in a sense controlled by the plants. I didn't love it. I was so used to walking into a grocery store and choosing the vegetables I felt like eating, or the ones that were on sale, or the ones I wanted for a particular recipe. But the plants growing in our yard didn't care about my tastes or my recipes. They were ready to eat when they were ready to eat. Some offered more flexibility than others: some, like the green beans, needed to be harvested within a day or two, while others, like the radishes, didn't seem to mind waiting a week until I felt like roasting them or putting them in a salad. But this was a new thing—this attention to what the plants were saying and when they wanted to be harvested. It was a new thing to let the plants determine what I ate.

I'm more used to this now. And I even kind of like it. What vegetable should we cook tonight? Well, the collard greens are (over)due for a harvest. Or maybe there are a couple of ripe cucumbers, but not enough for pickling; it's time for a cucumber salad. It can be fun. But it was a little jarring at first. I had to give up the illusion of control—both in the growing of the plants, and in the timing of their harvest. The garden has its own rhythms. These rhythms will continue with or without my attention—but we're all better off if I attend to them.

I find myself eating parts of plants I wouldn't have eaten before. Apparently, kale flowers and bok choy flowers are edible. Who knew? And when kale goes to seed in the early spring, about to complete its two-season life cycle (at least in our climate), it makes a ton of little broccoli-looking florets that are quite good to eat. Or, take radishes: some of my efforts at growing them have been more successful than others, but whether or not the root actually bulbs out into something resembling a radish, there's always an abundance of greens, and they're actually very tasty.

I see the time and attention and care that goes into the life of each plant, and I'm less likely to waste parts of it that could be eaten. I want to honor the plant's life—and my own efforts to keep it alive. Some waste is inevitable. But growing my own vegetables has encouraged me to branch out (pun intended), try new things, and have more appreciation for everything these plants have to offer.

I reflect on all of this because growing vegetables has been an important part of my journey toward becoming a healthy human. Gardening is a spiritual practice. And I reflect on it because there is so much going on in the natural world that we can learn from—so much that we need to learn from, and that many of us often ignore.

I think this is part of what it looks like to build new kinds of faith communities, and a new kind of world, together. Not that everyone needs to grow and pickle cucumbers, or grow sugar pie pumpkins to bake in autumn (although I'd highly recommend both of these things). The point isn't necessarily that everyone should garden, and definitely not that everyone should garden the same way I do. The point is to learn to notice the natural world, to think about what we eat and where it comes from, to receive these gifts thoughtfully and thankfully, to reconnect with Earth and all her creatures.

Humans, as the Genesis 1 story would tell it, are a part of God's very good creation. Christians have often focused on the "subduing" and "dominion"-exercising part of this story.[2] And well, here we are: in the middle of a climate crisis, disconnected, lonely, profit-driven, diseased and dying. What if, instead of reading the Genesis story and focusing on the subduing, we learned to read it and focus on the goodness of the natural world? Genesis paints a picture of light and darkness, dry land and seas, plants of all sorts, sun and moon, aquatic animals and flying animals, land animals and humans, woven together in life-giving, mutually-sustaining relationships.[3] As Kaitlyn B. Curtice writes, "We are not only made for community within our own species—we belong to all the creatures of the earth, our kin."[4]

I have heard preachers say that God did not declare the created world "very good"[5] until humans were made. This is true but potentially misleading. It may sound as if humans are, in and of ourselves, what is "very good"—while the rest of creation, including the plants and animals, are only "good." It may sound as if humans are better, separate, superior, dominant.

This is the opposite of what I see in the text. Really, it is not just humans who are "very good" on our own; rather, it is the whole of creation, all together. This includes humans but does not necessarily privilege us over others—and it certainly does not give us the right to do whatever we want at the expense of others. Humankind is not on its own. We are created in God's image, blessed by God, given the fruits and vegetables of Earth as a sacred gift. The animals, in turn, are given all the plants of Earth, also as a holy gift.[6] All of this—together, intertwined in relationships of giving and receiving, in cycles that could go on forever—is "very good."

God saw this. God was satisfied. And God rested.[7]

As we work to break down man-made patriarchal hierarchies, we find that they are tied to other hierarchies—hierarchies based on race, class, ability, sexuality, and other aspects of human identity. But not only that. We also find that human hierarchies are tied to hierarchies among species.

I appreciate Robin Wall Kimmerer's words in *Braiding Sweetgrass: Indigenous Wisdom, Scientific Knowledge, and the Teachings of Plants*:

In the Western tradition there is a recognized hierarchy of beings, with, of course, the human being on top—the pinnacle of evolution, the darling of Creation—and the plants at the bottom. But in Native ways of knowing, human people are often referred to as 'the younger brothers of Creation.' We say that humans have the least experience with how to live and thus the most to learn—we must look to our teachers among the other species for guidance. Their wisdom is apparent in the way that they live. They teach us by example. They've been on the earth far longer than we have been, and have had time to figure things out...Plants know how to make food and medicine from light and water, and then they give it away.[8]

I feel this hunger now to learn from plants. As Kimmerer writes, plants have been here longer than we have. We are their younger siblings. I like that—and I find it challenging, because it's so very different from how white U.S. American society tends to operate. But gardening is helping. (So is reading—and re-reading—*Braiding Sweetgrass*.)

It turns out that once we start poking at the power structures of patriarchy, if we're doing it right, we end up poking at all the oppressive power structures in our world. The ones that have degraded people of color. The ones that have degraded people living in poverty. And not just the ones that have degraded and marginalized people, but also the ones that have degraded animals, plants, waters, soils. It's all connected. And this is a good thing. As we aim to find ways of becoming healthy and whole women, we're really finding ways of becoming a healthy and whole humanity—and a healthy and whole web of interconnected beings of all sorts.

. . .

This may sound like a far cry from the Christianity most of us know. But if that's the case, it may be because the Christianity we know is a far cry from the Jesus of the scriptures. Jesus walked humbly as flesh on Earth. He spoke peace to the wind and waves.[9] Yes, he had dominion—but he was also God, not just any human, and he always used this dominion for the flourishing of all people. He used his authority to heal withered hands. He used his power to tell a marginalized woman from a people group who were enemies of his own people: God wants what you want. *Let it be done for you as you will.*

When he taught, Jesus used his authority to direct people's attention to other teachers—teachers who would be around in physical form much longer than he would. Teachers, that is, like plants and animals. I think of this well-worn text from the Sermon on the Mount:

> [25]*Therefore I tell you, do not worry about your life, what you will eat or what you will drink, or about your body, what you will wear. Is not life more than food, and the body more than clothing?* [26]*Look at the birds of the air; they neither sow nor reap nor gather into barns, and yet your heavenly Father feeds them. Are you not of more value than they?* [27]*And can any of you by worrying add a single hour to your span of life?* [28]*And why do you worry about clothing? Consider the lilies of the field, how they grow; they neither toil nor spin,* [29]*yet I tell you, even Solomon in all his glory was not clothed like one of these.* [30]*But if God so clothes the grass of the field, which is alive today and tomorrow is thrown into the oven, will he not much more clothe you—you of little faith?*[10]

Two observations might help us see this text in a new light. First, where v. 28 reads "*consider* the lilies of the field"—or, in other translations, "*see* the lilies of the field"—the Greek word translated as "consider" or "see" actually has its root in the word for learning. It's the same root behind the word for *disciple*. It might just as well be translated as *examine carefully* or *learn thoroughly*.[11]

Second, the word translated as "lilies" could also be read as "wildflowers." I like this, because it sounds a little more broadly relatable. We aren't talking about carefully cultivated lily bouquets sold at the grocery store or florist. We're talking about the subtle beauty of flowers that grow naturally in the fields, on the hills, in a clearing in the woods. *Learn thoroughly from the wildflowers*, Jesus says. Perhaps even—and this is a bit of a stretch, but not as big a stretch as one might think—*disciple yourself* to those flowers.

Jesus says, learn from the wildflowers, and from the birds, and from all the beings who, as Kimmerer writes, have been here longer than we have—and who, because of this, might know a thing or two about how to thrive in our world. What might we learn from the wildflowers—about worry, and about life in general? What might we learn about healthy relationships, about connectedness, about mutuality? About freedom from all sorts of hierarchies, all systems of domination and oppression?

Jesus invites us to learn from different kinds of teachers. He invites us to learn from the natural world, and to find ourselves as a part of it—interconnected, taken care of, and taking care of others. Disciple yourself to the wildflowers. Learn from the lilies.

The urgent impatience of our white supremacist patriarchal society has gotten us into the many messes we're in. But the birds and the wildflowers—and the people, often Indigenous people, who have been listening to them much longer and more deeply than I have—are pointing toward a better way.

Just as vegetables take *so long* to grow and mature and be

ready to harvest, often so does the work of God. Often so does anything worth doing.

I hope this mindset can help us persevere. Sometimes we jump into justice movements, and then, like Peter walking on water, we look around at all the waves and get discouraged and start to sink.[12] When this happens, like Peter, we can reach out and take the hand of the one who has been on this journey a long, long time—the one who created the birds and the wild-flowers, and who still invites us to learn from them. This one— this Jesus—will keep picking us up, encouraging us, inviting us, sustaining us in our long journeys toward wholeness.

The need for justice and liberation—for women and for all people—is urgent. But the work is long. We can recognize oppres-sive language and name oppressive systems. We can call out inequality where we see it. We can stubbornly live into our gifts and refuse to settle for anything else. When necessary, we can leave oppressive institutions that refuse to change. At the same time, though, on some level, we watch and wait and pray, like the farmer who doesn't really have a clue how her plants grow.

Maybe it is enough just to stay engaged—to do what we can and not give up. Maybe building a new kind of world involves paying more attention to this world that we have been given—a world that we have not taken good care of, but still could. And maybe, as we seek the restoration and healing of the land, we'll find our own restoration and healing, too—as women, as humans.

Jesus spoke of war, violence, and natural disasters as "the beginning of birth pains."[13] Paul wrote in his letter to the Romans that "the whole creation has been groaning as in the pains of childbirth right up until the present time."[14] This feels like the time we're living in. The world around us—this world that we are a part of and that is part of us—is groaning, that's for sure. What we have done to the natural world is not serving us well. Human domination over Earth is not serving us well. Systems of dominance and oppression among humans are not serving us well. They aren't serving women's flourishing, and they aren't serving anyone's flourishing. Our world is straining, trembling, falling apart, breaking.

And yet. Maybe these groanings are also labor pains. It's a terrifying time and an exciting time. As things fall apart, there is the chance to build something new. As old ways strain and shudder and tear open, there is room for something new to be born—however quietly, however subtly, however slowly. Out on the margins, where good things are usually born—like Jesus, to teen mom Mary in a dirty barn.

In our time, like midwives, we can watch for and perhaps catch the new world that is being born. We can welcome with open arms the new kinds of community that want to emerge, the new ways of being together that we so desperately need.

Women, let's respond to this. Women, let's lead this.

CLOSING WORDS AND PRAYER

The work of rooting patriarchy out of our faith communities—and our minds, hearts, souls, and ways of being—is no easy task. We can name the many faces of nice churchy patriarchy, grapple with them, and explore the ways we might build something different. And yet patriarchy may not exactly cease to exist so much as go into hiding, morph into new forms, come back to plague another generation in some of the same ways and some different ways we haven't seen yet. Nevertheless, the struggle is worthwhile. All progress, however small, is worth celebrating. All of our naming and wrestling holds power. And we can move forward, together.

As we do so, there is no easy road. There is no clear path; we chart our own. This can be both exciting and overwhelming. Often we are tempted by complacency. Sometimes we are lulled into stagnancy by the thought that change is too hard, or too disruptive, and there are so many other things we should be doing with our time and effort instead of arguing about controversial things like women's roles in church.

When this is the case, we can remind ourselves—and one another—that the status quo really is unsustainable. Or more precisely, that it could be sustained, but only at an absurdly high cost. We can remember, too, that we are not alone. We are surrounded by a great cloud of witnesses, from Bible times through two thousand years of Christian history to the present day. We are held in the courage and strength of women and communities around the world. We are part of a much larger struggle than the little bits of progress and anti-progress we might see.

I invite you again to attend to your thoughts and feelings as you reflect on these things. Consider sharing your reflections with a friend. Invite God into whatever mental, emotional, and spiritual space you find yourself in. Consider where God's Spirit might be moving, how she might want to mother you and love you in this time, where she might be guiding you.

Pay attention to this mothering, mysterious, cooking-up-justice Spirit. Honor her. Search her out and move with her. The entire patriarchal world may throw itself back against you violently when you push even a little bit against it. But you will still have God's Spirit, and you will still have a vast, diverse, gorgeous world of others who are trying to attend to her also. Together, we will move forward.

I'd love to end with a prayer—hopefully one that doesn't give an unduly masculine impression of God. Each stanza of the prayer pairs with a chapter in this book.

If you like, consider reading these words out loud. Feel free to embrace any parts that resonate with you and let the rest go. I hope maybe you've found God somewhere in these pages. I hope maybe you find God somewhere in this prayer. Most importantly, I hope you find God somewhere deep in your own spirit—guiding you, freeing you, bringing wholeness and peace.

Peace to you on this difficult journey that I would not trade for anything.

God who gives agency,
save us from the undue influence
of those who think they know what's best for us.

God of relationships,
a full and faithful life looks beautifully different for
    each person,
and, for those who have a partner, for each couple.
Give us courage to be exactly who you made us to be.

God of truth,
help us see through nice-sounding obfuscations.
Shine light on unjust practices, and help us try to
    make them right.

God who made women fully human,
save us from forces that would objectify and dehu-
    manize us.
Strengthen us to stand firm in our humanity.

God of equity,
help us know when we need to decrease and when we
    need to increase.
Help us be our full selves, embracing the gifts you've
    given us.

God who sees beyond outward appearances to the
    heart,
cut the ties that bind our appearance and our visual
    self-presentation

to our value and worth in this world.

God who breathes life,
meet us in our exhaustion as our value is debated.
Change the terms of these conversations
so that they no longer further wound those who are
*   already hurting.*
Help us remember we are free to excuse ourselves.

God who alone determines cans and can'ts,
help us speak more honestly with one another.
Remind us, as often as we need to hear,
that vague authoritarian claims have no hold on us.

God who plays no favorites,
help us recognize and undo double standards,
whichever side of them we find ourselves on.

God who takes things personally,
free us to bring our full selves to our faith—gut,
*   emotions, experiences, and all.*
This world is difficult and demands nothing less.

God of everyday things,
help us take our words seriously.
May we say things that build others up and do not
*   demean them,*
and may others do the same for us.

God of emotions,
help us not be afraid of the anger of the oppressed.
Give the powerless courage to speak, and soften the
*   hearts of those in power.*

God who heals,
may we no longer internalize words that keep us
  trapped in cycles of shame.
Remind us that our healing is tied to the healing of
  our communities.

God who honors household labor,
help us build relationships and communities
where work does not fall primarily on the backs
of those already bent over with too many burdens.

God of freedom,
lead us into spaces that feel like liberation.
Surround us with people who treat us as full fellow
  humans.

God who hears us,
let our words be heard in our communities.
Give us courage to call out interrupters—ours, and
  one another's.

God who is faithful and true,
guide us as we wade through mixed messages,
that we may find the kind of truth that breathes life
  into our bones.

God of Susanna, Joanna, and Mary Magdalene,
thank you for the women who were with Jesus from
  the earliest days of his ministry.
Help us remember them, honor them, and find
  ourselves in their stories.

God of Elizabeth and Mary,
help us bless one another freely.

Place your songs in our hearts—songs of justice,
*   reversal, hope, liberation.*
Unbind us from our imprisonment within cultural
*   notions of femininity.*

God of the persistent widow, of Miriam and
*   Shiphrah and Puah, of Priscilla and Junia,*
remind us that our words are nice enough for you.
Remind us that, if we have enemies, it doesn't neces-
*   sarily mean we did something wrong.*

God who is not a white man,
open up our thirsty hearts to receive living water
through the voices, pens, and keyboards of women of
*   color.*

God whose eye is on the sparrow,
your mothering presence sustained our ancestors in
*   the faith.*
Sustain us now, nourishing us from your body.

Brightly shining God, whom ten thousand metaphors
*   could not adequately describe,*
none of us knows every facet of your being.
Surprise and delight us with who you are;
expand the language with which we speak and think
*   of you.*

God of William Seymour, Jennie Evans Seymour,
*   and Clara Lum,*
your Spirit is egalitarian in all ways, poured out on
*   all flesh.*
May the oppressions we have faced make us compas-
*   sionate toward others.*

May we be radically open to the movement of your
    Spirit.

God of Marcela, Hildegard, Julian, Margaret, and
    Jarena,
you have always called women into ministry.
Remind us that we stand with a great cloud of
    witnesses,
a sisterhood that spans the whole of history.

God of desire,
connect and reconnect us with the longings of our
    hearts—
the ones that yearn toward justice, healing, and
    goodness.
Help us move us in the direction of these desires.

God who calls people to move,
help us know when it's time to leave.
Fortify us, because leaving is often not easy.
Surround us with true friends who will stick by us no
    matter what.

God of righteous anger,
help us get angry about the things you get angry
    about.
Show us what good we can do with our anger, and
    help us do it.

God who was executed by the state,
you are with us as we dissent from lies and injustice.
Help us listen to those who are quicker to dissent
    from these things than we are.

God who gives wisdom,
we need all the people you've made and all the
        wisdom you've given them.
Thank you for young leaders, leaders of color, female
        and queer and nonbinary leaders.
Make our communities worthy of them.

God of the seashells and the seashell collectors,
bless us with a deep sense of purpose.
Move us from judgment, striving, and fear into grace,
        mercy, and joy.

God of the birds and the wildflowers,
help us learn from the world you've made,
and from those who have been listening to this world
        for a long time.
Tap us into your work of justice that is both urgent
        and slow,
dismantling all systems of oppression
and building something new, together.

In the name of our Creator who made a very good
        world,
and of our mother Christ who sustains our lives,
and of the Holy Spirit who is still cooking up
        justice—
Amen.

ACKNOWLEDGMENTS

I would like to say a few hopelessly brief "thank you"s that can't even begin to capture the long journey that has brought this book into the world or adequately recognize the people who have been part of the process.

Thank you to the many, many wonderful people I met at "Faith Bible Church" in the Bay area and "Life Church" in Southern California. I want you to know that I remember the good stories as well as the not-so-fun ones, and that I stuck with Faith Bible for eleven years and Life Church for almost two years because I loved meeting you and spending time with you. I ended up needing to leave these organizations, but I am grateful to have met you.

Thank you to "United Evangelical Seminary" and my professors and classmates there, for an education that, although not always easy, was also rich, fascinating, and fruitful.

Thank you to Giles for believing in this book and sticking with it.

Thank you to John for all your work to bring this book into the world.

Thank you to Janeen for your thoughtful and thorough editing.

Thank you to the small (nonviolent) army of amazing friends and family who read and gave feedback on earlier drafts: Lisa, Rose, Yi, Bing, Yuhong, Christin, Andrew, Lisa Ann, Laura, Edric, Amy W, Marina, Jane, Jeff, April, Amy H, Jen,

Sam, Mindy, Grace, Janet, and Aimee. Your feedback was so valuable, and your encouragement sustained me.

Thank you to Virginia, Shirley, and Joan, for your consistent, kind, and honest critique that goes beyond writing technicalities and into the realm of wisdom, experience, and soul. Wise Women Writers, indeed.

Thank you to my current church community, "Peace Pres," for being a place where angst is welcome, justice is unapologetically central, and most of us are unlearning old ways and learning new ways of believing in God, reading the Bible, and being together in community.

Thank you to my parents, Joe and Cynthia, for making space for me to grow up into whatever kind of woman I wanted and needed to be.

Thank you to Ken for being here for the egalitarian marriage journey, being here for the post-evangelical journey, listening to all my "TED talks," and letting me write about you. And, most importantly, for doing your own laundry.

APPENDIX
RECOMMENDED READING

If you've enjoyed this book, you may also enjoy some of these female authors who have helped me think about patriarchy and many other things. I've quoted directly from many of these books; others have influenced my thinking in a more indirect way. I list them here to give them the credit they deserve for being an important part of my life, and to offer them to you as well.

Enjoy!

- Adichie, Chimamanda Ngozi. *We Should All Be Feminists*. New York, Anchor Books, 2015.
- Ahmed, Sara. *Living a Feminist Life*. Durham, Duke University Press, 2017.
- Allison, Emily Joy. *#ChurchToo: How Purity Culture Upholds Abuse and How to Find Healing*. Minneapolis, Broadleaf Books, 2021.
- Barr, Beth Allison. *The Making of Biblical Womanhood: How the Subjugation of Women Became Gospel Truth*. Ada, Brazos Press, 2021.

- Benbow, Candice Marie. *Red Lip Theology: For Church Girls Who've Considered Tithing to the Beauty Supply Store When Sunday Morning Isn't Enough*. New York, Convergent Books, 2022.
- Bessey, Sarah. *Jesus Feminist: An Invitation to Revisit the Bible's View of Women*. New York, Howard Books, 2013.
- Bessey, Sarah. *Miracles and Other Reasonable Things: A Story of Unlearning and Relearning God*. New York, Howard Books, 2019.
- Bessey, Sarah. *Out of Sorts: Making Peace with an Evolving Faith*. New York, Howard Books, 2015.
- Bolz-Weber, Nadia. *Accidental Saints: Finding God in the All the Wrong People*. New York, Convergent Books, 2016.
- Bolz-Weber, Nadia. *Pastrix: The Cranky, Beautiful Faith of a Sinner & Saint*. Nashville, Jericho Books, 2013.
- Bowler, Kate. *Everything Happens for a Reason: And Other Lies I've Loved*. New York, Random House, 2018.
- Bowler, Kate. *No Cure for Being Human (And Other Truths I Need to Hear)*. New York, Random House, 2021.
- Brown, Brené. *Braving the Wilderness: The Quest for True Belonging and the Courage to Stand Alone*. New York, Random House, 2017.
- Brown, Brené. *Daring Greatly: How the Courage to be Vulnerable Transforms the Way We Live, Love, Parent, and Lead*. New York, Avery Publishing, 2015.
- Brown, Brené. *The Gifts of Imperfection: Let Go of Who You Think You're Supposed to Be and Embrace Who You Are*. Center City, Hazelden Publishing, 2010.

- Brown, Brené. *I Thought It Was Just Me (but it isn't): Making the Journey from 'What Will People Think?' To 'I Am Enough.'* New York, Avery Publishing, 2007.
- Brown Taylor, Barbara. *An Altar in the World: A Geography of Faith.* San Francisco, HarperOne, 2010.
- Brown Taylor, Barbara. *Holy Envy: Finding God in the Faith of Others.* San Francisco, HarperOne, 2019.
- Brown Taylor, Barbara. *Learning to Walk in the Dark.* San Francisco, HarperOne, 2014.
- Brown Taylor, Barbara. *Leaving Church: A Memoir of Faith.* San Francisco, HarperOne, 2012.
- Burke, Tarana. *Unbound: My Story of Liberation and the Birth of the Me Too Movement.* New York, Flatiron Books, 2021.
- Burke, Tarana, and Brené Brown, Editors. *You Are Your Best Thing: Vulnerability, Shame Resilience, and the Black Experience.* New York, Random House, 2021.
- Cleveland, Christena. *God Is a Black Woman.* San Francisco, HarperOne, 2022.
- Cooper, Brittney. *Eloquent Rage: A Black Feminist Discovers Her Superpower.* New York, St. Martin's Press, 2018.
- Curtice, Kaitlin B. *Native: Identity, Belonging, and Rediscovering God.* Ada, Brazos Press, 2020.
- Davis, Angela. *Women, Race, and Class.* New York, Vintage Books, 1983.
- Doyle, Glennon. *Untamed.* New York, The Dial Press, 2020.
- Everhart, Ruth. *The #MeToo Reckoning: Facing the Church's Complicity in Sexual Abuse and Misconduct.* Westmont, IVP, 2020.
- Finch, Jamie Lee. *You Are Your Own: A Reckoning with the Religious Trauma of Evangelical Christianity.* Independently published, 2019.

- Garza, Alicia. *The Purpose of Power: How We Come Together When We Fall Apart*. New York, One World, 2020.
- Gay, Roxane. *Bad Feminist: Essays*. New York, Harper Perennial, 2014.
- Gay, Roxane. *Hunger: A Memoir of (My) Body*. New York, Harper Perennial, 2018.
- Hamad, Ruby. *White Tears/Brown Scars: How White Feminism Betrays Women of Color*. New York, Catapult, 2020.
- Hatmaker, Jen. *Fierce, Free, and Full of Fire: The Guide to Being Glorious You*. Nashville, Thomas Nelson, 2020.
- Held Evans, Rachel. *Faith Unraveled: How a Girl Who Knew All the Answers Learned to Ask Questions*. Grand Rapids, Zondervan, 2014.
- Held Evans, Rachel. *Searching for Sunday: Loving, Leaving, and Finding the Church*. Nashville, Thomas Nelson, 2015.
- Held Evans, Rachel. *A Year of Biblical Womanhood: How a Liberated Woman Found Herself Sitting on Her Roof, Covering Her Head, and Calling Her Husband "Master."* Nashville, Thomas Nelson, 2012.
- Hong, Cathy Park. *Minor Feelings: An Asian American Reckoning*. New York, One World, 2020.
- hooks, bell. *All About Love: New Visions*. New York, William Morrow Paperbacks, 2001.
- hooks, bell. *Feminism is for Everybody: Passionate Politics*. Cambridge, South End Press, 2000.
- hooks, bell. *Feminist Theory: From Margin to Center*. Cambridge, South End Press, 2000 (2nd Edition).
- hooks, bell. *The Will to Change: Men, Masculinity, and Love*. New York, Washington Square Press, 2004.

- Kendall, Mikki. *Hood Feminism: Notes from the Women That a Movement Forgot.* New York, Viking, 2000.
- Khang, Kathy. *Raise Your Voice: Why We Stay Silent and How to Speak Up.* Westmont, IVP, 2018.
- Kidd, Sue Monk. *The Dance of the Dissident Daughter: A Woman's Journey from Christian Tradition to the Sacred Feminine.* San Francisco, HarperOne, 2016 (Updated edition).
- Kimmerer, Robin Wall. *Braiding Sweetgrass: Indigenous Wisdom, Scientific Knowledge, and the Teachings of Plants.* Minneapolis, Milkweed Editions, 2015.
- Kim-Kort, Mihee. *Outside the Lines: How Embracing Queerness Will Transform Your Faith.* Philadelphia, Fortress Press, 2018.
- Klein, Linda Kay. *Pure: Inside the Evangelical Movement that Shamed a Generation of Young Women and How I Broke Free.* New York, Atria Books, 2019.
- Kobes Du Mez, Kristin. *Jesus and John Wayne: How White Evangelicals Corrupted a Faith and Fractured a Nation.* New York, Liveright, 2020.
- Lorde, Audre. *A Burst of Light: and Other Essays.* New York, Ixia Press, 2017.
- Lorde, Audre. *Sister Outsider: Essays and Speeches.* Berkeley, Crossing Press, 2007 (Reprint edition).
- Lythcott-Haims, Julie. *Real American: A Memoir.* New York, Henry Holt and Co., 2017.
- Moraga, Cherríe, and Gloria Anzaldúa, editors. *This Bridge Called My Back: Writings By Radical Women of Color.* Albany, SUNY Press, 2015 (4th edition).
- Nikondeha, Kelley. *Defiant: What the Women of Exodus Teach Us about Freedom.* Grand Rapids, Eerdmans, 2020.

- Oluo, Ijeoma. *Mediocre: The Dangerous Legacy of White Male America*. New York, Seal Press, 2020.
- Oluo, Ijeoma. *So You Want to Talk About Race*. New York, Seal Press, 2018.
- Pagels, Elaine. *Why Religion? A Personal Story*. New York, Ecco, 2018.
- Perry, Imani. *Breathe: A Letter to My Sons*. Boston, Beacon Press, 2019.
- Perry, Imani. *South to America: A Journey Below the Mason-Dixon to Understand the Soul of a Nation*. New York, Ecco, 2022.
- Rankine, Claudia. *Just Us: An American Conversation*. Minneapolis, Graywolf Press, 2020.
- Riley, Cole Arthur. *This Here Flesh: Spirituality, Liberation, and the Stories That Make Us*. New York, Convergent Books, 2022.
- Rodgers, Julie. *Outlove: A Queer Christian Survival Story*. Minneapolis, Broadleaf Books, 2021.
- Rothaus, Kyndall Rae. *Thy Queendom Come: Breaking Free from the Patriarchy to Save Your Soul*. Minneapolis, Broadleaf Books, 2021.
- Schuller, Kyla. *The Trouble with White Women: A Counterhistory of Feminism*. New York, Bold Type Books, 2021.
- Solnit, Rebecca. *Hope in the Dark: Untold Histories, Wild Possibilities*. Chicago, Haymarket Books, 2016 (Second edition).
- Solnit, Rebecca. *Men Explain Things to Me*. Chicago, Haymarket Books, 2015 (Updated edition).
- Solnit, Rebecca. *The Mother of All Questions*. Chicago, Haymarket Books, 2017 (Third Printing).
- Solnit, Rebecca. *Recollections of My Nonexistence: A Memoir*. New York, Penguin Books, 2021 (Reprint edition).

NOTES

Words of Introduction

1. Ephesians 6:12.
2. Rebecca Solnit, *A Short History of Silence*, in *The Mother of All Questions* (Chicago: Haymarket Books, 2017), 18-9.
3. Mostly Western Christian history—not because this is the only kind of Christian history or the most important kind, but because it's the tradition I inhabit and therefore the one I want to interrogate.
4. Galatians 3:28 (NRSV).
5. Galatians 3:26, among lots of other places.

1. What's Best For Them

1. See, for example, *Emerging Adulthood: The Winding Road from the Late Teens through the Twenties* by Jeffrey Jensen Arnett (Oxford University Press 2006).
2. There are a few different Presbyterian denominations; PC(USA) is the more progressive major denomination among them. It's considered a mainline denomination rather than an evangelical one, if you're interested in that kind of distinction.

2. Tell Me, What Must I Be?

1. I was unable to find the exact talks that I remember—I think they were informal recordings from a retreat, making the rounds among some of my Christian friends—but they seem to be earlier versions of conservative pastor Voddie Baucham's more recent sermons "What He Must Be if He Wants to Marry My Daughter" (28 Aug 2020, see https://www.youtube.com/watch?v=WuT3dQt6A2E) and "What She Must Be" (6 Apr 2022, see https://www.youtube.com/watch?v=XlCtfzoo6Kg).
2. Brittney Cooper, *Eloquent Rage: A Black Feminist Discovers Her Superpower* (New York: St. Martin's Press, 2018), 202.
3. Cooper, *Eloquent Rage*, 202.
4. This is a fun word used by the Protestant Reformers back in the 1500s to try to say that the meaning of scripture can be understood by all, no

priest or pope needed. Which is great, in theory, but also complicated. Some parts aren't the least bit clear, and many parts might seem to clearly mean one thing to one person and another thing entirely to someone else.

5. If you're looking for a book that reflects more on the experience of growing up in an evangelical home—and then unlearning, as an adult, the damaging gendered messages taught there—consider Linda Kay Klein's *Pure: Inside the Evangelical Movement that Shamed a Generation of Young Women and How I Broke Free* (Atria Books, 2019), as well as Jamie Lee Finch's *You Are Your Own: A Reckoning with the Religious Trauma of Evangelical Christianity* (independently published, 2019).

6. See Matthew 23:36-40, for example.

7. I use the phrase "Paul's letters" as shorthand for both the letters Paul likely wrote and the letters he probably didn't write but are often attributed to him.

8. Rachel Held Evans, *A Year of Biblical Womanhood* (Nashville: Thomas Nelson, 2012), 295.

9. Brené Brown, *I Thought It Was Just Me (but it isn't): Making the Journey from 'What Will People Think?' To 'I Am Enough* (New York: Avery, 2007), 278.

10. For example, 1 Corinthians 12, where Paul writes of spiritual gifts given to each person for the good of the community.

3. Soft Complementarian, Hardly Grateful

1. Jen Hatmaker, *Fierce, Free, and Full of Fire: The Guide to Being Glorious You* (Nashville: Thomas Nelson, 2020), 21.

2. Hatmaker, *Fierce, Free, and Full of Fire*, 21-2. (As Jen writes next, "What. In. The. Actual. Hell.")

4. Stand Up and Turn Around

1. Not that Jesus Followers wasn't sometimes disturbingly authoritarian in its own way, but Aaron's talk was still a little different from our norms.

2. Rebecca Solnit, *Recollections of My Nonexistence* (London: Penguin Books, 2021), 48.

5. Who's Leading the College Ministry?

1. I initially shared a version of this story and reflection at https://lizcooledgejenkins.com/2019/12/13/i-must-decrease-or-must-i-part-1-of-3/.

2. John 3:30 (NRSV).
3. Are we also supposed to follow the part about living out in the wilderness, eating locusts and wild honey (à la Mark 1:6)? The wild honey part doesn't sound bad, but I'm not so sure about those locusts.
4. Or, I guess, teaching college students, but without the title or salary that a pastor would receive for doing the same work.

6. Preaching in Jeans

1. Cooper, *Eloquent Rage,* 222.
2. Cooper, *Eloquent Rage,* 222-3.
3. I speak from my (dominant U.S.) cultural context; other cultures may have different ideas. The point is not so much the specifics of the One Right Way, but the idea that there is one at all.
4. Drawing on 1 Samuel 16:7.

7. At the Church Picnic

1. 1 Timothy 2:11-12 (NRSV).
2. 1 Timothy 5:13 (NRSV).
3. I call the author of 1 Timothy "Paul" here for convenience, although it's likely the letter was written by someone else in Paul's name. This was standard practice at the time and was not considered dishonest. It just meant that the author intended to write in the same spirit as Paul.
4. Julie Rodgers, *Outlove: A Queer Christian Survival Story* (Minneapolis: Broadleaf Books, 2021), 124.

8. What Can Women Do?

1. From *Sister, You Can Be Anything God Desires You to Be,* by Kara Triboulet. Published in the CBE International newsletter, Jan 16, 2020. Also published by CBE International at https://www.cbeinternational.org/resource/sister-you-can-be-anything-god-desires-you-be/, Jan 15, 2020.
2. David M. Scholer's article on women in ministry, available at https://www.fuller.edu/womeninministry/#article, is a great place to start. Consider also: *Rediscovering Scripture's Vision for Women: Fresh Perspectives on Disputed Texts* by Lucy Peppiatt (IVP Academic 2019); *Paul and Gender: Reclaiming the Apostle Paul's Vision for Men and Women in Christ* by Cynthia Long Westfall (Baker Academic 2016); and *Women in the Church: A Biblical Theology of Ministry* by Stanley J. Grentz (IVP Academic 1995).
3. Like Miriam, Deborah, Junia, Priscilla—more on these women later.

9. Some Weird Stuff About Blood Moons

1. See Matt 24:36, Mark 13:32, and Luke 12:40.
2. Never mind that several major Christian denominations had already headed in the LGBTQ+ affirming direction, and others were (and are) considering it, or were at least divided over it. Surely, these denominations were gravely mistaken, capitulating to secular culture rather than letting the scriptures be their guide.
3. Ijeoma Oluo, *So You Want to Talk About Race* (New York: Seal Press, 2019), 16.
4. On the question of LGBTQ+ affirmation, one side would say, *of course we take the Bible seriously. And y'all clearly don't, because you aren't willing to follow the morality it clearly teaches in the passages that say homosexuality is sin.* The other side would say, *of course we take the Bible seriously. And y'all clearly don't, because you aren't considering all the cultural and historical context behind those passages you think are so very clear.*
5. For example, the woman is called a "helper" to the man (Gen 2:18), and the woman is made after the man, from the man's rib (Gen 2:21-23).
6. Rebecca Solnit, *Men Explain Things to Me* (Chicago: Haymarket Books, 2015), 60.
7. Barbara Brown Taylor, *Leaving Church: A Memoir of Faith* (San Francisco: HarperOne, 2012), 106.

11. He Never Quite Figured It Out

1. The MDiv is a three-year degree usually pursued by people looking to go into pastoral ministry.
2. Which is more than we can say for some modern-day complementarian pastors (see, for example, John Piper's 2015 article *Should Women Be Police Officers?*—available at https://www.desiringgod.org/interviews/should-women-be-police-officers).

12. This is Why It's Hard to Talk About Money

1. Matthew 21:12-13, Mark 11:15-18, Luke 19:45-47, and John 2:13-16. (You can tell it's important because it's in all four Gospels.)
2. Acts 2:42-47, 4:32-37.
3. Matthew 25:31-46.
4. Kaitlin B. Curtice, *Native: Identity, Belonging, and Rediscovering God* (Ada: Brazos Press, 2020), 105.

13. Have You Considered Therapy?

1. Brown, *I Thought It Was Just Me,* 100.
2. Brown, *I Thought It Was Just Me,* 99.

14. You Do Your Own Laundry?

1. Of course, it would help if men and women were paid equally in the workplace; otherwise, when the wife is making less than the husband, it can be hard, pragmatically speaking, to justify prioritizing her career over his. I'd recommend Kate Mangino's book *Equal Partners: Improving Gender Equality at Home* (New York: St. Martin's Press, 2022) for a deep dive into all of this.

15. Men Can Do Better

1. This is just what swimmers call a normal gym workout—mostly strength training and the like.
2. Ruby Hamad digs deep into this idea of white damsel womanhood in her book *White Tears/Brown Scars: How White Feminism Betrays Women of Color* (New York: Catapult, 2020).
3. Roxane Gay, *Hunger: A Memoir of (My) Body* (New York: Harper Perennial, 2018), 13.
4. Yoga and strength training, by the way, are more accessible these days than they've ever been. I love following along with *Yoga with Adriene* on YouTube, for example, which is free. There's also a lot you can do at home with an inexpensive set of adjustable dumbbells and various free workout apps.
5. With perhaps a side helping of *oh no, is this what I was like when I used to invite people to church stuff all the time?*

16. Thank You, Mr. Vice President

1. Mikki Kendall, *Hood Feminism: Notes from the Women That a Movement Forgot* (London: Penguin Books, 2021), 2.
2. Kendall, *Hood Feminism,* 2.
3. Kathy Khang, *Raise Your Voice,* 139.

Words of Transition

1. Acts 2:37.

17. Submit to One Another...But Mostly in One Direction

1. Ephesians 5:21 (NIV). As with 1 Timothy, I call the author of Ephesians "Paul" for convenience.
2. Ephesians 5:24 (NIV).
3. 1 Corinthians 11:5 (NIV). Actual Paul, this time.
4. 1 Corinthians 14:34 (NIV).
5. Held Evans, *A Year of Biblical Womanhood,* 281.
6. Acts 2:17-18.
7. As suggested by Galatians 3:28: "There is no longer Jew or Greek, there is no longer slave or free, there is no longer male and female; for all of you are one in Christ Jesus" (NRSV).
8. Ephesians 5:21 (NIV).
9. I use brackets to indicate a translation of a Greek word that exists in some manuscripts but not others.
10. I use parentheses to indicate a word that is not directly stated in the Greek text but seems to be implied.
11. I use "y'all" to clarify that it's a plural "you" in Greek, not a singular one. Greek distinguishes between plural "you" and singular "you," but English doesn't. So, often, in English translations, "you" might seem to refer to an individual, when actually it was meant to refer to a whole community. Using "y'all" is perhaps a small step toward reclaiming the communal mindset in which so much of the Bible was written.
12. Ephesians 5:21-33 (my translation).
13. I shared a version of the following reflections on my blog; see https://tinyurl.com/footnote17-13.
14. Galatians 3:28.
15. 1 Corinthians 14:34-35 (NIV).
16. Or, literally, "The women, let them be silent in the churches," using a command form.
17. 1 Corinthians 14:33 (NIV). A literal translation would be "all the churches of the holy ones," or "all the churches of the saints."
18. 1 Cor 14:33-37 (NIV, with quotation marks added).
19. 1 Corinthians 11:5 (NIV).
20. 1 Corinthians 11:13 (NIV).
21. It's probably also worth pointing out that not very many modern-day evangelical churches take this passage about hair and head coverings

literally—even the ones that talk a big game about the Bible's inerrancy and how we should follow all its instructions literally.

22. 1 Corinthians 12:8-10.
23. 1 Corinthians 12:28.

18. When the Anonymous Disciple is a Man

1. Drawing on Galatians 5:22.
2. Plus, people often talk about the larger group of (mixed gender) disciples and the smaller group of twelve (male) apostles as if they're the same group of people, which tends to erase female disciples from the picture.
3. See John 4:1-42.
4. See Luke 24:1-12; Matthew 28:1-10.
5. Luke 10:38-42.
6. Luke 8:1-3.

19. Blessed Are You

1. Luke 1:42 (NRSV)
2. Luke 1:48 (NRSV).
3. Kendall, *Hood Feminism*, 135-6.
4. See Luke 1:5-25.
5. This is the gist of Luke 1:26-38.
6. Christians for Social Action published a version of these reflections (3 Jan 2022). See https://tinyurl.com/footnote19-6.
7. Luke 1:39-45 (NRSV).
8. Luke 1:15.
9. Luke 1:67.
10. Acts 2:4.
11. Acts 4:8, 13:9.
12. Ephesians 4:31.
13. Luke 1:5.
14. Kendall, *Hood Feminism*, 92.
15. Kendall, *Hood Feminism*, 4.
16. Kathy Khang, *Raise Your Voice: Why We Stay Silent and How to Speak Up* (Westmont: IVP, 2018), 139.
17. Kendall, *Hood Feminism*, 135-6.
18. Luke 1:46-55 (NRSV).
19. The lyrics were written by Mark Lowry in 1984, and the music by Buddy Greene in 1991. It's been recorded by everyone and their choir since then, but the original recording was by Michael English in 1991.
20. Luke 1:32.

21. Luke 1:33.
22. Luke 1:35.
23. Luke 1:42.
24. Luke 1:43.
25. Luke 1:45.
26. Luke 1:48.
27. Luke 1:51-2.
28. Luke 1:53.
29. Luke 1:54-5.
30. Luke 2:8-20.
31. Luke 2:25-35.
32. Luke 2:36-8.
33. Luke 2:19.
34. Kelley Nikondeha, *Defiant: What the Women of Exodus Teach Us About Freedom* (Grand Rapids: Eerdmans, 2020), 176-7.
35. Glennon Doyle reflects on this idea of Knowing throughout her book *Untamed* (The Dial Press, 2020). Perhaps Mary has learned, in Doyle's words, to "choose what [she] Know[s]" (251), to "do the next thing [her] Knowing guides [her] toward" (60), to hear the "whisper" of her Knowing (70).

20. Those Pesky Bible Women

1. Luke 18:1-7 (my translation). As before, words in parentheses are not explicitly present in the original Greek but are implied.
2. Ruth Everhart, *The #MeToo Reckoning: Facing the Church's Complicity in Sexual Abuse and Misconduct* (Westmont: IVP, 2020), 94-5.
3. Everhart, *The #MeToo Reckoning*, 98.
4. This wild story is found in Exodus 1:15-22.
5. See Exodus 2:1-10.
6. See Exodus 15:20-21.
7. Nikondeha, *Defiant*, 76.
8. Romans 16:7 (NIV).
9. Acts 18:26.
10. This isn't exactly stated in Acts, but it seems to be implied.
11. Acts 18:26.
12. Acts 18:27.

21. Bookshelf Math

1. I recognize that this was a highly privileged experience of those early days of the pandemic, and that too many people had to deal with prob-

lems much bigger than boredom or isolation in a safe and comfortable home.

2. Check out the Appendix at the back of the book for reading suggestions.

3. For example, the biography of Ella Baker for my class on Martin Luther King, Jr., and a community organizing book for my class on urban ministry.

4. Mostly just a handful of books by Augustine—who, for the record, was from Hippo in northern Africa.

5. I included editors and co-editors if they are named on the front cover of the book. I did not include writers who contributed individual chapters to an anthology.

6. It felt right to give these authors more credit—if I've read multiple books by them, they've probably influenced my thinking quite a bit. All in all, sixteen authors show up at least twice, one author shows up three times (Dr. Brenda Salter McNeil), and one shows up four times (C.S. Lewis).

7. For those who don't mind even more detail, if we break it down by race, we find that 16 authors (11%) are Black, 6 authors (4%) are Asian or Asian American, 4 (3%) are Latinx, and 3 (2%) are Indigenous—and those three Indigenous authors were all co-authors of the same book. If we're talking female authors, 8 (6%) were Black women, 1 (1%) was a Latina woman, 1 (1%) was an Indigenous woman, and none were Asian or Asian American women.

8. I learned only near the end of my time in seminary that at least a couple of my peers had made a habit of speaking with their professors about their reading lists at the beginning of the quarter, pointing out the over- whelming maleness and/or whiteness of it all, articulating why this was a problem, and asking if they could replace some of the books on the list with books written by women and/or people of color. It had never occurred to me that one could do this, but apparently it worked in some cases.

9. Most of my professors were still white men, but I tried.

10. For example, *Race and Theology in America, Sexuality & Ethics*, and *Women in Church History and Theology*.

11. I counted the number of non-white-male authors who wrote on topics other than race (for the authors of color) or gender (for the female authors). I came up with 17; that is, 34% of the 50 total non-white-male authors. That means that 66% of the non-white-male authors on my bookshelves wrote books mostly limited to the topics of race and/or gender.

12. Phew. For a second there, I thought Khang was going to say, *if you are a man, listen to women preach; if you are a woman, listen to men preach.* I'm glad that went in a different direction.

13. Khang, *Raise Your Voice*, 67-8.

14. Check out the appendix for a fuller list of recommendations.

15. I've written some related reflections on this fasting experience in *I Fasted from White Authors for Lent*, originally published by Christians for Social Action (March 3, 2022). See https://tinyurl.com/footnote21-15.

16. Same deal—check out that appendix.

22. Her Eye is On the Sparrow

1. Lyrics included with Megan Moody's permission.

2. From Exodus 3:14, when Moses asks God for God's name.

3. Come to think of it, maybe this should be part of every pastor's job description: "Help your parishioners deal with their deep-seated patriarchy." And their racism, heterosexism, ableism, classism, etc. After all, pastors are supposed to build community, and all these dominance systems get in the way of that.

4. These are mostly things I learned in my Women in Church History and Theology class, taught by Dr. John Thompson.

5. *The Paedagogus*, Book I, Chapter 6.

6. Tractates on the Gospel of John, Tractate 124.

7. Genesis 1:27.

8. A classic dehumanization technique that came up again during the time of U.S. chattel slavery. Were enslaved people *really* full image-bearers of God? In other words, how can we use the Bible to justify our desire to keep enslaving them and stealing their labor for our economic benefit?

9. Isaiah 49:14-15.

10. Hosea 11:4 (NRSV).

11. Hosea 13:8.

12. Matthew 23:37, Luke 13:34 (NRSV).

13. Luke 15:8-10.

14. Dr. Marianne Meye Thompson points this out in her article *Speaking of God* (*Catalyst* 17.3, 1991) and it kind of blew my mind.

15. John 3:4 (NRSV).

16. John 3:5-6 (NRSV).

17. See Exodus 1:8-22.

18. Nikondeha, *Defiant*, 40.

19. Sarah Bessey, *Miracles and Other Reasonable Things: A Story of Unlearning and Relearning God* (London: Darton, Longman, and Todd Ltd, 2019), 170.

20. Bessey, *Miracles*, 172.

21. Bessey, *Miracles*, 173.

22. Sue Monk Kidd, *The Dance of the Dissident Daughter* (San Francisco: HarperOne, 2016), 138.

23. Brightly Shining God

1. Luke 9:35.
2. After all, Jesus said "When you are praying, do not heap up empty phrases as the Gentiles do; for they think that they will be heard because of their many words" (Matt 6:7, NRSV)—or, I might add, because of their eloquent, perfectly planned words.
3. Mihee Kim-Kort, *Outside the Lines: How Embracing Queerness Will Transform Your Faith* (Minneapolis: Fortress Press, 2018), 160.
4. If you're tempted to say, "well, actually, the biblical image of a shepherd is kind of masculine," I'd invite you to consider the biblical shepherd Rachel (see Genesis 29:9), as well as the seven female shepherds in Exodus 2:15-17.

24. Brother Seymour and His Sisters

1. By "charismatic," I mean a Christian tradition that emphasizes miraculous movements of the Holy Spirit, like physical healing, supernatural words of knowledge, speaking in tongues and interpreting tongues, and other "signs and wonders" from God. These kinds of things are considered *charisma*, from a Greek word that means "gift." This is not to be confused with "charismatic" in the sense of a likable, compelling leader (although charismatic churches often have their share of those, too).
2. A disturbing guest speaker in 2015 made me less excited about going back to visit, and then the senior pastor's 2016 article about why he voted for Trump sealed the deal of my breakup with that church. Later I would learn that in many ways Miracles had never been a healthy environment, especially for many queer people and people of color (which, in my straight white privilege, I had been blissfully unaware of).
3. It feels strange to write these things now, like all of this was in another lifetime. I am now skeptical of an entire world I once enjoyed.
4. The idea is that God's glory appears physically, looking something like a cloud full of little golden particles. It's loosely based on Bible verses like 2 Chronicles 5:13-14 ("the house, the house of the LORD, was filled with a cloud, so that the priests could not stand to minister because of the cloud; for the glory of the LORD filled the house of God," NRSV).
5. Cecil M. Robeck, Jr, *The Azusa Street Mission & Revival: The Birth of the Global Pentecostal Movement* (Nashville: Thomas Nelson, 2017), 125-6.
6. Gaston Espinosa, "Ordinary Prophet: William J. Seymour and the Azusa Street Revival," in *The Azusa Street Revival and its Legacy*, ed. Harold D. Hunter and Cecil M. Robeck Jr (Cleveland: Pathway Press, 2006), 35.
7. Specifically, *Azusa Street: An Eyewitness Account to the Birth of the Pentecostal Revival*, by Frank Bartleman.

8. This didn't happen until in the 1950s in the United Methodist Church and in the denomination that later became the Presbyterian Church (USA), and not until the 1970s in the Lutheran Church in America (the predecessor of the Evangelical Lutheran Church in America) and the Episcopal Church.

9. Estrelda Y. Alexander, *Black Fire: One Hundred Years of African American Pentecostalism* (Downers Grove: IVP Academic, 2011), 146.

10. Alexander, *Black Fire*, 147.

11. Alexander, *Black Fire*, 144.

12. Estrelda Alexander, "The Role of Women in the Azusa Street Revival," in *The Azusa Street Revival and its Legacy*, ed. Harold D. Hunter and Cecil M. Robeck Jr (Cleveland: Pathway Press, 2006), 75.

13. Estrelda Alexander, *The Women of Azusa Street* (Cleveland: The Pilgrim Press, 2005), 153.

14. William Seymour, "The Holy Spirit Bishop of the Church," September 1907. In *Azusa Street Sermons by William J. Seymour: The Complete Azusa Street Library*, Volume 5 (ASS), p. 70.

15. See John 4:1-42.

16. William J Seymour, *Azusa Street Sermons*, 30-1.

17. See Genesis 24 for the story of Rebekah becoming Isaac's wife.

18. William J Seymour, *Azusa Street Sermons*, 58.

19. William J Seymour, *Azusa Street Sermons*, 61.

20. When, really, women were not legally allowed to initiate divorce, implying that her husbands must have either divorced her and/or died.

25. Dreaming Through Two Thousand Years

1. Just one province, even though it sounds like two.

2. This section draws on my Introduction to the New Testament class, taught by Dr. Bruce Hansen.

3. This section draws on my Women in Church History and Theology Class, taught by Dr. John Thompson.

4. Although it does include several notable stories about women leading in the early Christian movement, and these things often aren't preached and talked about enough.

5. Elizabeth Clark, *Women in the Early Church: Message of the Fathers of the Church* (Collegeville: Liturgical Press, 1983), 77.

6. Clark, *Women in the Early Church*, 78.

7. Substantial excerpts of which are found in Clark's *Women in the Early Church*, 78-88.

8. *Acts of Paul and Thecla* 10.

9. *Acts of Paul and Thecla* 22.

10. *Acts of Paul and Thecla* 22.

11. *Acts of Paul and Thecla* 26.
12. *Acts of Paul and Thecla* 26.
13. *Acts of Paul and Thecla* 27.
14. *Acts of Paul and Thecla* 34.
15. *Acts of Paul and Thecla* 40.
16. Clark, *Women in the Early Church*, 205-6.
17. Clark, *Women in the Early Church*, 206.
18. Clark, *Women in the Early Church*, 207.
19. Clark, *Women in the Early Church*, 207.
20. Clark, *Women in the Early Church*, 207.
21. Clark, *Women in the Early Church*, 208.
22. Clark, *Women in the Early Church*, 207.
23. Luke 8:1-3.
24. Clark, *Women in the Early Church*, 207. See John 10:11-18.
25. Clark, *Women in the Early Church*, 207. It sounds quite a bit like Dr. King's famous line from *I Have a Dream*, about people being judged not by the color of their skin but by the content of their character.
26. Not entirely unlike Zechariah in Luke 1.
27. This section draws Dr. John Thompson's Women in Church History and Theology class.
28. The fact that women's ordination needed to be expressly prohibited in 1215, as Dr. Thompson liked to point out, says something about what must have been happening up until that time.
29. Not unlike the "inner light" emphasized in the Quaker movement a few centuries later.
30. Not unlike the ethos of the Azusa Street Revival, where human credentials and qualifications were bypassed in favor of the direct leading of the Holy Spirit.
31. Much of this history—or, should I say, herstory—is from Barbara MacHaffie's book *Her Story: Women in Christian Tradition* (Minneapolis: Augsburg Fortress Publishers, 2006), pp. 141-5.
32. This section draws on Dr. Jeff Waldrop's American Church History class.
33. MacHaffie, *Her Story*, 143.
34. MacHaffie, *Her Story*, 144.
35. MacHaffie, *Her Story*, 144.
36. This essay is included in Barbara MacHaffie's book *Her Story: Women in Christian Tradition*, pp. 156-158.
37. A version of these reflections on Margaret Fell was published by Feminism and Religion (14 Jan 2022). See https://feminismandreligion.com/2022/01/14/womens-speaking-justified-reflections-on-fell-feminism-and-history-by-liz-cooledge-jenkins/.
38. MacHaffie, *Her Story*, 156.
39. MacHaffie, *Her Story*, 157.
40. MacHaffie, *Her Story*, 158.

41. MacHaffie, *Her Story*, 158.
42. This section draws on Jarena's own autobiography, as recorded in the chapter entitled *Jarena Lee: A Female Preacher Among the African Methodists* (pp. 164-184), in the book *African American Religious History: A Documentary Witness* (Durham: Duke University Press, 2000), edited by Milton C. Sernett.
43. Lee, *A Female Preacher*, 166.
44. Lee, *A Female Preacher*, 167.
45. Lee, *A Female Preacher*, 167.
46. Lee, *A Female Preacher*, 172.
47. Lee, *A Female Preacher*, 173.
48. Lee, *A Female Preacher*, 174.
49. Beth Allison Barr, *The Making of Biblical Womanhood: How the Subjugation of Women Became Gospel Truth* (Ada: Brazos Press, 2021), 84.
50. As Hebrews 12:1 puts it.
51. Drawing on Rebecca Solnit's book *Hope in the Dark: Untold Histories, Wild Possibilities*, where Solnit beautifully explores this idea of an uncertain future that we then have power to shape.

26. Let It Be Done For You

1. Matthew 6:10a (NIV).
2. Matthew 6:9-13 (NIV).
3. Matthew 15:21-28 (NIV).
4. Matthew 20:21 (my translation).
5. Matthew 20:32 (my translation).
6. Matthew 23:37 (my translation).
7. Matthew 26:39 (my translation). The "will" part of what is usually translated "as you will" is implied in Greek but not stated directly.
8. Matthew 15:26.
9. And not just in church, but in our patriarchal world in general. Sara Ahmed dives deep into feminism and "willful" women in *Living a Feminist Life* (Duke University Press, 2017) if you want to read more.

27. I Left a Church

1. Barring more extreme situations of control—which do happen but are probably a topic for a different book, since these forms of churchy patriarchy couldn't exactly be considered "nice."
2. Which is perhaps in itself a reason to leave!
3. Romans 13:8.

4. Linda Kay Klein, *Pure: Inside the Evangelical Movement that Shamed a Generation of Young Women and How I Broke Free* (New York: Atria Books, 2019), 168.

28. Y'all, Be Angry

1. A word that could also just mean something like "accuser" or "slanderer."
2. Ephesians 4:26-7 (my translation). Again, probably not actually written by Paul, but we'll call him that for simplicity.
3. Kim-Kort, *Outside the Lines*, 197.
4. I shared a version of the following reflections at my blog; see https://tinyurl.com/footnote28-4.
5. Four quick translation notes, for the real Greek geeks out there: 1) If you find the "y'all" distracting, try perhaps: "Let the sun not set on your collective rage." 2) I know "let the sun not set" isn't really how we talk these days, but I wanted to clarify that this is a third person singular ("he/she/it") command—referring to the sun—and not a second person plural command directed toward Paul's hearers (like "be angry" and "do not sin"). 3) I use the word "rage" to reflect how this word comes from a different root from the word used for "be angry." 4) The word I'm translating as "rage" could also be translated as wrath, indignation, or exasperation.
6. I stole that from Romans 12:18.
7. Ephesians 4:31 (NIV).
8. One last exception for a male author!
9. Willie Jennings, *After Whiteness: An Education in Belonging* (Grand Rapids: Eerdmans, 2020), 28. Italics in original (indicating it's a poetic interlude in his book).
10. Audre Lorde, *The Uses of Anger: Women Responding to Racism.* In *Sister Outsider: Essays and Speeches* (Berkeley: Crossing Press, 2007), 127.
11. Mark 3:5a: "He looked around at them with anger" (NRSV).
12. Mark 3:6: "The Pharisees went out and immediately conspired with the Herodians against him, how to destroy him" (NRSV).
13. Kim-Kort, *Outside the Lines*, 197.

29. Oh, So That's a Heresy

1. Hatmaker, *Fierce, Free, and Full of Fire*, 155.
2. Sarah Bessey, *Out of Sorts: Making Peace with an Evolving Faith* (Brentwood: Howard Books, 2015), 41.

30. Please Welcome Your New Ruling Elders

1. Which is maybe what I did just now, but I wanted to give a brief sketch of who these elders are, because they're awesome.
2. Austin Channing Brown, *I'm Still Here: Black Dignity in a World Made for Whiteness* (New York: Convergent, 2018), 79-80.
3. Ijeoma Oluo, *Mediocre: The Dangerous Legacy of White Male America* (New York: Seal Press, 2021), 224.

31. Maybe Do Waste Your Life

1. John Piper, *Don't Waste Your Life* (Wheaton: Crossway, 2003), back-cover excerpt.
2. Of course, these are only some of the many factors involved in college admissions. There's also legacy status (huge), for example, and economic privilege (also huge). For me, I was able to do so many things in high school in part because I had the economic privilege of not needing to work to help support my family.
3. To borrow from Psalm 19:1.
4. This story can be found in Matthew 26:6-13 and Mark 14:3-9; there are also similar stories in Luke 7:36-50 and John 12:1-8.

32. Learn from the Wildflowers

1. Mark 4:26-27 (NRSV).
2. Genesis 1:28.
3. Genesis 1:4,10,12, 18, 21, 25, 31.
4. Curtice, *Native*, 105.
5. Genesis 1:31.
6. Genesis 1:29-30.
7. Genesis 2:1-3.
8. Robin Wall Kimmerer, *Braiding Sweetgrass: Indigenous Wisdom, Scientific Knowledge, and the Teachings of Plants* (Minneapolis: Milkweed Editions, 2015), 9.
9. See Mark 4:35-41.
10. Matthew 6:25-30 (NRSV).
11. I've shared some related reflections at https://lizcooledgejenkins.com/2021/10/08/learn-from-the-wildflowers-a-mini-sermon-on-matthew-625-34/.
12. See Matthew 14:22-33.
13. Matt 24:6-8 (NIV).
14. Romans 8:22 (NIV).

ABOUT THE AUTHOR

LIZ COOLEDGE JENKINS is a writer, preacher, and former college campus minister who lives in the Seattle area with her husband Ken and their black cat Athena. She has a BS in Symbolic Systems (Stanford University) and a Master of Divinity degree. Her writing has appeared in *Sojourners*, *Christians for Social Action*, *Feminism and Religion*, and *Red Letter Christians*. She can be found at lizcooledgejenkins.com (blog) and @lizcoolj and @postevangelicalprayers (Instagram). When not writing, Liz enjoys swimming, hiking, attempting to grow vegetables, and drinking a lot of tea.

9 781958 061404